D0394106

THE PROFESSOR
IN THE CAGE

ALSO BY JONATHAN GOTTSCHALL

The Storytelling Animal: How Stories Make Us Human

Graphing Jane Austen: The Evolutionary Basis of Literary Meaning

Evolution, Literature, and Film: A Reader

Literature, Science, and a New Humanities

The Rape of Troy: Evolution, Violence, and the World of Homer

The Literary Animal: Evolution and the Nature of Narrative

THE PROFESSOR
IN THE CAGE

WHY MEN FIGHT AND
WHY WE LIKE TO WATCH

JONATHAN GOTTSCHALL

PENGUIN PRESS
New York
2015

PENGUIN PRESS
Published by the Penguin Publishing Group
Penguin Random House LLC
375 Hudson Street
New York, New York 10014

USA • Canada • UK • Ireland • Australia
New Zealand • India • South Africa • China

penguin.com
A Penguin Random House Company

First published by Penguin Press, an imprint of Penguin Publishing Group,
a division of Penguin Random House LLC, 2015

Grateful acknowledgment is made for permission to reprint "Small Poem About
the Hares and the Hounds" from *Alive Together* by Lisel Mueller. Used by
permission of Louisiana State University Press.

Illustration credits appear on page 287.

LIBRARY OF CONGRESS CATALOGING-IN-PUBLICATION DATA
Gottschall, Jonathan.
The professor in the cage : why men fight and why we like to watch / Jonathan Gottschall.
pages cm
Includes bibliographical references and index.
ISBN 978-1-59420-563-7
1. Gottschall, Jonathan.   2. Violence in men.   3. Hand-to-hand fighting.   4. Fighting (Psychology)
5. Aggressiveness.   6. Spectators—Psychology.   I. Title.
HQ1090.G684   2015
155.2'32—dc23   2014036665

Printed in the United States of America
1   3   5   7   9   10   8   6   4   2

DESIGNED BY NICOLE LAROCHE

In memory of Nathan Singo

Reader, have you ever seen a fight?

William Hazlitt, "The Fight," 1822

CONTENTS

THE PROFESSOR
IN THE CAGE

It's the night of March 31, 2012, and I am standing half naked in a chain-link cage. I'm bouncing restlessly from foot to bare foot, trying to vent the tension building at my core. I'm surrounded by a swarm of men in Tapout T-shirts who are hooting at me over cups of beer. I can see the young man coming through the crowd to break my face, to strangle me to sleep. It's like a nightmare.

I'm thirty-nine years old. I'm an English teacher at a small liberal arts college. My first book, *The Rape of Troy*, focused on the science of violence—from murder to genocidal war—but I learned all I know from an armchair. I've never experienced real violence, never even been in a fight. But that's about to change.

As I dance and pace, I watch them smear the young man's face with Vaseline, watch them slip a mouthpiece between his lips. He's making fists in his fingerless gloves, and I can hear my own gloves creaking as I do the same. People have the wrong idea about the gloves. They think they civilize the sport, but they are the soul of its barbarism. The fine bones of the hand are no match for a heavy skull. Knuckles shatter on heads. But if you wind the hand in ribbons of gauze and tape, then armor it in foam and leather, you turn the fragile fist into a fearsome club.

The young man strides up the steps to the cage, sinews writhing beneath his skin like snakes. The steel door clangs shut behind him, and they drive the bolts home, locking us in to battle until one of us can't. The referee moves to the center of the cage. We will be fighting very soon, and I'm so relieved that I don't feel the fear that I expected. There's fear, but not the kind of terror that might unman me, might tempt me to hop the fence and run for home. Mainly I feel a sharpness of focus that I've never felt before. There's nothing in the world except the young man—no sound or scent, no wife squirming in her seat, no cornerman murmuring soothingly at my back.

The referee stands sideways between us. He shouts to each of us in turn, "Fighter, are you ready?" We nod. In the next heartbeat civilization will melt away, the law will disappear, and we will meet at the center of the cage to try to kill each other. I have never seen the young man before, and I feel nothing for him but respect. And yet the crowd will cheer as I try to shut down his brain with punches, to wrench his joints, to throttle his neck until his eyes roll blindly in their sockets.

The referee yells, "Fight!" And so we do.

IT WAS THE CULMINATION of a journey that began two years earlier when I was sitting in the cubicle I shared with other English Department part-timers, mulling the disappointments of my academic career. I had a PhD, my name was on the cover of a few books, and I had already lived my fifteen minutes of fame (or what passes for it among university types), but I was still a lowly adjunct making $16,000 per year teaching composition to freshmen who couldn't care less. My career was dead in the water. I'd known it for a long time. Whether this was because my effort to inject science into the humanities was before its time (the narrative that gets me through the day) or because that effort was wrongheaded (the more popular narrative in English departments) wasn't the question. The question was whether I could summon the courage to move on to something new, or at least to provoke my bosses into firing me.

As I paced between my cubicle and the adjoining lounge, a streak of motion caught my eye, and I went to the window. There used to be an auto parts shop directly across the street from the English department. But now a new product was on display in the building's big showcase windows. There were two young men in a chain-link cage. They were dancing, kicking, punching, tackling, falling, and rising to dance some more. There was a new sign on the building: MARK SHRADER'S ACADEMY OF MIXED MARTIAL ARTS. I stood at the window for a long time, peeping at the fighters through the curtains, envying their youthful strength and bravery—the way they were so alive in their octagon while I was rotting in my cube.

I began to fantasize. I saw myself walking across the street to join them. The thought of my peace-loving colleagues glancing up from their poetry volumes to see me warring in the cage filled me with perverse delight. It would be such a scandal. *That's how I'll do it,* I thought with a smile. *That's how I'll get myself fired.*

Over the next months, I began to plan a book about a cultured English professor—a lifelong specialist in the art of flight, not fight—learning the combat sport of mixed martial arts (MMA). The book would be part history of violence, part nonfiction *Fight Club,* and part tour of the sciences of sports and bloodlust. It would be about the struggles—sad and silly and anachronistic though they may seem—that men endure to be men.

One day, not long after noticing the cage fighting studio across the street from my office, I met my family for lunch. When I ordered a salad, my wife gave me a skeptical look. "Salad?" she asked. "Are you okay?"

"Yeah," I said. "But I'm so fat. Gotta get in shape."

When she asked why, I told her—a little shamefacedly—my whole dumb plan for becoming a cage fighter. "Why would you do that?" she asked. I fumbled for an honest answer. "You'll be killed," she pointed out. "You have no skills."

Learning that my wife had no respect for my skills hurt, but it hurt worse to see how casually she learned to treat my danger. Much later, when I was having trouble getting a fight here in Pennsylvania (the state commission does not make it easy for older fighters), she recommended that I fight in Las Vegas, where her brother lives. "Anthony knows a lot of fighters," she said. "I bet he could help get you a fight."

The very idea made me clammy. "Vegas is the fight Mecca of the whole universe," I explained to her. "I'm not exaggerating. Those guys would end my life. They would send me home to you in buckets." A big part of me wanted her to talk me out of my whole suicidal plan. I wanted her to seize my hands and tell me through her big, pretty, man-slaying tears that it was just too dangerous and that she couldn't stand the thought of scars on my handsome face. But instead she stared off into space like a prisoner dreaming of freedom.

"Yeah," she said, "you should definitely fight in Vegas."

But my wife's question was a good one. Why did I *really* want to do this? Was I having a midlife crisis? I didn't think so. Did taking up MMA—a sport where the whole point is to violently incapacitate the other guy before he can violently incapacitate you—seem like fun? It didn't. Did I actually think that the cage could free me from the cubicle? Yes, I was just desperate enough to hope that it could. But there was more to it than that. I wanted to fight because I was simply fascinated by fighting, and I wanted to learn about it—and write about it—from the inside. I wanted to fight because I'd always admired physical courage, and yet I'd never done a brave thing. I wanted to fight, I suppose, for one of the main reasons men have always fought: to discover if I was a coward.

So in January 2011 I finally made the short walk from the brick and leaf of my college to the grit and stink of the local fighting academy. Beneath the English Department's windows, I began studying the fighting arts alongside students, soldiers, frackers, an actuary, a busboy, a rock singer, a tree trimmer, and the occasional young woman. And each night I carried home, along with my bruises and abrasions, powerful insights into why violence is so attractive—and so repulsive.

When I crossed the street to try to become a fighter, I never stopped being a professor. I never stopped noticing the basic questions that hang in the humid air of an MMA gym, and I never stopped trying to answer them. There were the biggies: Why do men fight? Why do so many people like to watch? And why, especially when it comes to violence, do men differ so greatly from women? And there were the questions that seemed small at first but ended up having large implications: Why do human beings spend (waste?) so much energy on sports? Are traditional martial arts such as karate and kung fu sheer hokum? Why do fighters try to stare each other down? And why do nonhuman primates do exactly the same thing?

When I first joined the gym, I expected to write a book about the rapid rise of cage fighting in America and what its massive popularity says about us—not just as a nation, but as a species. I thought MMA was bad for the athletes who did it and bad for society at large. I saw cage fighting as a metaphor for something darkly rotten at the human core. But my library research convinced me that MMA tells us nothing particularly interesting about our place or time; everywhere and always, people have loved to watch men fight. And my gym research—sparring, interviewing, and finally fighting myself—upended all my other preconceptions. In short, I set out to write about the darkness in men, but I ended up with a book about how men keep the darkness in check.

One big idea threads through all the chapters to come: While always anchored in MMA, *The Professor in the Cage* is about the duels of men, broadly defined. Most historians trace the origins of the duel back to Europe in the 1500s. But far from being a Western invention, the duel is not even a *human* invention. Animals have their fights, too, and biologists refer to them tellingly as duels, sports, tournaments, or, most commonly, ritual combat. *Ritual combat*—think of elephant seals clashing in the surf, or deer locking antlers—establishes dibs on all good things through restrained contests that diminish risk. The same is true of human contests, only more so. Humans, especially men, are masters of what I call the monkey dance—a dizzying variety of ritualized, rule-bound competitions. These events range from elaborate and deadly duels (pistols at dawn), to combat sports such as MMA or football, to the play fights of boys, to duels of pure language (rap battles, everyday pissing contests). They often seem ridiculous and sometimes end in tragedy. But they serve a vital function: they help men work out conflicts and thrash out hierarchies while minimizing carnage and social chaos. Without the restraining codes of the monkey dance, the world would be a much bleaker and more violent place.

ONE

THE RIDDLE OF THE DUEL

The trouble with this country is that a man can live his entire life without knowing whether or not he is a coward.

John Berryman

The first cage fight in the history of the Ultimate Fighting Championship (UFC) occurred on November 12, 1993, pitting karate against sumo. There were no rules. There were no rounds. There were no weight classes. There were no gloves. There was no mercy. There was also no ring.

The UFC's creators wanted the fighting space to drive home the whole point of the sport—which was that it *wasn't* a sport. It was, in the words of its first announcer, Rich "G-Man" Goins, "combat in its most basic equation: Survival or destruction." The creators considered locking the fighters in an electrified cage surrounded by a moat full of famished alligators, but they decided that was a bit much. Instead, the men would fight in a chain-link octagonal cage, which one announcer likened to the "pits" used in dogfighting. Once the fighters entered the cage, officials would bolt the door behind them, and the only way out would be through the other man. To quote the G-Man again: "The rules are simple—two men enter, one man leaves." (It's probably no coincidence that in Mel Gibson's 1985 dystopian fantasy *Mad Max Beyond*

Thunderdome, the crowd chants "Two men enter; one man leaves" as gladiators fight inside a steel cage.)

The first fighter to step into the UFC cage was a mountainous Hawaiian sumo wrestler named Teila Tuli. He walked through the crowd wearing traditional island garb resembling a checkered muumuu, paired with a ski hat. He handed his hat and gown to his cornermen, then danced around the cage in his Hawaiian skirt, looking loose and confident. Teila Tuli was six feet two, sleekly bald, and massively obese. At more than four hundred pounds, he was fat in all the ordinary places—thick in the hams, belly, and jowls. But at some point he maxed out the fat-storage capacity of the ordinary places, and so his body started laying in cellulite bags wherever it could. Tuli had several bags pinned between his chest and upper arms, as well as a blubbery roll fitted like a pillow to the back of his neck. Even so, he was a magnificent animal, with huge muscles twitching beneath the fat. Despite the bulk, he moved as nimbly as a dancer and dropped effortlessly into deep stretches. Teila Tuli was a formidable athlete.

Tuli's opponent was a Dutch karate black belt named Gerard Gordeau, and compared with the Hawaiian he wasn't much to look at. Gordeau was tall and skinny, with a buzz cut and scraggly chest hair. With his thin arms and almost defiantly unripped torso, he didn't look like an athlete at all. Instead, he looked exactly like what he was: a guy who made his living as a school janitor, while competing in karate tournaments on the side. Gordeau walked to the cage wearing karate pants and a white towel draped over his shoulders. Though he was only moments away from fighting an athlete who was double his size, he looked about as troubled as a guy walking from the shower to his bedroom.

When Gordeau entered the cage, Tuli's mask of serene confidence—of manly insouciance—began to slip. Tuli moved nervously in his corner, sucking down huge lungfuls of air and spewing them out again. As the camera panned to Gordeau's corner, it was clear why. Gordeau didn't look like a man who was about to be sacrificed to a giant. He just stood there, flat-footed, slump-shouldered, and breathing normally through his nose, as if he were running a pulse of about forty. And he watched Tuli not with the "mean mug" of a fighter trying to intimidate, but with a serial killer's blank stare. His look said to Tuli, not unkindly, *This is nothing to me. You are nothing to me.*

The bell rang, and after a few seconds of circling and feinting Tuli tipped himself toward Gordeau and let gravity take over. Gordeau pivoted like a matador and stung Tuli with a hard punch as he charged by. Unbalanced, Tuli crashed face-first into the bottom of the fence. As the huge man struggled to rise, Gordeau stepped in, wound up, and soccer-kicked Tuli, full power, in the mouth. The crack of the blow was so terrible, the spray of blood and slobber so dramatic, that the referee jumped in to stop the fight. But not before Gordeau crouched down for a haymaker that spun Tuli around and left him sagging against the fence. The fight lasted twenty seconds. Tuli hauled himself upright and shuffled out of the cage, complaining through the gory hole of his mouth that he wanted to fight on. Gordeau left the cage with a fractured right fist and one of Tuli's front teeth broken off inside his foot. Gordeau had punted Tuli's other front tooth straight through the chain-link cage, past the announcers' heads, and into the crowd.

I DIDN'T SEE Gordeau fight Tuli live. I saw the fight a few years later at a party when a friend cracked open a Blockbuster video case and jammed a tape into a VCR. He said, "Check this out. You guys won't believe it." I didn't believe it. Watching Gordeau punt Tuli's face, then watching replays of him punting it again and again, from multiple super-slo-mo angles, made me sick to my stomach. And listening as my friends yelped and giggled through the onslaught—watching as men in the Denver crowd screamed through conniptions of bloodlust—sickened me even more. I asked myself, *What kind of savage would want to watch this?* And then the next pair of fighters strode into the cage, and I found that I couldn't look away.

That night we gorged ourselves on raw violence. When it ended, with a skinny Brazilian choking Gordeau into submission in the final fight, I staggered home feeling exactly like I'd felt after seeing my first porno as a teenager. The porn tape, like the UFC tape, was a fleshy catastrophe that raised serious ethical issues. After both experiences I lay awake trying to erase the images of swollen flesh and spattering fluids strobing in my mind. And in both cases I awoke still feeling disgusted and disturbed—but also wanting to see more. And soon. In the ensuing months I frequently visited the video store, where I guiltily lurked through the section that included UFC tapes, professional wrestling tapes, and tapes from an infamous video series called Faces of Death.

I told myself that unlike the blood-drunk men raving in the UFC crowd, I had a good reason for watching. In my early twenties I was a devoted, if basically inept, karate student, and the UFC was an education about what worked in a real fight and what absolutely didn't. I watched the tapes in a scholarly spirit, rewinding over and over to study particularly cool moves—etching them in my mind so I could drill them with my karate friends. But I didn't try too hard to fool myself. I watched the tapes to learn, but also because I was a lot like those UFC fans cheering for carnage—I just had the good taste not to show it. I watched because the fights excited me. I watched because fighting was real, high-stakes drama with no acting and no artifice. I watched because I envied the manly excellence and courage of the fighters. I watched because—God help the human race—there's nothing harder *not* to watch than two men fighting.

And I watched because I was deeply confused. As I took in the footage of Gordeau shattering Tuli's teeth, the questions of this book were already forming in my mind. Why do men fight? And why are seemingly decent people drawn to watch? I didn't know it at the time, but that night I began a research project that would last almost twenty years and culminate in this book.

EN GARDE!

To begin, I have to take you back more than two hundred years to tell the story of a different fight—a story you only think you know.

Before dawn on November 23, 1801, Hamilton, his second, and his surgeon eased aboard a wobbly dinghy, and a ferryman rowed them away from Manhattan (and its laws against dueling) to the Jersey side of the Hudson River. Hamilton crunched through the forest into a clearing, where his adversary was already busy with his own second, clearing away branches and pacing off the agreed distance—ten paces, or around thirty feet. Hamilton stood off to one side, eyeing his opponent through the slanting dawn light, feeling no hatred toward him. He was thinking, *How strange and stupid this is.* He was thinking, *Don't let your hands shake.* He could hear the seconds droning through their last, pro forma attempts at reconciliation. Although both Hamilton and his opponent had much to be sorry for, neither could say so for fear of appearing cowardly.

The two men would fight with a pair of dueling pistols that belonged to Hamilton's uncle. The pistols were handcrafted, gorgeously filigreed objects of art and death. With dark walnut stocks and gleaming barrels, they were about the size of sawed-off shotguns, and with their .54-caliber balls they could open a man about as wide. The seconds loaded the weapons, each using a ramrod to pack in powder, ball, and wadding, then handed them to the duelists by the barrels. Hamilton took his place and tried to avoid his adversary's gaze. It was his first duel, and he could not believe how close together they were standing. They could almost duel by spitting.

We don't know for sure, but the men may have arranged themselves in classic dueling stances that were designed to shrink the profile and shield the vital organs. If so, they would have positioned themselves sideways to each other, sucking in their bellies and tucking their chins to hide their necks. They would have turned their hips in hopes of taking a low shot in the buttock and not the groin. Thus contorted, they would have stood with their pistols dangling, awaiting the command to fire. When the command came, they would not have fired with their arms extended to full length. Instead, they would have fired with their right elbows cramped tight to their ribs so their pistols and arms could shield their torsos.

"Present!" said one of the seconds, commanding the duelists to raise their weapons and fire. But neither man did. They just stared at each other across the stillness of the clearing, their breath clouding the morning air. They stared at each other for a long time, perhaps hoping that someone might still call this madness off and they could embrace and part as friends. After a full minute had passed, Hamilton raised his weapon. The clearing erupted with two near-simultaneous explosions. The two lead balls passed each other in flight, one sizzling wide into the trees, and the other steering around Hamilton's gun arm to bite into the soft flesh beneath his ribs. The ball punched a fist-size hole through his innards before exiting through his left side and lodging in his opposite arm. Hamilton fell face-first to the earth. Once back in Manhattan, he lay in bed for more than twenty-four hours, writhing in agony and trying to die bravely.

And now we come to the part of the story you probably don't know. When Hamilton's father received news of the catastrophe, he raced to his son's bedside. The father—Alexander Hamilton, the man whose handsome face still graces the ten-dollar bill—climbed carefully into bed with his doomed son Philip and gave vent to his grief. One of Philip's friends was looking on and said that Alexander's sorrow "beggared all description." The nineteen-year-old Philip was Alexander's eldest and favorite child, the one he'd doted on as a baby and later called "the brightest, as well as the ablest, hope of my family." When Philip was buried, Alexander had trouble walking to the graveside; as one observer wrote, he had to be half carried to "the grave of his hopes."

And yet, less than three years later, still mourning Philip and knowing he was in the wrong, Alexander had himself rowed away from Manhattan to the Jersey banks of the Hudson, directly across the river from Forty-second Street. There, at Weehawken, on a lovely summer morning, he was greeted by the vice president of the United States, Aaron Burr. When the two men fired, Hamilton fell, perhaps cut down by the very same pistol that had killed Philip. (Hamilton and Burr certainly used the same *set* of pistols.) Gut shot like his son, Hamilton's death throes lasted thirty-eight hours. His agony was, according to his surgeon, "almost intolerable" and not much deadened by opium.

Philip Hamilton was killed by one of his father's many political adversaries, a twenty-seven-year-old lawyer named George Eacker. One night at the theater, young Philip, possibly drunk, stormed Eacker's private box with a friend and abused the lawyer for criticizing his father in a speech. Afterward Philip wouldn't apologize for his insults. He was too enraged over the way Eacker had insulted him in reply, calling him a "damned rascal." These were, quite literally, fighting words. A man called someone a rascal—or a puppy, a jackanapes, a coxcomb, or a liar—only if he specifically wished to provoke a duel.

Aaron Burr called out Alexander Hamilton for more serious affronts. Hamilton was outwardly friendly to Burr when they met on the street or socialized in each other's Wall Street homes. In later years Burr would sometimes speak of "my friend Hamilton—whom I shot." But Hamilton deeply distrusted Burr's politics and character and said that he felt "a religious duty to oppose his career." Rather than confront Burr openly, however, Hamilton opted, in the parlance of the day, to slit Burr's throat with whispers. Hamilton may have had a hand in newspaper accounts that accused Burr of, among other depravities, treason, being named as the best customer of no fewer than twenty whores, and twirling buxom girls at a "nigger ball." Burr believed that Hamilton was smearing him, and his suspicions were confirmed when Hamilton was quoted in a newspaper calling Burr a "profligate" and a "voluptuary in the extreme," with implications that he had said far worse.

On the eve of his duel, Hamilton tried to put his affairs in order. He updated his will and wrote a letter to his wife, Elizabeth, whom he addressed as "best of wives, best of women." The letter explained that he was fighting Burr with the greatest reluctance and only after exhausting all other options. This was true. Burr and Hamilton had traded endless letters back and forth through their seconds, with Hamilton working lawyerly dodges and splitting verbal hairs, trying to weasel out of the mess on a technicality. He was reluctant to fight because he didn't hate Burr and he felt that dueling was radically at odds with good Christian behavior. Moreover, Hamilton knew that if he died, his family would struggle to pay their debts.

So why, when they had so much to live for, did the Hamiltons, father and son, recklessly risk their lives over such paltry stuff? Alexander Hamilton was a co-author of *The Federalist Papers* and the architect of the American financial system. Couldn't he do the cost-benefit math?

To us moderns the killing of a former Treasury secretary by a sitting vice president seems fantastically exotic. (Remember the uproar in 2006 when Vice President Dick Cheney accidentally wounded a friend in a quail-hunting accident? Well, imagine the hullabaloo if Cheney had killed Clinton's former Treasury secretary Robert Rubin in a shoot-out on the Virginia side of the Potomac, and had then gone on the lam.) But a little more than two centuries ago, there was nothing particularly strange about the Burr-Hamilton affair—not the high social and political status of the combatants, nor the way that the effect (a deadly gunfight) seemed so out of proportion to the cause (gossip). Throughout the five-hundred-year history of Euro-American dueling culture, aristocratic men were generally prepared to kill each other at the drop of a hat. In sharp contrast to modern times, in those days it was educated, rich, and powerful men—blue bloods, newspaper owners, congressmen, future presidents, British prime ministers—who were most likely to shoot or stab each other over disses.

It's easy to see why men fight over precious and necessary things such as food, wealth, or the love of a woman. But duelists so often killed, and were killed, over trifles—loose words, rumors, impertinent looks. Duelists imperiled their lives for something they couldn't touch, see, or even precisely define: their personal honor. This is the riddle of the duel: how could intelligent men risk so much over what seems like so little?

HONOR

Killing a man in cold blood because he has called you a voluptuary or ruined your night at the theater seems deranged. But that's because most of us today don't fully grasp the historical importance of honor. In the Hamiltons' time, honor represented the entirety of a man's social wealth. Honor wasn't some trivial thing; it was precious coin that bought the best things in life. And if this coin was devalued, a man's prospects—and the prospects of his entire family—were devalued as well.

Muscular cultures of honor still exist today, and where they do, it's easy to see honor's value. Take prison. If a mad scientist wanted to run an experiment that plunged deep down to the roots of masculine aggression, he could do no better than to take many hundreds of frustrated young men, isolate them from the softening influence of women and children, see that they are armed with all kinds of ingeniously improvised weapons, and cage them together for years on end in circumstances that give them little hope of ever prospering outside the walls. Prisons are the most extreme honor cultures currently in existence. The harder the prison, the harder the culture of honor. And what emerges from such cultures is a lot of violence. In prison, inmates fight over tangible things such as control of a black-market economy in drugs, booze, and other contraband. But as frequently they fight over honor, although they usually don't call it that. They call it respect. But *honor* and *respect* are different words for the same thing. They represent a group's estimation of a man's ability to inflict harm and confer benefits—of his power, in other words.

It may seem odd to think of a prison as an honor culture, because for us honor has noble connotations. But a culture of honor can tolerate extremely ignoble behavior—from Alexander Hamilton's profane gossip to the rapes and murders in modern American jails. A culture of honor is really nothing more than a culture of reciprocation. A man of honor builds a reputation for payback. In a tit-for-tat fashion he returns favors and retaliates against slights. Consider the case of Jimmy Lerner, a corporate number cruncher who got locked up for killing a friend in a fight and afterward wrote a prison memoir called *You Got Nothing Coming*. Early in his sentence a massive inmate called Big Hungry approached Lerner in the crowded lunchroom, lifted a banana from Lerner's tray, and sauntered away as he peeled it. On a second occasion Big Hungry wordlessly cut in front of Lerner in the phone line. On both occasions Lerner was more chagrined than annoyed, and he let the slights pass with a shrug.

Lerner was lucky in having a formidable cell mate named Kansas, who was still a young man but old in the ways of prison. After the phone incident Kansas told Lerner that he had no choice but to kill Big Hungry.

"Kansas, that seems a little extreme, don't you think? *Stabbing* a guy over a phone call?" Kansas replied, "It ain't about the phone call, O.G. It's about *Respect*." Lerner explains: "Ask any convict who has been down a few days for his definition of a 'man' and the concept of 'disrespect' will surface quicker than stank on shit . . . 'A man,' Kansas might say, 'is someone who tolerates no disrespect! A real man, a *stand-up* man, seeks out disrespect and destroys it!'"

A different convict, a thirty-five-year-old armed robber named Peter, explains why. "You can tell the rabbits . . . They bring this guy in and he is doing time for some punk-ass white-collar rip-off, and right away I figure this guy's got no heart." So Peter gives the new guy a "heart check" by harassing him on little things—stealing his books in the same way Big Hungry stole Lerner's banana. By failing to retaliate, the new guy fails the heart test, just as Lerner did. Peter says, "I mean, c'mon, a righteous motherfucker would have stuck me, 'cause he's gonna know that if he lets me take his law books, I'm coming back for his ass next. I'm no fool. A few days later, I go up to this dude and tell 'im we are forming a partnership. He's gonna do my laundry for me and buy me whatever I want from the commissary and that's just how it's gonna be . . . You see, that's how it is with rabbits. You ever wonder what they are good for, or why God made them? They're food."

In a tough prison, you can either be a "righteous motherfucker"—a missile programmed to seek out and destroy disrespect—or you can give up your ass, often literally but figuratively, too. If you fail the heart test, the other inmates will take your food, exploit your commissary privileges, extort your relatives, and make you a slave. The prison equation is ruthlessly simple: yielding on the smallest thing (a banana, a book) is equivalent to yielding on the biggest. Not fighting over a banana or a book is the same as declaring *I am a rabbit. I am food.*

In prison men defend honor because honor is necessary to life. The most respected prisoners have the best lives, while the least respected have no lives at all. Prison culture provides an exaggerated—and thus clarifying—insight into why men like the Hamiltons were willing to risk so much over honor. In the upper strata of European and American society, *not* dueling in defense of honor was a form of suicide. Men risked death or injury (throughout history, most duelists managed to walk or limp away afterward) to avoid the certainty of social annihilation. Some historians have speculated, lamely, that Hamilton fought Burr because he was suicidally depressed over Philip's death, a daughter's mental illness, political setbacks, and constant money problems. But this is wrong. Hamilton desperately sought a face-saving way out of the duel and fought Burr not because he wanted to kill or die, but because he so much wanted to live.

To dodge the fight Hamilton would have had to apologize to Burr and effectively admit to a history of low and dirty lies. If Hamilton simply refused to fight, Burr would have instantly "posted him," literally printing the news that Hamilton was a coward. To be seen as a duel dodger was, in many ways, a fate worse than death. Backing down would have jeopardized Hamilton's political ambitions, his position of social eminence, and his business as a lawyer. Hamilton's family would have been tainted as well—his wife unable to show her face in society, his children's prospects diminished professionally and romantically. Hamilton fought not because he was brave, but because he was scared of what it would cost him *not* to fight. As one of Hamilton's friends wrote after his death, "If we were truly brave, we should not accept a challenge; but we are all cowards."

BRAIN DAMAGE

Two centuries after the Hamiltons tromped through the New Jersey woods to their deaths, I was crossing an octagonal cage to face mine. I tapped fists with my coach, Mark Shrader. We circled away from each other, then reengaged.

I was a few months into my MMA adventure, and I was already getting impatient. I knew that for a book with a "memoir stunt" component to

Mark Shrader (right) posing with champion boxer Roy Jones Jr. Shrader served as a sparring partner for Jones as the latter prepared for his 2008 fight against Felix Trinidad. Note the enormous size of Shrader's left fist and then read on.

work, I'd need to get hurt and humiliated, early and often. From George Plimpton's forays into professional sports to the gentler stunts of A. J. Jacobs (such as spending a year living as an extreme biblical fundamentalist), the formula is pretty much set: ordinary schmuck enters an exotic world; suffers humorous setbacks, agony, and shame; learns a lot along the way. But so far I'd hardly been hurt or humiliated at all. The guys at the gym seemed to be treating me gently, either because I was new or because they feared for my ancient, chalky bones. So one day I blurted to Coach Shrader that I wanted to boost my training. I was writing a book about fighting, and I had to know what it was like to be hit.

I actually said that. It was a foolish thing to say and, as I would learn, an even more foolish thing to say to Mark Shrader. Mark is black-haired and handsome, with just a touch of what the boxing writer F. X. Toole calls "the monkey look"—the pugilist's scar-thickened eyebrows and fist-flattened nose. He has a quick, charismatic smile and the infectious energy of a boyhood martial arts fanatic who grew up to do exactly what he wanted with his life. But Shrader's also had more than thirty fights as an amateur boxer, kickboxer, and MMA fighter. And as he was edging into his late thirties, he was going through a hard transition—from being an ambitious fighter who simply *must* dominate everything that moves in a gym to being a teacher whose job is building up, not beating down.

The round began, and I moved forward with my gloves high. We played a bit of patty-cake, pecking each other with jabs and catching them in the palms of our mitts. He started to throw another jab, and I reached out to block it with my right glove. Mark had repeatedly warned me not to reach out to intercept punches, and now he showed me why. The jab was just a feint, and he lunged forward, hooking his fist around my outstretched glove and caving it into the right side of my face. Mark likes to quote Sun Tzu: "All warfare is based on deception."

Earlier that week, I'd held the focus mitts during class while Mark hammered them with punches, demonstrating a two-three combination: right cross followed by atomic left hook. Mark was showing us the brutal, simple physics of hitting. He was twisting his whole body in one direction, then untwisting it the other way; coiling up his life force and uncoiling it as a death force—coiling and uncoiling. Mark says that a fighter's fist is "just the messenger" because its job is to deliver energy generated by the whole body. And the energy it can deliver is enormous, greeting the skull like a twelve-pound mallet moving at twenty miles per hour and imparting as many as one hundred Gs of force. Feeling Mark rip those Gs through the focus mitts and into my arms made me marvel

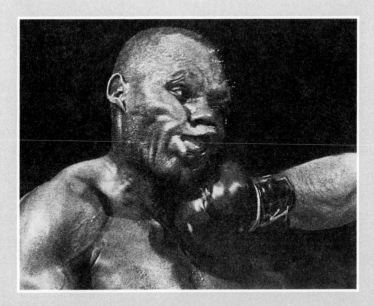

Rocky Marciano's right cross greets Jersey Joe Walcott's chin. You can't see it, but the same shock wave deforming Walcott's face is also rolling and twisting through the soft stuff of his brain.

at the toughness and resilience of the human skull, brain, and neck—that men can be clubbed with such heavy punches and keep living. Now I'd taken one of those punches, and I was still alive.

But just barely. With the punch pain detonated inside my brain. Gloved punches don't hurt your face all that much, unless they flatten your nose or crush a tooth through your lip. The padding distributes the force and dulls the pain. But the full shock wave of the punch still passes through the skull to slosh and jiggle the brain in its casing, just like Jell-O in a mold. Neuroscientists don't fully understand the physiology of a knockout, but here's the gist. The brain is a soggy, fatty, gelatinous meat computer, with chemicals and electrical signals running through its trillions of wispy connections. The shock wave from a heavy blow rolls through the brain like a tsunami, shearing connections and disrupting signals. Effectively the brain shorts out. And the man falls stiff and twitchy to the mat until the brain can reroute the signals and get back online. Feeling that instantaneous brain pain was a eureka moment for me. It made me really *get*—in a way that just watching fights can't—that the main object of fighting sports is to temporarily shut down the other guy's brain. Head punches hurt what they are designed to hurt: not the face, the brain.

Simultaneous with the brain pain my consciousness flickered out, and I started to tip like a chopped tree. But in the next moment I realized that it was just my perception of the world that was tipping, not my actual body, and when I blinked, the world heaved itself upright. I realized that I was reeling across the cage and Shrader was pursuing with a predatory look in his eyes. I backpedaled, weaving here and there, bouncing off the cage. A few times I literally turned my back on Mark in panic and ran for it. But no matter how fast I fled, he was always right there hitting me. The barrage never stopped. Shots to the belly, shocks to the arms, whip-crack jabs, bomb crosses, and the terrible concussive explosions of his left hooks going off inside my brain—filling the cage with a snow of glinting, golden flakes. I tried to fight back, flailing my arms in Mark's general vicinity, but he seemed almost offended that I had the gall to try to hit him, and he stung me with counterpunches.

After what seemed like forever, Mark backed off to let me gasp. Hiding behind my gloves, I flicked my eyes at the clock. The sight crushed me. There were still nearly two minutes left in a three-minute round, and I was already worn-out from the punches, the running, and the fear. Realizing that I was almost helpless from fatigue after just sixty seconds was a second eureka moment. Unless you've fought in the cage, it's hard to grasp how exhausting it is. MMA fans know that fighters have to be strong and skilled, but few really appreciate how freakishly fit the best guys are. MMA demands a sprinter's explosiveness and a marathoner's stamina. When the pace is hot, when the match mixes the constant footwork of striking with the heavy exertion of grappling, the experience feels like sprinting uphill, like drowning in a sea of air. Fighters call it gassing out. And when you gas out, that's it; you're done. Your brain sends commands, but your body can't respond, or it responds so sluggishly that it's useless.

In MMA, as in other sports, it is conventional to speak of "heart." A man with a lot of determination and fighting spirit, a man who never quits, is said to have a lot of heart. This is meant as a metaphor, but it's also literally true. The quality of the physical heart—its ability to push oxygenated blood through the veins—is the best indicator of fighting spirit. A guy in great shape is literally great-hearted. Fighters break when their hearts break—when the heart muscle can't keep up with the body's demand for oxygen.

My heart was sorely taxed, but it wasn't broken, and so when Mark came forward again, I tucked my chin and raised my fists against him, just as he'd taught me. When the round finally ended, Mark gave me a little half hug and apologized: "Sorry, man, that first hook got away from me."

"That's okay," I said, meaning it. He'd given me only what I was stupid enough to ask for. And besides, he'd also just given me the most intensely educational three minutes of my life.

Mark tousled my hair with a gloved hand and said, "Now you know what it's like!" I watched him cross back to his side of the cage. I was thinking, *I'm alive right now only because he likes me better this way.*

Afterward I felt concussed. For the rest of that day and into the next, my vision and thinking were hazy, like someone had thrown a translucent blanket over my head that dulled my perception and slowed my mind. My head throbbed in rhythm with my heart, and when I cleared my sore nose, clots of black blood appeared in the tissue. The whole left side of my face felt as if it had been pushed in by that first left hook, from my right eyeball down to my swollen lip. One of the punches seemed to have knocked most of the feeling out of my mouth, except that touching my aching right eye was like pushing a button that delivered an electric jolt of pain to my front teeth.

Midway through sparring with Mark and feeling him attack my brain again and again, it occurred to me that this was very reckless and stupid. *I make my living trying to think smart thoughts. I'd better cry uncle while I still know my alphabet.* But I didn't cry uncle. Why? It had something to do with honor—something to do with the other guys in the gym, lazing around the cage, watching. So when the bell rang signaling the end of our round, I had one minute to bend over, grip my knees with my hands, and suck wind. And then the bell sounded again. I had two more rounds to go.

FEAR

Fighting deadly duels over slights and gossip might seem stupid and barbaric. But we should avoid falling for a self-flattering narrative that portrays us as the enlightened ones. "Leviathan" is the name the English philosopher Thomas Hobbes (1588–1679) gave to the huge apparatus of state power, from the laws to the judges to the enforcing cops, prison guards, and executioners. The formal duel arose in Europe when Leviathan was weak and men were largely responsible for getting their own justice. A duelist wasn't behaving stupidly when he fought over an insult—because he wasn't really fighting over the insult. The insult was spilled milk. He fought to keep the next guy from even thinking about spilling his milk. So there is a certain madness to the duel. Duelists risked so much for so little. But it was totally sane and smart, too. By dueling, a man demonstrated in a moment of intense risk that he would literally fight to the death anyone who crossed him. And this gave other men excellent reason not to cross him.

Neither was the duel barbaric. The duel wasn't about authorizing unfettered violence. To the contrary, it was about fettering violence—locking it up in tight rules that were as clear and fair as the rules of tennis. The duel system evolved to civilize savage passions. It helped limit conflict to two aggrieved parties and kept it from metastasizing into what you get when you have an honor culture without a dueling system: Hatfield-McCoy–style vendettas, prison shankings, and inner-city drive-bys.

The European duel's greatest civilizing innovation was simple delay. Offense was often given and challenges delivered in hot blood. But duel etiquette demanded a delay between the challenge and the actual duel so the seconds could try to negotiate a peaceful way out. As time passed, rage tended to give way to fear, and men would look for a way out.

On the dueling grounds, the great adversary wasn't really the other duelist so much as the fear. To win a duel you didn't need to shoot straight or slash gracefully. You didn't need to kill your opponent or hurt him worse than he hurt you. You didn't even need to survive. A duel was a bravery contest far more than a skill contest. To win all you really needed to do was show up and not show fear, even if you were mortally wounded. As one dueling manual explained, "I cannot impress upon an individual too strongly, the propriety of remaining perfectly calm and collected when hit: he must not allow himself to be alarmed or confused, but summoning up all his resolution, treat the matter coolly; and if he dies, go off with as good a grace as possible."

Most duelists stewed through a nerve-racking waiting period ranging from a couple of days to a couple of weeks. The waiting period for my MMA duel began the moment I decided to write this book and lasted until my actual fight, more than two years later. For most of that period I lived with a sense of mild anxiety occasionally punctuated by stabs of

The French short story writer Guy de Maupassant (1850–1893). Maupassant's story "A Coward" describes a man on the eve of a duel, struggling with his fear—not of death but of fear itself. The story ends with the coward sitting at his desk before dawn, inspecting his dueling pistol: "He looked at the little black, death-spitting hole at the end of the pistol; he thought of dishonor, of the whispers at the clubs, the smiles in his friends' drawing-rooms, the contempt of women, the veiled sneers of the newspapers, the insults that would be hurled at him by cowards. He still looked at the weapon, and raising the hammer, saw the glitter of the priming below it. The pistol had been left loaded by some chance, some oversight. And the discovery rejoiced him, he knew not why. If he did not maintain, in presence of his opponent, the steadfast bearing which was so necessary to his honor, he would be ruined forever. He would be branded, stigmatized as a coward, hounded out of society! And he felt, he knew, that he could not maintain that calm, unmoved demeanor. And yet he was brave, since the thought that followed was not even rounded to a finish in his mind; but, opening his mouth wide, he suddenly plunged the barrel of the pistol as far back as his throat, and pressed the trigger."

terror. I had set out on a journey that would most likely end with a martial arts master splashing my face across the cage—hitting me in the brain as hard and as fast and as savagely as he could, until he laid me down in a dreamless sleep. But my big fear wasn't of a concussion, or a broken nose, or a torn knee. As in Maupassant's short story, my central fear was of fear itself. What if I panicked cageside and refused to climb the stairs? What if I unconvincingly faked a last-minute injury? What if, once the fight started, I turned and ran—sprinting in circles around the perimeter of the cage while my opponent gave chase? What if, in short, I showed myself to be a coward?

So, like many duelists, I spent a lot of time and energy trying to negotiate a way out of my mess. I negotiated almost exclusively with myself, constantly fondling all of the reasons I shouldn't fight (pain, disfigurement, brain damage, paralysis, disgrace). And then I argued the other side of it. I told myself that MMA wasn't all that dangerous. Look at how many fights I'd seen in which no one died. Plus, in Pennsylvania's amateur divisions, striking the head of a down man—the signature MMA maneuver of "ground and pound"—is against the rules. But then I recalled how many bloody amateur scraps I'd seen—with all the full-force nose punching, gut kneeing, strangling, body slamming, and testicular hazard—which looked unpleasant enough.

Unlike most duelists, I had not only to prepare for my fight but also to steep myself to saturation in the science and history of mano a mano conflict. Fighting can be seductive. It seduces men, and it helps men seduce women, who have always been drawn to the blood on a duelist's hands. But the more I immersed myself in the history and social science of men's fights, the less seduced I felt. I've claimed that the duel was not barbaric. But of course the duel *was* barbaric. It was just that the duel's restrained violence was *less* barbaric than the alternative, which wasn't peace, love, and understanding, but unrestrained violence. The story of the duel is one of (usually) young men getting themselves killed over nothing, or getting their noses cut off by swords, their penises nipped off by bullets, or their brains bashed into comas over spilled beers. How sad it is that the Hamiltons, father and son, got themselves killed. How selfish of the young Russian poet Alexander Pushkin (see chapter 2) to waste his life in a duel when he still had decades' worth of poetry locked inside him. Wasn't there more nobility by far in *not* fighting than in fighting?

About nine months into my training I was pondering these questions as I hobbled around on crutches thanks to a kick to the calf that had temporarily crippled me. I was worried about the long-term damage the sparring might be doing to my brain, about all the ibuprofen I was taking for headaches. I was tired of hurting all the time—of the way my whole body had become a road for migrating pain. I was exhausted from the training and constantly famished from the dieting I was doing to lose weight. And I was a little queasy from all the fights I'd been watching, not on TV but at local MMA events.

Seeing men fight in person is different from watching on TV. Sitting cageside, you can hear the raw smack of the gloves on meat, the grunting and wheezing as the men give blows and receive them; you can feel the body heat radiating from the cage and the occasional spritz of sweat or blood flying into the crowd. One night I sat cageside and watched Tony, one of the toughest fighters at my gym, get pounded to the mat by an even tougher man, and then I followed my staggering friend to the locker room, where he fell to the concrete floor to writhe in his own sweat and vomit. I was almost forty years old. I was an English professor. Did I really want to be part of this world? Did I really want to be in a cage fight? No, I was pretty sure I didn't.

When all my doubts about fighting were reaching their peak, the journalist Matt Polly came out with a book about his own experience as a fortyish intellectual who learns about MMA by taking an actual fight. Polly's book followed on the success of Sam Sheridan's incisive book about fighting, *A Fighter's Heart*, in which the author also trained as a fighter and competed in an MMA contest. And Sheridan was himself late to the party, as decades earlier George Plimpton had written to great acclaim about sparring the light heavyweight champion Archie Moore in

Shadow Box. Even Plimpton had to acknowledge that many other writers had beaten him to the punch, including the crazy sportswriter Paul Gallico, who stepped through the ropes with Jack Dempsey just so he could describe to his readers—in his classic essay "The Feel"—what it's like to be clouted by one of history's greatest heavyweights.

Since Polly's book was published, even the jokey *Time* magazine columnist Joel Stein had gotten into the cage with UFC legend Randy Couture, for a playful sparring match reminiscent of Plimpton's stunt. As I've worked on this book, Hollywood has also put out two movies—*Warrior* (2011) and *Here Comes the Boom* (2012)—that basically tell my story: desperate teachers become cage fighters to stave off financial catastrophe. In short, the hook for my book, which seemed sharp enough when I began planning, seemed to have gone blunt.

So I decided to let it go. I'd watch fights. I'd read every book about fighting, every article. I'd train at the gym. I'd interview fighters. I'd still get an insider's view of MMA. But there was no point in fighting myself. If it hadn't already been done to death by other writers, it had at least been done.

When I told one of the guys at the gym my whole rationale for not fighting, he listened patiently and then replied, half jokingly: "So you're pussying out, in other words?" That's pretty much what the next guy said, too. And in their voices I heard the secret disdain of fighters for the milksop life of every ersatz male who isn't brave enough to fight.

I intended to enter MMA culture as a sort of detached anthropologist who'd live as the natives lived yet always remain somewhat aloof. But I soon found my detachment slipping. I was no longer an observer of the warrior society I'd set out to study. I was its captive. I couldn't back out of my fight without losing face—not just at the gym but among my family, friends, and acquaintances as well. When I told people I was writing this book instead of my usual stuff for English lit nerds, they looked at me differently. And when I showed up at an academic conference with a purple hammock of blood sagging under one eye, I found that somehow,

Jack Dempsey, "the Manassa Mauler." In "The Feel," Paul Gallico writes, "When it was over and I escaped through the ropes, shaking, bleeding a little from the mouth, with rosin dust on my pants and a vicious throbbing in my head, I knew all there was to know about being hit in the prize ring . . . I knew the sensation of being stalked and pursued by a relentless, truculent professional destroyer whose trade and business it was to injure men. I saw the quick flash of the brown forearm that precedes the stunning shock as a bony, leather-bound fist lands on cheek or mouth . . . I learned that as the soldier never hears the bullet that kills him, so does the fighter rarely, if ever, see the punch that tumbles blackness over him like a mantle, with a tearing rip as though the roof of his skull were exploding, and robs him of his senses. There was just that—a ripping in my head and then sudden blackness, and the next thing I knew, I was sitting on the canvas covering of the ring floor with my legs collapsed under me, grinning idiotically . . . I held on to the floor with both hands, because the ring and the audience outside were making a complete clockwise revolution, came to a stop, and then went back again counter-clockwise."

in some very elemental dimension, I outranked all the other men present. And now and then a woman looked at me in the way—or so I've imagined—women look at men who are dashing.

So I decided to fight after all. I fought because I was trapped in a real, live affair of honor. If I fought, I'd gain honor; if I didn't, I'd lose it. I fought out of fear of what people would think and say. I fought because—just like Alexander Hamilton—I was too much of a coward *not* to fight.

And though it may seem like a contradiction, I also fought for all the times, long ago, when I was too much of a coward *to* fight.

TWO

MONKEY DANCE

The male disposition to duel, once it comes on line in development, just keeps going and going. It has no end, only moments of temporary satiation.

John L. Locke

I was a sophomore in high school, I think, screwing around with the other guys at tennis practice. Normally we didn't screw around at practice because we were afraid of our coach. But one of the parents had stopped by, and Coach was chatting with him. So we ran around and joked and whacked balls at one another. A senior named John zinged a ball in my direction. I dodged it and fired back with a joking insult, but the joke flew wide, while the insult tagged him square. John was a hero of the football team who dabbled with tennis in the off-season. He was a shitty tennis player, but he almost made up for it with his linebacker speed and power. When my jibe hit him, he came for me, levitating over the net as he closed the distance. I retreated to the fence, palms up. "I'm sorry," I said. "I'm sorry. I was just kidding."

John seized my T-shirt in both hands, twisted, and jammed his fists up painfully under my chin, yanking me left and right, bouncing me against the jangling chain-link fence. When he let go with his right hand and raised it toward my face, I cowered as low as I could go. But he just shook the hand at me, punctuating his threats with stabs of his index finger. "Okay," I said. "I'm sorry. I didn't mean it."

John walked away, leaving me sagging and red-faced against the fence. All the other players were staring at me, and so were the two men standing cross-armed outside the fence. One was our coach, and the other was my father, the parent who had stopped by on his way home from work. Soon after, practice resumed, and my father went home. We never spoke of it. I think we were both too ashamed of my behavior. My father probably felt that he shouldn't be ashamed of me, but how could he help himself?

I chose this story of being roughed up by John from a big pile of candidate humiliations. From grade school through high school, I attracted bullies. And I don't think I ever stood up to one. There was no amount of being hip checked in the hall, titty twisted, slammed up against the lockers, or called a pussy in front of giggling girls that I would not swallow. I never fought back because I calculated—quite accurately, I have no doubt—that I would have been stomped by my mustachioed, Camaro-driving tormentors. Linebacker John, for example, was older, bigger, and meaner than me, and much, much stronger. My only hope of winning a fight against John would be to viciously attack his fists with my face, maiming his knuckles so badly that he'd have to surrender. (Lest this all sound like a sob story, I can't really blame the guys who pushed me around. They were just alpha predators in a jungle. I probably would have behaved the same way if I'd had the fangs and the claws for it. I wasn't a good kid, just a weak one. In high school I occasionally managed to identify someone even weaker and more isolated than me, and I did my small part to make his life even harder and sadder than it already was.)

I didn't fight back because I couldn't win. But what does winning or losing have to do with it? The movie *Braveheart* opens with the bullying, rapacious English army on the march and the outmatched Scots weighing their options. One chieftain points out that they can't possibly defeat the English, and another replies, "We don't have to defeat 'em. Just fight

Most of us see adolescent bullying as a kind of disease—the result of a bad upbringing or some sort of failure of the culture as a whole. But bullying is as natural as ragweed and cancer. Bullying is a problem, especially among adolescents, in every human society that's ever been studied—from the simplest hunter-gatherers to the most complex industrial societies. Biologists have also identified bully-like behavior as a "relatively common social adaptation in the animal world." Bullying is ubiquitous because it pays. If you are a strong lion, why not take the runt's share of the kill? If you are a strong boy, why not take the wimp's lunch money? We'd like to think that bullies pay a price, and often they do. (Among hunter-gatherers, the worst bullies were sometimes assassinated by coalitions of fed-up victims.) But bullies—especially the ones who are skilled enough to choose victims wisely—actually thrive in adolescence. They are more popular than non-bullies, and they have more dating success.

'em!" I couldn't have beaten the bullying football player, but I could have fought him. I could have taken the sort of brave beating I'd be proud of someday—a beating that would have won me respect from the other guys looking on, that might have made a father proud of his son. When it comes to bullies, all men and boys know by instinct what the Scottish chieftain expressed out loud.

Having acted the coward so many times as a young guy, I began to suspect that I actually was one. And whenever I have walked away from a fight as an adult, I've felt ashamed, even though I knew it was the civilized thing to do. Once I walked away from a stinking, raving homeless guy who wanted to fight me in Atlantic City. I thought less of myself for months. Once a driver—foaming with road rage—tried hard to fight me at a traffic light. I wasn't about to oblige him. I had my three-year-old daughter in the backseat. Driving away, I told myself that nothing good comes from violence and that good men should do everything in their power to avoid it. I knew with absolute certainty that I was doing the right thing. But nothing about it *felt* right, and when I got home, I couldn't stand looking in the mirror. Part of me—and not a small part—felt that the right thing was to burst out of my car and fight the ruffian in the turning lane. If this sounds insane, if it sounds like I'm captive to a barbaric version of masculinity, I plead guilty. My only defense is that I'm not alone. As we'll soon see, this barbaric masculinity is typical of our species, not just our culture.

So I joined the gym to learn about fighting from the inside, but also in search of redemption. I wanted to go into the cage and stand up to guys who outclassed me in strength, skill, and youth—and to get back up every time they knocked me down. I wanted to take the beatings I should have taken decades ago. I never actually dreamed of becoming good at cage fighting. I never thought I could become anything like one of the martial arts demigods in the UFC. For once I just wanted to do a courageous thing. I wanted to show myself and (Christ, don't you think I know how pathetic this sounds?) anyone who might still be watching from high school that I may have been a cowardly boy, but I had grown into a brave man.

FIGHT CLUB

Boxers say that one of the hardest things about becoming a fighter is summoning the nerve to walk through the gym door for the first time. It's pretty easy to approach the door and loiter outside. It's much harder to seize the knob and turn it. In my case, I spent several weeks staring at the door of the MMA gym from the safety of the English Department. When I finally worked up the courage to cross the street and go inside, I stood among the guys milling around before class and felt a wave of relief wash over me. Aside from their youth and tattoos and good hairlines, they were just like me. Far from being the grunting, heavily muscled Neanderthals I expected, most were smallish guys with average or slight builds. There were some fat kids, too. And guys whose eyeglasses and haircuts somehow gave them away as *Lord of the Rings* fanatics. At five feet nine and almost two hundred pounds, I was on the big side for the gym, and on the strong side, too, even if I was pushing forty.

In some ways the other guys were just like I expected them to be. They were not a diverse bunch. They were overwhelmingly young, white, unmarried, and working-class. Like young guys everywhere, they liked farting on one another and calling one another gay and bragging about girls. A few of them were aggressively uneducated, in a "fuck your Kenyan president" sort of way. Aside from me, there have been no married guys at the gym who've lasted more than a few months, no graybeards, very few college boys, and only a handful of women.

But in the most crucial respects the guys at the gym were nothing like I expected. Going in, I expected to find a gang of high school bully types honing their terroristic skills. But I didn't. In fact, in my three years at the gym I've never heard of anyone getting in a fight outside the cage.

Most of the guys have been distinctively nice. Many have been downright sweet. And several have become close friends.

There have been a few scary guys, however. We had a cop who could bench-press 450 pounds. We've had boys who flew around the cage like banshees, seemingly numb to pain or fear. We've had ex-boxers, like Shrader, who could make you feel as helpless as a punching bag. We've had giants who could dominate through bulk and huge crushing strength. We've had standout wrestlers who didn't know what it was like to be tired and could sweep you off your feet and spike you like a football. Every MMA gym has men like this, men who are strong and tough and athletic. And those are the types of guys you see fighting on TV and who shape the public image of what an MMA guy is like.

But they are the anomalies. Most guys at most MMA gyms just aren't like that. They aren't the best athletes you knew from high school, and they aren't the bullies either. Football captains and bullies don't need martial arts. They already know they are strong and tough. Guys turn to martial arts when they fear they are weak.

In *Fight Club*, the novelist Chuck Palahniuk paints the club as a kind of support group for damaged men. And there's an element of that at my gym. Not every guy signs up because he was traumatized by bullies. But many do. Coach Shrader himself was a skinny kid who grew up in a hardscrabble neighborhood full of hardscrabble boys. As a teenager he took up karate, boxing, and kickboxing when the intimidation got old. Or take my friend Nick Talarico, who joined the gym after losing a fight to his girlfriend's ex. Everything about the episode shames Nick. The way he dodged the fight, even though the bullying ex kept calling him out. The way he agreed to fight only after getting drunk enough to drown his fear. The way he got laid down and pounded out before he could throw a single punch. The way practically everyone who mattered—his coworkers, his girlfriend, even his girlfriend's family—knew he was dodging the fight and then actually saw him lose it. "It totally demoralized me," Nick says. "It crushed me bad. I felt like less of a man."

Soon after, Nick shipped out to Iraq with his National Guard unit.

Between street patrols and guard duty, Nick ate like crazy, swallowed supplements like crazy, and heaved weights like crazy. Nick got big and Nick got strong. And when he came home from the war, he signed a contract at the gym. It was expensive for him, but he forked over because "I knew, as a man, I couldn't afford for something like that to happen again."

Five years after losing the fight to his girlfriend's ex, Nick is now one of the toughest, bravest fighters at my gym. He told me the story of his beatdown one day over lunch. When I asked him if the wounds still hurt, he chewed his sandwich and studied the ceiling for a while. He swallowed and said, "I don't think about it every day no more."

DUELISTS IN THE CAGE

I've come to see an MMA gym as a kind of dueling society, much like the ones that existed in Europe into the twentieth century. In France, for example, men joined dueling societies to learn proper swordsmanship in preparation for fighting real duels in the outside world. The same pretty much applies to your average MMA gym. Most MMA guys aren't training to win sport fights. Only a tiny fraction of them will ever compete in an actual sport fight. They train for a lot of reasons, including fun, exercise, and camaraderie. But you can get all that stuff playing pickup basketball, without getting punched in the jaw. The guys at my gym are of an age when physical aggression between men is most common, and of a class in which backing down from a challenge still comes with stiff social consequences. They came to martial arts for the same reason Shrader and Nick did—for the same reason I took up karate after college. If they are challenged to a "duel"—if someone provokes them to fight—they want to be able to handle the situation and not dishonor themselves.

This is how it is at my small-town gym, but honor and dishonor play a big role even at the highest levels of MMA. The UFC is a corporation; like Walmart or Starbucks, its main goal is to make a profit. But even in the

UFC, the fighters are very much driven by honor. Recently I watched the light heavyweight phenom Jon "Bones" Jones massacre last decade's light heavyweight phenom Mauricio "Shogun" Rua. Jones—young and strong and scary—long dominated Shogun from beginning to end, beating him up, tiring him out, lumping his face with sharp elbows. It was soon clear to everyone—fans, announcers, and probably the fighters themselves—that Shogun was hopelessly outclassed. But he hung on bravely as Jones smeared him around the cage. I stood up and started muttering at the TV, as I often do, "Stop the fight. Stop it. Stop it." But the ref didn't stop it. And Shogun wouldn't stop it himself by tapping out. Why not? It's because fighters compete for more than money. MMA's unwritten code duello dictates that even if you are being dangerously kicked, kneed, and punched, it is dishonorable to "tap on strikes" (that is, quit). By taking his beating manfully, Shogun enhanced his honor even in defeat. If he had tapped, he would have been like the boxer Roberto Duran, remembered less for his many displays of almost superhuman tenacity than for the one time Sugar Ray Leonard made him say *no más*.

To speak of MMA as training for duelists, and to lump MMA fights and street fights together with formal duels, might seem like a stretch. But here's why it isn't: MMA, and other forms of prizefighting, are directly descended from a British form of the duel. While aristocrats blazed holes through each other over kerfuffles, working-class Brits hashed out beefs with their fists. But the fights weren't wild melees. They were formal duels, carefully restrained by rules and rituals. Here's how one observer described working-class duels in London around the mid-eighteenth century:

> [If two men have a disagreement] that they cannot end up amicably . . . they retire into some quiet place and strip from their waists upwards. Everyone who sees them preparing for a fight surrounds them, not in order to separate them, but on the contrary to enjoy the fight, for it is great sport to the lookers-on, and they

judge the blows and also help to enforce certain rules used in this mode of warfare. The spectators . . . form a big circle around them. The two champions shake hands before commencing, and then attack each other courageously with their fists, and sometimes also with their heads, which they use like rams . . . Should one of the men fall . . . those who have laid their bets on the fallen man generally encourage him to continue till one of the combatants is quite knocked up and says that he has had enough.

As this accounts suggests, prizefighting traditions—such as having a ring (initially a circle of people, later a "squared circle" of posts and ropes), seconds (as in aristocratic duels) to negotiate for the fighter and work his corner, a preliminary handshake, rounds, time limits for a fallen man to regain his feet (as in modern boxing), and a spirit of fair play (enforced by the spectators at first and referees later on)—weren't drawn up by some committee. They go back hundreds of years to the dueling codes of British workingmen.

The modern age of prizefighting dawned when some clever hustler— an old-time Dana White or Don King—realized that people got more excitement out of watching fights than they got out of almost anything else. This ur-promoter saw that the public's hunger for fights far outstripped the supply of fights to be seen. So he took the whole ritual of the fistic duel and literally put it on an elevated wooden stage, then sold tickets to the show. People came in big mobs, often traveling ridiculous distances and braving arrest (for much of its history, prizefighting was illegal), to stand and watch men hurt each other in a barn or a muddy field. Prizefighting's kinship with the formal duel is evident even today in the way promoters always try to manufacture some kind of beef between combatants. They don't hype the size of the purse at stake; they hype the size of the beef. This is because, in fighting, what *really* sells isn't sport but a counterfeit theatrical duel. The more the promoter spins us a story about animosity between fighters, the more we'll pay to see them scrap.

The blurry line between dueling and sport is evident in the way all the main Western dueling forms eventually evolved into sport versions: dueling with fists, swords, and pistols became boxing, fencing, and even Olympic pistol dueling. In the 1906 Olympic Games in Athens, men fired standard dueling pistols at twenty and thirty meters, aiming for the bull's-eye on the chest of a frock-coat-clad plaster dummy. In the 1908 Olympic Games in London, wax bullet dueling was an unofficial, exhibition sport, with competitors squaring off in heavy canvas overcoats, face masks, and trigger guards (as above) to protect their hands.

Still, most of us think of a sport like MMA as something like the opposite of a duel. After all, traditional duels were fought with deadly weapons, and an MMA contest is an unarmed, and almost always non-lethal, form of combat. (Although no UFC fighter has yet died in the cage, several have died in smaller promotions.) But do these distinctions actually hold up? While it's true that duels were extremely bloody and dangerous in some periods (e.g., France in the late sixteenth century), in others they were almost comically safe (e.g., France around the turn of the twentieth century). Often a duel came down to two men scratching each other's arms with their swords or purposely aiming their pistols wide, with both walking away as winners simply because they'd been brave enough to take the field.

But is an MMA fight actually unarmed combat? Not exactly. Padded gloves were introduced into boxing and MMA in an honest effort to civilize the sports. Reformers thought they were weakening fighters' weapons. In reality, however, they were exponentially increasing the danger of those weapons. This is partly because of the not-negligible weight of the gloves (most boxing gloves weigh about the same as the head of a standard hammer). But it is mainly because the tight wraps and padding make the fist and wrist all but invulnerable to damage. Bare-fisted, a fighter had to carefully aim and measure his blows, throwing far more punches into the padded torso. Gloved-up, a fighter can throw punches with wild abandon, as hard and as often as he is able. If a bare-knuckle fighter threw punches like a gloved fighter, he'd quickly reduce his hands to sleeves of shattered bone. (That's why old-time fighters threw such funny punches from such funny stances. Bare-knuckle fighting required entirely different offensive and defensive techniques.)

Boxing was dangerous in the bare-knuckle era for a lot of reasons: for instance, referees didn't stop lopsided fights, and there were no time limits—fights could stretch on for hours in the heat of the day, with both fighters swilling down brandy like Gatorade. By far the safest thing about bare-knuckle boxing was the bareness of the knuckles. Padded gloves turned boxing from a contest of grit and stamina (what the old-timers called "bottom") into a test of a fighter's ability to inflict brain damage—and to absorb it (that's what it means to say that a fighter has "a good chin").

The famous *Boxer at Rest* (ca. fourth century BC). From the earliest days of combat sports, gloves were weapons. Ancient Roman boxing gloves were like brass knuckles, sometimes studded with spikes. (Virgil's *Aeneid* has a vivid description of a pair of these gloves, stained with blood and spattered brains.) Thai boxers used to dip their hand wraps in resin, then roll their fists in shards of broken glass. Ancient Greek pugilists padded their hands with oxhide straps that protected their knuckles while slashing their opponents' faces. The *Boxer at Rest* was excavated in Rome in 1885. On his hands you can see the Greek-style leather straps, and his face, lumpy with scar tissue, shows the damage they could do. His ears are cauliflowered. His sunken lips suggest a toothless mouth. His nose shows signs of multiple breaks.

Although it's true that classic duels were fought over real disputes between men and MMA fights mostly are not, if we look more closely, even this distinction begins to dissolve. Men who fought duels always commanded massive respect. So over the five-hundred-year history of the European-style duel, many men swaggered around looking for any pretext—no matter how thin—to call another man out. On German college campuses this kind of faux dueling was institutionalized in the *Mensur*. Originally, these duels were based on authentic disputes between students. But as time went on, the supply of real disputes couldn't satisfy the demand of young men to show their courage in a duel. So fights became based on fake, ritualized insults that would give them some pretext for a fight. For the *Mensur*, students wore goggles and a neck guard and madly hacked at each other's faces with razor-sharp swords. They didn't bother much with parrying or defensive footwork. This was both because defense was considered cowardly and because it interfered with the main goal of the fight, which wasn't so much to demonstrate skill as to incur an ugly "bragging scar" that would forever advertise the participants as men of courage, who would suffer no affront.

THE END OF THE DUEL?

In 1897 the great French novelist Marcel Proust exchanged errant pistol shots with a critic who had savaged one of Proust's books and called the author "a pretty little society boy who has managed to get himself pregnant with literature." More than a century later, when a reviewer at a certain tony magazine took the opportunity to fart aristocratically in the direction of my last book—and then to spend several pages luxuriating in the pungency of his own aroma—I thought with some nostalgia of the days when one literary man might squeeze off an honorable shot at another.

Part of the riddle of the traditional duel is why we stopped fighting them. Over the course of roughly a century, from the early 1800s to the end of World War I, the duel disappeared in one country after another. With unusual speed, cultural norms flipped. In most places, the change was so sudden that where fathers might have politely arranged a murder appointment over some slight, their grown sons would not. What happened? Why did these cultures change so quickly?

It's a long story, but I'll abridge. The duel faded away because the culture of honor faded away. And the culture of honor faded away because Leviathan started doing the honor culture's job. In centuries past, men ferociously defended their honor because they were, in reality, defending their lives, families, and property. But when Leviathan started guaranteeing retaliation for crimes against everyone's life and property, the deterrent value of personal honor declined, and risking everything over a slight just wasn't worth it. Leviathan stood up in all its power, allowing individual men to stand down.

This is a conventional story about the end of the duel, and though it's true as far as it goes, it's still misleading. The rise of Leviathan eliminated only one stiff, elaborate form of the duel. To say that the duel died with the formal European-style duel is like saying music died because disco did. Just as music survived the end of disco, honor conflicts survived the end of the formal duel. (If you object that disco never really died, that makes my point about the duel even stronger.) In fact, the duel—in the sense of an escalating conflict over honor—is now what it has always been: the world's leading cause of homicide.

If you don't believe it, go to a bar and start banging shoulders with the guys you pass, muttering, "Watch it, asshole!" When someone protests, scoff, "What's a pussy like *you* going to do about it?" If he still won't hit you, say something appreciative to his girlfriend about her figure or her lustful mouth. Then see how long it takes to get pounded by a man who feels—whether he would put it this way or not—that he would be dishonored and diminished if he allowed your insults to go unpunished.

Let me make two points about this little thought experiment. First, research shows that it is much more likely to work if the whole scene plays out in front of an audience, since no one likes backing down in front of witnesses. Second, men's honor differs from women's, so this experiment is most likely to work when both parties are male. Women sometimes engage in honor-based violence, too, but the insults have to be different. As another experiment, go back to that bar, approach a man, and say, "'Sup, slut?" The man is unlikely to take offense. Maybe he'll slap you a high five or just walk away thinking, *Yeah, deep down I really am a dirty, dirty slut.* Then go up to a woman and call her a wimp. She'll probably just look at you quizzically, wondering what you are about. But if you reverse the insults—calling the woman a slut (or better yet a whore) and the man a wimp (or better yet a pussy)—you will stab at the heart of their honor, and you should be ready to run. For men honor is still inseparable from strength and bravery, which is why the most dangerous insults (pussy, faggot, cocksucker, girl, bitch, and so on) are intended to imply their lack. And for women honor is still tied to ancient notions of sexual propriety. On the rare occasions when women and girls do fight each other, it is most frequently due to insults about sexual behavior.

RITUAL COMBAT

The European dueling system seems, at first blush, so stunningly unnatural—as bizarre and culture specific as Chinese foot binding. But far from being a Western thing, duels are not even a strictly human thing. They are just an embellishment of a natural conflict resolution pattern found across animal species. Historians usually date the beginning of dueling to about five hundred years ago in Europe, but that's millions of years too late.

To see why, consider this perfectly ordinary slice of chimpanzee life. I was at the San Diego Zoo with my wife and infant daughter, staring into the chimp enclosure as the animals peaceably groomed each other's fur and dandled their youngsters. Suddenly the whole space erupted with the hooting energy of a school-yard fight. Two big males—bristling like

The way an audience pressures men to fight is illustrated by the duel between the Russian poet Alexander Pushkin (pictured) and Georges d'Anthès. The two men fought only in the presence of their seconds. But the real reason they fought was because *everyone* was watching. D'Anthès was a charming young military officer who, sick with love for Pushkin's wife, pursued her recklessly until the news spread through society. Pushkin and d'Anthès tried to avoid fighting. D'Anthès wrote that neither man "wanted a bloody denouement, and the point was how we were all to extricate ourselves from this stupid situation without losing our dignity." But one day fashionable St. Petersburg found a scurrilous announcement in the mail: "The Most Serene Order of *Cuckolds . . . have unanimously nominated Mr. Aleksandr Pushkin coadjutor to the Grand Master of the Order of Cuckolds.*" Pushkin suspected that he might be a cuckold, but it was another thing to be publicly taunted over it. He immediately scrawled out his challenge to d'Anthès, charging that the latter's "cowardice and servility" were astonishing (and adding that d'Anthès's second was a "pimp" and an "obscene old woman"). And so Pushkin, one of the world's great poets, was shot through the bowels and died very slowly and painfully at the age of thirty-seven.

porcupines—were having a disagreement. At first they kept their distance from each other, jawing back and forth, baring their teeth, punching dirt, drop-kicking tree stumps. When neither chimp could back the other down with threats, one charged, dragging a big leafy branch behind him. As the other chimps scattered, the two males raced around, screaming. When they finally engaged, it was a fast and seemingly indecisive fight. They rolled in the dirt like conjoined tumbleweeds, and then one chimp broke away in a sprint. That was it. The fight was over.

The main features of this chimpanzee fracas are applicable to other species in at least three respects. First, physical confrontation between members of the same species is usually a male thing. Female chimps do fight, but not with the frequency or ferocity of males. Second, although there's an incredible amount of conflict and competition in a chimpanzee troop, actual violence is comparatively rare. Chimps try to back each other down with bluffs, bluster, and angry screams that roughly translate as *Do you want a piece of this? You do not want a piece of this!* Most frequently, one chimp sees that he is outmatched and backs down without a fight. Third, when neither chimp will back down their fights can be loud, frenetic, and scary to behold, but one chimp will generally tap out before either is severely injured. The same goes for other species. For example, while combat between one-ton elephant seals looks brutal, the bulls are feeling each other out, measuring the strength and sharpness of each other's teeth, and the heft and drive of the bulk behind them. When the weaker bull realizes he is outmatched, he will cut his losses and flop off in retreat.

I'm describing the marvel of ritual combat.* Across a stunningly

---

* The term "ritual combat" has gone a bit out of style, replaced by fuzzier terms like "agonistic behavior" or simply "aggression." Scientists still believe that animals engage in elaborate behaviors to mitigate the risks of conflict, but they no longer believe, as many once did, that animals altruistically refrain from harming members of their own species. They now recognize that animals hold back not for the "good of the species," but simply because they don't want to risk being injured or killed themselves. I'm sticking with the term "ritual combat" because it is still the term general readers will know best, and because it nicely conveys the predictable, dancelike patterns we find in human and animal conflict.

diverse array of species—from beetles to birds to bears to mantis shrimp—the same sort of conflict patterns prevail. The patterns are so strong, and the "etiquette" so unvarying, that some biologists explicitly compare them to duels. These duelly systems prevail across species for a simple reason: ritual combat works. It allows animals to resolve conflicts and thrash out dominance hierarchies without the extreme risks of fighting with no holds barred.

It's the same for people. I used to play in a lunchtime basketball league at the college where I taught. Even though many of the players were middle-aged, the play could get surprisingly fierce, with some trash talk and hard fouls. One day I was guarding one of the college's legion of young football coaches. He posted up on me, pushed off with one hand, and laid the ball in with the other. "Push," I muttered, not calling the foul but letting him know his gains were ill-gotten. "Fuck you," he replied. Something about the contemptuous way he extended his insult as he backpedaled on defense—"*Fuuuuck* you"—made me instantly insane, and I ran after him screeching, "*Fuck you!*"

That was it. That was all. He decided to play defense, and I decided to play offense, and we both let it go. (Or did I? Absurdly, just writing this has quickened my pulse.) Afterward I felt embarrassed. Here I was, a literature professor who'd been raised in the feminized (or at least androgynized) world of left-wing academia and the Unitarian Church. And yet I could have easily fought the guy over . . . what? I had so much to lose—certainly my job, probably my teeth—and so little to gain. And yet, for a furious moment, I was ready to risk everything just to prove, I suppose, that I'd risk everything.

This is a book about the "monkey dance," a term I use to encompass all of the wild and frequently ridiculous varieties of ritualized conflict in human males. But the term isn't original to me. I've adapted it from the self-defense expert Rory Miller, who uses it in a more limited sense. In his day job as a corrections officer, Miller sees macho confrontations on a daily basis. Usually they fizzle before they get violent, just like the confrontation between the football coach and me. But sometimes they don't.

Miller explains that a standard fistfight is like a dance that always follows the same pattern. "The Monkey Dance," Miller writes, "is a ritual, with specific steps. The dance, I believe, is innate. The steps may be cultural. In my culture:

Eye contact, hard stare.
Verbal challenge (e.g., 'What you lookin' at?').
Close the distance. Sometimes chest bumping.
Finger poke or two-handed push to the chest.
Dominant hand roundhouse punch."

Reading the history of men's fights is like reading the same tragically hackneyed script over and over again—the same old story acted out by men who think they are being original. Of course, the whole point of ritual combat is to thrash out disputes in a way that diminishes risk. But diminishing risk isn't, as researchers used to believe, the same as eliminating risk. In many animals, ritual combat is a leading cause of male mortality despite its safeguards. And the same goes for human males. Social scientists have shown that most homicides begin in "altercations of a relatively trivial origin"—someone gets jostled in a bar, flips somebody off in traffic, or tells someone to fuck off playing basketball.

But Miller is right. The monkey dance wasn't invented by any culture; it really is etched in the DNA of our species. The duel is flexible: it allows all kinds of different rules, weapons, and rituals. But there's also a deep structure—a game of move and countermove, dare and double dare—that characterizes all duel forms. As Miller himself suggests, dancing is universal. Different cultures may invent different styles and steps, but it is always obviously dancing. There would seem to be an enormous difference between a jail-yard or barroom fistfight and the duels of Euro-American aristocrats. But there isn't. Or, more properly, dueling codes just formalized and elaborated the standard moves of the human monkey dance—in the same way the opera formalizes and elaborates the universal attraction of humans to melody and beat.

Samurai photographed around 1890. Different forms of the duel have emerged all over the world, but they are still recognizably duels. Always they begin with some sort of trespass or slight, and they are settled according to rules and rituals that limit the carnage. For example, among the Yanomamö Indians of South America, duelists whipped down long roof poles from their huts and took turns smacking each over the head until one man fell. Like the Yanomamö, the Inuit also took turns bashing each other, whether with head butts or roundhouse punches. In Japan, affronted Samurai dueled with swords. Among the Ona of South America, men settled disputes with wrestling challenges. In the Micronesian state of Truk, they did so with fistfights.

We reflexively think of humans as more complex than other animals, and in many respects we are. But when it comes to conflict between males, a standard duel (or fight) runs perfectly parallel to animal versions of ritual combat. When bruisers square off in a bar—or boys on a soccer pitch—the escalating pattern of provocation and retort (the monkey dance) is every bit as hardwired as rams squaring off on a hillside or chimps screaming and brawling in the jungle. When animals fight, the moves are strongly stereotyped. They lock horns; they wrestle; they rise up on their hind legs and spar with their hooves. Everything is instinctive. But the same is more true of people than not. Hollywood has given us the sense that men are competent, even creative, fighters. But in the main we aren't. Before the rise of elaborate systems of martial arts, all fights pretty much looked the same: bluster, push, punch, tackle, gouge.

And there's a good chance that any fight would have started with the eyes.

DUELLY EYES

In the months leading up to my fight, I worried about everything. Worry is what I *did*. Worry is what I *was*. I worried constantly about the weight I needed to lose to squeeze down into my weight class. I worried that I'd get hurt and not be able to fight. I worried that I'd stay healthy and have no excuse *not* to fight. I worried about what might happen to me on fight night. I worried about my opponent: how could I live with myself if, by some fluke, I really hurt him? Above all, I worried that I'd find some way to chicken out in the end, either dodging the fight at the last minute or doing nothing but dodging and running during the fight itself. And then how would I bear the shame?

These were all very good and reasonable things to worry about, because they all bore directly on my physical and mental health. But I also worried about this: what would I do if my opponent came into the cage and stared right at me? This seems like a pointless concern. If you are about to be in a cage fight, the last thing you should worry about—possibly the single least relevant thing—is the direction of your opponent's eyes. Let him look at his toes, or scan the crowd, or stare hard into your eyes. Why should you care?

Here's why. When a guy stares at you before a fight, he's directly challenging you to a staring duel. He's trying to use the weight of his eyes to push yours *down*. And according to fight lore, if you lose the prefight staring duel, you are well on your way to losing the actual fight. Take Mike Tyson, a stare-down master who thrived on intimidation. He always tried to break his opponent with his eyes in order to soften him for his fists. When his opponent looked away—if only for a tenth of a second—Tyson felt that the man had "lost the fight before he even got hit." This is because fighters read gaze aversion as a signal of submission and fear.

So I worried about my opponent's gaze because I was sure I could not hold it. And if I folded in the stare-down contest, I thought I'd feel so defeated and intimidated that I'd fold in the actual fight. In the end, it didn't go down that way. My opponent and I carefully avoided eye contact until the fight was over. But my seemingly irrational anxiety about my opponent's eyes got me thinking about the weird force of the gaze and the most memorable stare-down contest of my life.

When I was a teenager, I visited a zoo with my family. (I promise this is my last zoo story.) I can't recall which one, but I do remember the signs tacked to the glass of the gorilla enclosure: PLEASE DON'T STARE AT THE GORILLAS. *That's dumb,* I thought. *Aren't we here to stare at gorillas?* So I maneuvered around to the side of a salt-and-pepper male who was slumped against the glass, picking at his splayed toes. I fully intended to challenge him to a stare-down duel. But when he turned his face to mine, I stared into eyes that were so liquid and large, so brown and sad, that I was overwhelmed by a sense of kinship. I pressed my hand to the glass, and he raised his hand, too. For a thrilling moment I thought he would press his palm to mine. But then the glass wall boomed as he tried to punk-slap me through it. I stood with my hand on my throbbing heart as he swaggered away, leering back over one shoulder.

As we drove away from the zoo, I pondered the strangeness of it: *How can these crazy apes take mere eye contact as an intolerable affront?* At the time it didn't occur to me that the gorilla enclosure's warning signs would be as apt in any tavern: PLEASE DO NOT STARE AT THE MEN (unless you are a woman, then maybe it is okay). Only there's no need, since everyone knows not only that it is impolite to stare, but it can be dangerous. In the history of dueling, from aristocrats crossing sabers to jailhouse dustups, it's amazing how many fights trace back to the direction of a man's gaze.

People are masters at tracking eyes: at conversational distance we can detect a gaze shift of just one centimeter. And we are extremely touchy about prolonged staring: when a set of pupils lingers on us from across the room, it can feel like an act of physical trespass. If you are skeptical, go to a bar and pick someone out who's your size or bigger (why not make it sporting?) and simply put your eyes on him. Feel free to lean into your stare a little, but with zero malice on your face. There's an excellent chance that the other guy will feel confused at first, then flustered, then angry. Deep in his primate brain he's going to recognize, just like the zoo gorilla did, that you are making the first move in a monkey dance. And he'll feel obliged to make the next move—either fleeing the scene or joining the dance with a stock challenge: "What do you think you're looking at?" Or at least an edgy "Can I help you?"

We find extended eye contact so uncomfortable that we generally avoid it, even with friends. When we converse with a friend, we mostly don't look at each other; we look at the wall, at the clouds, at our wrist freckles. When we do look at our conversational partners, we steal glances mainly when they aren't looking back. In conversation our direct eye contact is glancing. Like magnets touching pole to pole, our eyes meet briefly and then push away after an average of just one or two seconds. There are cross-cultural variations, but in all cultures too much eye contact is taken as a signal of anger, intimidation, or disrespect. This explains why elevator passengers spontaneously orient toward the door. And it probably also explains the long bars in drinking establishments: they allow strangers to drink side by side without the awkwardness—or the danger—of inadvertent eye contact.

Women like to "girl watch," which is generally interpreted as a way to measure the competition. Men are also inveterate watchers of their own sex. But while women are evaluating each other's beauty, men are literally sizing each other up, assessing the most critical predictors of formidability: height and muscular bulk. Men scan each other's faces for cues of toughness and each other's bodies for signs of athleticism or klutziness. And when men feel that they are being sized up, they may subtly inflate themselves so they seem like harder targets. Like other animals, a man who feels threatened stands a little straighter, puffs out his chest, and holds his arms out a little from his sides, all of which make him look taller and thicker. Men are so good at sizing each other up that they don't even need to see each other's bodies to do it. In a 2009 study, the psychologist Aaron Sell and his colleagues showed people photographs of men's faces, with even their necks cropped out. Based solely on facial information, men made quite accurate judgments of who was strong and who was weak.

It's different for women. Females—from baby girls to grown women—hold
eye contact longer than males, especially in same-sex settings. Researchers
have found that the least amount of mutual gazing occurs when men interact with men, and the most occurs when women interact with women. In
addition to prolonged gazing, women are comfortable with other forms of
body language that men find unwelcome or aggressive. For instance, women
demand much smaller circles of personal space. When women converse,
they sit or stand closer together than men do, and they are comfortable
pointing their heads and bodies directly at each other, while men like to
angle off to one side.

When men watch each other, they do so carefully and covertly. It's about as awkward to be caught sizing up a man as it is to be caught dressing down a woman. When a man is caught in the act, he quickly shifts his gaze away. He has been caught ransacking another man's body for information—doing hostile reconnaissance. And if he doesn't look away, the other man will feel that some sort of response is called for, from a verbal challenge to a return of hard eye contact.

The stare-down contest is great evidence for the theory of evolution. In primates, dominance hierarchies are managed less by fights than by duelly eyes. Male monkeys and apes compete in contests of "staring endurance." One monkey starts pacing back and forth, staring unwaveringly at his rival. If the other monkey takes up the challenge, they will both swagger back and forth along parallel lines, holding eye contact even when they change directions. This goes for humans as well. In the prefight stare downs of boxing or MMA, fighters often pace back and forth on parallel lines, holding eye contact just as monkeys do. When they are brought to center ring for the formal stare-down ritual, pacing isn't practical, but a monkeyish swaying from side to side is extremely common.

Sustained eye contact is as stressful for other primates as it is for humans. As monkeys pace through their stare-down duels, the stress hormone cortisol floods their blood. If neither monkey looks away, there's a good chance of escalation to an actual fight. But usually the painfully unpleasant stress builds until one monkey breaks his gaze, effectively admitting subordinate status. At bottom, a primate stare-down duel is a stress-tolerance duel: which monkey can tolerate the unpleasant sensations that come with all that cortisol in the blood?

The same goes for men. Imagine two business rivals debating across a boardroom table. One man stares at his rival as he forces his point home, and his rival holds his gaze. Both men are instantly aware that they are in a macho duel and that whoever looks away first will lose. As with other primates, a human staring contest is also a stress-out duel. When lab subjects are shown images of staring faces, more dominant

individuals tend to stare back, and more submissive types feel an unpleasant spike in stress and thus avert their eyes, granting dominance to
the photograph.

MONKEY DANCERS FOR PRESIDENT

Men's dominance dances may seem like macho nonsense, but that
doesn't keep them from mattering a lot. Nowadays politicians don't fight
deadly duels against their political rivals. But they do compete in formal verbal duels, in which what they say with their bodies matters as
much as what comes out of their mouths. If you were to read over the
transcripts for the first presidential debate between Mitt Romney and
Barack Obama in 2012, you might come away thinking that both men
had their stumbles along with their winning flourishes, and that the
contest was more or less a draw. But as Richard Nixon learned when he
took on John F. Kennedy in the first televised presidential debate in 1960,
there's more to a verbal duel than words. Nonverbal elements such as
posture, facial expressions, perspiration, and gesticulation all affect
the score. The consensus among people who watched the first Obama-
Romney debate—both Republicans and Democrats—was that Romney
won big. He was more energetic, and his gestures were typical of dominant individuals in that they were large and sweeping, demanding more
space. Obama's body language was more typical of a subordinate: he
kept his elbows tucked close to his ribs, making little *T. rex* gestures
with his forearms and hands. Most important, in contrast to the president, who spent an inordinate amount of time frowning down at his
lectern, Romney held direct eye contact with the camera, with the moderator, and with Obama himself. On the occasions when Obama did
meet Romney's gaze, he was almost always the first to look away. In the
course of the ninety-minute debate, Obama made the submissive move
of looking down five hundred times more than Romney did.

Obama was roundly panned by his own side following this debate, and his lead in the polls eroded. He knew he needed a stronger showing in the second debate, not only when it came to matching Romney's aggressive rhetoric but also in matching the virility of Romney's nonverbal cues. What ensued was the most fascinating and anxiety-provoking presidential debate in recent memory. It was a massive contest for male supremacy, waged with tough words, forceful gestures, and challenging eye contact. Obama was more energetic and engaged, and was armed with sharper rhetorical darts. But he also came prepared to literally stand up to Romney. Unlike in the first debate, where the candidates were entrenched behind lecterns, now they were free to roam around a large circular stage. The result was, as many pundits noted, like a pantomime fight, with the two men physically circling, squaring off, and trading rhetorical blows. Often they closed almost to within punching distance, gesticulating, accusing, and making strong eye contact. As Sarah Kaufman commented in the *Washington Post*, "At times, the thinly veiled aggression grew so hot—with President Obama and Mitt Romney closing in on each other like street fighters—that you wondered if the two would come to fisticuffs." (And then what would have happened? A bench-clearing brawl between rival Secret Service details?)

Obama lost the second alpha male contest as well. Romney was more likely to fire his answers and questions directly into Obama's face, while the president more often addressed the moderator or the crowd. And Romney kept striding forcefully into the neutral zone dividing the two halves of the stage, invading Obama's territory. Like a savvy prizefighter, Romney physically claimed the center of the ring, pushing Obama to one side of the stage and holding him there like a boxer pummeling an opponent against the ropes. And all the while, Romney bore into Obama with his fierce gaze (though he usually managed to mask the fierceness with a frozen smile).

Obama made forceful displays of his own, striding up to within a few feet of Romney so they could both gesticulate and try to talk over each other. Obama and Romney are the same height, but Obama's build is slighter than Romney's, and Obama acted like the smaller man: whenever they came together, Obama broke contact first. And when their eyes met, Obama almost invariably looked away first.

So if Obama came in second in this alpha male contest, why was there such a strong consensus that he had won the second debate, and why did he—not Romney—win the election? My point isn't that the more dominant candidate always gets to be president. (If he did, guys like Chuck Norris or Mr. T would always be elected president.) My point is that deep, duelly primate dynamics are absolutely relevant to who gets to be president. In the second debate Romney probably overdid the macho stuff (as he had in the primary debates, where in an effort to shut Rick Perry up, he'd reached out and put a hand on Perry's shoulder). Just as important, Obama made up for a performance in which he seemed weak with a performance in which he seemed plenty strong enough, without sacrificing any of his likability or reputation for class. If Obama hadn't been able to make such a strong nonverbal display, Romney might have become president.

Now, sticking with the subject of masculine display, let's talk muscle.

THREE

TOUGH MEN

*The greater size, strength, courage, and pugnacity of
the male, his special weapons of offence, as well as his
special means of defence, have all been acquired or
modified through that form of selection which I have
called sexual selection.*

Charles Darwin

I was at the college fitness center with my friend the poet. We were racing along shoulder to shoulder on our treadmills, cutting furtive glances at each other's speedometers. Neither of us much cared to win this cardiovascular duel, but we were both anxious not to lose it.

Since I first went to work at the college, the poet and I had been meeting for regular sparring sessions. Sometimes we played basketball at the gym (I always crushed him) or swam laps at the pool (he always crushed me), but mostly we just argued. We'd meet at our favorite bar, order bourbon backed by beers, and charge straight into a war of words, mostly about things we knew nothing about.

The poet was a useful friend for a scholar like me to have because he had a talent for being wrong in intelligent ways and the stamina to defend his errors to the last. Arguing with the poet always sharpened my thinking. But he got raw from being my whetstone, and so he man-dumped me for a Muppet-headed horn blower in the college music department. It

Academic life may seem comfortable and sedate from the outside, but it's fiercely competitive. Professors gain advancement not only by thinking newer and smarter thoughts but also by mastering verbal forms of the duel. I'm drafting this paragraph at 35,000 feet, flying back from a conference in Europe that brought together twenty scholars and scientists (mainly men) to argue about the nature and nurture of violence. It got violent. No one got punched, but as the academics argued, there was a lot of hard eye contact, tightly clenched jaws, sarcastic eye rolling, and dismissive stage sighing. In two days of debate I don't think any of us significantly modified our positions. It was just a verbal battle royal—a contest to see who could display a bigger peacock's tail of learning and verbal razzle-dazzle while most efficiently disemboweling the other guy's argument. I stumbled early in the fight and got hammered down by a hooting primatologist. Then, before I could gain my feet, an elderly historian from Oxford doddered over to drag his blade across my throat. I don't think anyone actually won the battle, but a bespectacled, velvet-voiced literary theorist named Joseph Carroll clearly walked out with the biggest wad of scalps steaming on his belt (including, I'm glad to report, the silvery pelt of the elderly historian).

wasn't a formal breakup. In the spineless way of males, the poet just stopped calling. And whenever I invited him out for a drink, he'd text back that he was already out with the horn blower.

I can't blame him. For all his intelligence and argumentative stamina, the poet is just a poet, trained to make beauty out of words. He's not what I am: a battle-scarred academic pit fighter, who's been training for twenty years in all the forms of rhetorical judo. When it comes to the verbal duel, the poet is beneath my weight class, and I don't think I ever let him stagger from the bar with anything more than a Pyrrhic victory.

Not long after he man-dumped me, I found the poet pounding away on a treadmill at the fitness center. I climbed on the adjacent machine, and we huffed along, making small talk while discreetly monitoring each other's speed. We asked after each other's families. We discussed classes and writing projects. We avoided arguments. We noticed the college girls, all pertness and ponytails, bouncing on the elliptical machines or waving small pastel dumbbells over their heads. We noticed the college boys, all muscle and machismo, loading bars with huge steel disks and driving them up with groans. The girls wanted to be smaller. The boys yearned to take up more space in the world.

I was already in the early stages of planning this book, and I'd begun the long process of working myself into something like fighting shape. I knew from watching the UFC that it's no fun gassing out in a cage fight. When a guy gasses, he stops being a real competitor and starts being a helpless assault victim. Fighters say that "fatigue makes cowards of us all," and it does. In sparring, I've been so helplessly exhausted that lying on my back being battered by punches, I've almost hoped for that anesthetic punch that would put me to sleep. It's like that terrible moment in the nature documentary when the gazelle, having run from the lion and struggled in its jaws, finally goes limp. You can see from the eyes that the gazelle is still alive, but it's so tired that it succumbs to the fangs almost with relief.

So I made it a main priority to be in top cardiovascular condition, spending a lot of time running on treadmills and trails, or out at the football field, gasping through Mark Shrader's draconian MMA calisthenics or plodding up and down the stadium steps. I also needed to sweat my richly marbled flesh down to something like fighting weight. Going into this project, I weighed about 200 pounds. Since MMA fighters compete in defined weight classes, I could either hit the doughnuts even harder and take on the 205-pounders (light heavyweight), or I could diet down to 185 (middleweight) or even 170 (welterweight). Because it's no fun being the little fat guy in a cage fight (and since I'm even more chicken than I am glutton), I decided to cut all the way to 170. Light heavyweights are enormous men—natural heavyweights who have temporarily starved themselves down to 205. Fighting them would be a bid for martyrdom. But most 185ers are pretty enormous, too—tall, gristly guys who also have starved themselves to make weight. At five feet nine, I'd be a soft and stubby middleweight. By doing my cardio work and cutting to 170 lean pounds, I'd dodge the big guys and up my odds of achieving my primary fight goal: survival.

And so the poet and I gerbilled along side by side, trying to undo the fatty ravages of our ultrasedentary occupations. The poet was watching the young men heaving and posing, watching them hold a casual flex as they swaggered past the girls on the way to the water fountain. Quoth the poet: "Do they really think that's what a man is? They don't know what masculinity is." The poet didn't so much say it as sneer it.

He was probably groping toward a good point. He was probably saying that masculinity is more than a muscular facade. He was probably suggesting that the boys were putting on an external show of masculinity while neglecting deeper dimensions. And he probably also had a good point about how men are falling now, almost as hard as women, for whatever the magazine covers say we ought to be. The poet would later call this new masculine look—with the swollen pecs, sharp abs, and smoothly shaved torso—"a porno aesthetic." But the poet was also circling back toward one of the most contentious topics of our tavern sparring sessions. He was flirting with the modern truism that concepts such as "masculinity" have no natural basis. Gender isn't real. It's a game, a charade, something people made up. The young men were muscled dupes, straining after an arbitrary cultural ideal.

I didn't agree. I had once been one of those small boys who yearned to be big—heaving metal, forcing down protein shakes, packing heavyweight meat on my lightweight bones. I couldn't help myself; I flung down the gauntlet. "Poet," I said, "can you name a single society in world history where physical strength *wasn't* part of the masculine ideal?" Before he could answer, I provoked him a little further. "We didn't invent masculinity. It's not a cultural thing. It's not even a people thing. Watch an alpha chimp or a silverback gorilla strut around. They're macho!" And we fell into our familiar ritual—our all too *masculine* ritual—of competitive disputation, where the point is less to be right than to win the fight.

The poet was, like me, a husband and father closing fast on forty. I told him that he'd forgotten what it was like to be a young man competing for his place in life. I said he'd lost sight of how useful it is for a male *Homo sapiens* in almost any walk of life to be big and formidable. The boys were pumping themselves up in obedience to a primordial law of nature: *The big get their way, while the small give way.*

I knew this law because I had lived it. When I let linebacker John rough me up on the tennis court, I did so because he was so far out of my weight class that resistance wouldn't have just been futile, it would have been hilarious. But here was my problem. When I was young, everyone was out of my weight class. By the time I got to college, I had matured into a factory-standard human male—perfectly average in height and build. But my growth came very late, and through all my schoolboy years I was always a class runt.

Everyone knows that it's no fun being the heavy, unattractive girl. The other girls give you looks, and the boys don't look at you at all, except to taunt you. I think fewer people understand that being a small, weak boy can be equally hard. The girls don't look at you, and the other boys don't look at you much either, except to stare you down.

So I understood what the boys at the college gym were after, and I sympathized. I don't think they were chasing a porn aesthetic so much as they were chasing respect. The culture of ordinary young men really isn't so different from that of prison. As in prison, strength equals respect in its most basic dimension: when you are strong, guys don't fuck with you. One of the most reliable findings in the social sciences is that exploiters—from school-yard bullies to parking-lot rapists—like their victims meek and weak. Bullies and criminals aren't looking to test themselves in fair fights. So young men bulk up on the weights for many reasons. They want to look good. They may want to improve in sports. But they are also building up an arsenal of deterrence. Muscle is a bold advertisement: *I am not a rabbit. I am not food.*

WHY MEN ARE THE WAY THEY ARE

The poet's views on masculinity were shaped by powerful authorities. For about half a century academic thinking about gender has been guided by the theory of the "sex/gender system." According to this theory, sex—in the sense of ovaries and testes, penises and vaginas—is biological. But gender—all of the attributes we typically describe as "masculine" or "feminine"—is purely cultural. We all emerge into the world as genderless blobs that parents, media, and teachers torture into culturally appropriate shapes. The act of taking the soggy mass of human raw material and mashing it into a rigid gender mold has been called "boying" and "girling."

Outside the win-at-all-costs context of manly disputation, I doubt the poet would go this far. Most people who have met actual men and women, boys and girls, know that the sex/gender theory can't be entirely true. And science is very much on their side. Researchers haven't found support for all of the stereotypical sex differences. In fact, as Melvin Konner argues in *The Evolution of Childhood*, most sex differences claimed as natural and universal turned out to be "not real." But scientists have found very real and robust sex differences in the areas that are central to this book: competitive and violent behavior.

Indeed, the basic foundations of masculinity and femininity are much older than humanity. With some exceptions I'll get to in a moment, the basic masculine and feminine traits—males more competitive and aggressive, females more peaceable and nurturing—extend across diverse animal species. Over the past few decades biologists have determined that masculinity and femininity are rooted in something very simple: how fast the two sexes can reproduce (biologists call this the "maximum reproductive rate"). In the main, the maximum rate of reproduction in female animals is much slower than in males. For example, the most fertile woman in history was an eighteenth-century Russian named Mrs. Feodor Vassilyev, who is said to have given birth to sixty-nine children. (She specialized in litters of triplets and quadruplets.) That's impressive, but most healthy young men, given the opportunity, could conceivably produce that many pregnancies in a month or two.

Look at it this way: in the course of their lives, men produce sperm in astounding abundance—trillions of guppylike cells lashing through gallons of semen. By contrast, women produce only four hundred eggs in their entire lives. An average man produces 255 million sperm per ejaculation. That means that a man who averages two ejaculations per week for fifty-five years produces roughly 1,458,600,000,000 sperm, or 3.6 billion times more sex cells than the average woman. (If you lined up one man's lifetime sperm production head to tail it would circle the equator twice; a woman's eggs would circle a ping pong ball once.) Men manufacture this superabundance of sperm in hopes of offering it, as generously as possible, to women. But here's the rub: women are distinctly uninterested in absorbing all the semen men have to offer. And so there is sharp competition—economic, physical, social—among the world's billions of eager sperm donors to be favored by the world's less eager sperm receivers. Moreover, because of pregnancy, because of the way nursing infants suppresses fertility, because menopause lops decades off women's reproductive lives, and because of a worldwide tendency toward polygamy

An Inuit woman. Across species, most male aggression is ultimately tied to a shortage of female reproductive supply relative to male demand. Here's one test of whether the same thing is true of humans: When the default shortage of fertile women is exaggerated, do males become even more ornery? Yes, they do. Wherever you find shortages of young women—due to female infanticide, polygamy, or other factors—you always find the same thing: men behaving badly. As the political scientists Valerie Hudson and Andrea den Boer concluded in their book *Bare Branches*, the relationship between shortages of women and violence in males is "substantiated by empirical evidence so vast and so compelling as to approach the status of social science verity." Among the Inuit, for example, high rates of female infanticide in the past meant that there were not enough marriageable women to go around, which resulted in pitched competition among the men and high rates of male mortality. The Inuit themselves were aware of this relationship, saying that "boys will have to kill each other" in order to win wives. The reference to "boys" is telling. Universally, young *unmarried* men are responsible for the lion's share of violence. The fact that marriage pacifies young men is a good clue to what unmarried men are so worked up about.

(some guys always hog more than their fair share of the women), there are always *far* fewer fertile females in circulation than fertile males. This is true today, and the discrepancy was even larger in the past. Before the invention of reliable means of birth control, sexually mature females ovulated much less frequently, because they were usually pregnant or nursing.

The history of sharp male reproductive competition is written into our DNA. Genetic studies show that each of us has twice as many *different* female as male ancestors. What this means—as a genetic fact, not a theory—is that maleness has always been a high-stakes competition. In the past men were twice as likely as women to die childless. But those men who competed well won big, reproducing with multiple women. (An extreme example is Genghis Khan, who left behind hundreds of children and, according to modern genetic studies, is now the paternal ancestor of about sixteen million people.) Women also had to compete for the best mates, but because men make such unstinting sperm donors, women rarely faced total reproductive failure. This started men and women down different strategic paths. For women, dangerous risk taking usually made less sense, because they were betting heavily on a limited upside. With their low risk of total reproductive failure and their low likelihood of Khan-like (or even Vassilyev-like) reproductive success, women were smart to play it safe. But for men, the path of intense reproductive competition was the only path available. Men who sat out the competition might have long lives, but they were likely to be celibate lives. All men alive today are descended from ancestors who, for uncounted thousands of generations, succeeded in the intense competition just to become someone's grandfather.

This competition to attract mates and defeat rivals is what Darwin called sexual selection. And in males the suite of features shaped by generations of consistent high-risk, high-reward competition for mates is what we call masculinity. As Darwin indicated, these features consist of being bigger, stronger, more bellicose, more willing to take risks, and more sexually eager. They also include slower sexual maturation in

A female phalarope. The shortage of female reproductive supply relative to male demand is the rule across species. But in species in which males invest more in reproduction than females, typical sex roles may be reversed. In a shorebird called the phalarope, for example, the drably colored males incubate the fertilized eggs and take care of the hatchlings, while the brightly colored females fight over the males, attempt to mate promiscuously, and take no part in rearing the young. In such sex-role-reversed species, the males take on typically female characteristics: they are smaller, less aggressive, and much pickier in mate selection. The females take on typically male characteristics: they are more promiscuous, more aggressive, and strongly conspicuous in courtship displays. This shows that masculinity and femininity are *not* essential products of "maleness" and "femaleness." Females are "feminine" when reproduction costs them more; in the rare cases where males invest more in reproduction, they exhibit "feminine" traits.

males, higher male mortality, and more male infants born (to make up for that higher mortality). All these factors apply not only to human males but also very broadly across the animal kingdom, including to most mammals and nonhuman primates. This is because precisely the same reproductive pressures have applied in other species. Put baldly, this means that masculinity has an overriding purpose. Whether in men or musk oxen, masculinity is for prevailing in the competition for mates. It's about being big and fierce enough to win fights, or to intimidate a rival into yielding without a fight.

That intense mating competition has powerfully shaped the males of other species is not controversial. Male gorillas are about twice as big as female gorillas. This is because gorillas are a harem-holding species: a male passes on genes only if he can outfight or intimidate a horde of angry, horny bachelors. But have human males been shaped by a similar history of intense mate competition? The most conventional answer is no, not so much. Size differences between men and women are usually deemed "modest." The average man is only about 10 percent taller than the average woman, and 20 percent heavier, suggesting relatively minor male-male sexual competition. (I must point out, however, that a 20 percent weight advantage is highly significant. In weight-class-governed combat sports—wrestling, boxing, powerlifting, MMA—there's nothing "modest" about a 20 percent weight difference. In MMA terms, it would be like sending a 135-pound bantamweight into the cage to get mauled by a 170-pound welterweight.)

But these blunt size comparisons are highly misleading in the human case because women are fatter than men. Delightfully fatter, I hasten to add. In modern societies, chronic obesity and fashion's vagaries have teamed up to give fat a bad name. We tend to think of fat as unattractive. But nature has fattened women up not only to maintain their fertility but also for the sheer sensory delight men take in women's shapeliness. The artful distribution of female fat—swelling out here, crimped in there; plumping the buttocks, hips, breasts, lips, and cheeks—is the essence of women's physical beauty. When the fat-free body mass of men is compared with that of women, men are 40 percent heavier than women and have 60 percent more lean muscle mass, 80 percent more arm muscle mass, and 50 percent more leg muscle mass. Thus, when it comes to working brawn—not overall weight—humans show massive sex differences.

How large is the difference? As the biological anthropologist David Puts observes, "The sex difference in upper-body muscle mass in humans is similar to the sex difference in fat-free mass in gorillas, the most sexually dimorphic [sexually differentiated] of all living primates." When it comes to upper body strength, only one in a thousand women can outlift the average man.

WOMEN ARE WONDERFUL

About two years ago I was eating breakfast at a diner with my two daughters, Abigail, age eight, and Annabel, age five. Abigail accidentally dropped a bite of pancake in her dollop of ketchup. "Dare you to eat it," I said.

"No way."

"Come on," I thoughtlessly prodded, "be a man."

Abby replied, "I'm not a man," and she pushed the pancake daintily to the rim of her plate. I was a little chagrined that she was taking me so literally, and so I asked her, "What does it mean when I say 'Be a man?'"

"Be tougher," she said.

Little Annabel was swinging her hand above her head in a kindergartner's *I know, I know, I know* fashion. "What does it mean," I asked her, "to be a man?"

"Being strong," she said.

From the mouths of babes. There's nothing complex about masculinity. Masculinity is simply strength and toughness—of body and mind. There are many valid ways to be a man, things that cultures respect or disrespect, but there is no masculinity without strength. This isn't just a Western thing. In a study of thirty cultures—including New Zealand, Finland, Zimbabwe, Malaysia, Pakistan, Bolivia, and Trinidad—definitions of masculinity and femininity hardly fluctuated at all. As a rule, people said they did not believe that men and women differed in all respects, and they did not view one sex as superior to the other. But in every culture, men were seen as more active, adventurous, dominant, forceful, independent, and strong. And in every culture except for one (but not always the same one), males were seen as more aggressive, autocratic, daring, enterprising, robust, and stern. Given the domineering tendencies implied in these lists, it's no wonder that studies uniformly show that *both* sexes find women more likable than men. Psychologists describe this as the "WAW Effect": Women Are Wonderful (at least in comparison with men).

These studies of what people *think* men and women are like are consistent with studies of what men's and women's personalities actually *are* like (men more dominant, women more tender and friendly). They are also consistent with evidence showing that children begin developing masculine and feminine traits before they even know the difference between boys and girls. (Boy toddlers, for example, are much more likely than girl toddlers to hit, push, and bite.) Just as crucially, the evidence goes against the typical socialization arguments for the origins of gender roles. Far from endorsing masculine play patterns, for instance, schools have harshly cracked down on "boy" forms of play for decades, enacting zero-tolerance policies toward all forms of real and pretend aggression (such as gunplay or swordplay) and most forms of rough-and-tumble play (such as wrestling and tackle football). And contrary to popular belief, parents do not actually differ much in the way they treat their sons and daughters. Summarizing the findings of a massive psychological study, Anne Campbell reports that evidence for "differential treatment was virtually nil." Parents strain at least as hard to inhibit aggressive and boisterous behavior in boys as in girls.

We are all trained to think of stereotypes as stupid, lazy, and mean. But stereotypes about masculinity became so entrenched for a reason:

Girls having a tea party. Studies of sex hormones also support a strong biological component of masculinity and femininity. For example, "female monkeys exposed to androgens [e.g., testosterone] early in development are masculinized with respect to sexual behavior, rough play, grooming, and some learning abilities." And the same goes for people. There is a condition called congenital adrenal hyperplasia (CAH) that occurs when female fetuses are exposed to abnormally high doses of male hormones in utero. Compared with unaffected girls, CAH girls are much more like typical boys in their levels of pretend and real aggression, their liking for sports, their attraction to rough-and-tumble play, their tendency to seek out male playmates, their liking for toys such as guns and trucks, and their indifference to toys such as dolls and dress-up clothes. When they grow up, CAH women are also more aggressive, less empathic, and more likely to report sexual attraction to other women.

they are mainly true. To be timid, muscularly weak, and emotionally shaky is now and has always been unmasculine. Masculinity is not a cultural invention. It is not the result of a conspiracy by men against women. It is a real thing that has evolved over millions of years as a response to the built-in competitive realities of male life. This isn't to suggest that masculinity is entirely innate, leaving no room for cultural variation. In Ancient Greece, for example, one's status as a manly man wasn't compromised by public weeping or having sex with boys. And obviously the brawny masculinity you'd find in a warrior society is a lot more, well, masculine than what you'd find in a middle-class American suburb. But the differences would be of degree, not kind.

And there's another thing about "being a man" that Annabel and Abby left out. Being a man has always required more than a penis. To earn the status of a *real* man, not an ersatz one, a guy must prove he has the right stuff.

RITES OF PASSAGE

The natives swarm together in the shape of a ring. Then the prettiest maidens escort two young braves to the center, where, to the rhythm of drums and the howl of song, the braves fly at each other with their fists. An elder circles the braves, watching for fouls and periodically making them stop and rest. While the braves squat down to gasp and smear blood from their eyes, the maidens move to the center and shiver their abundance to jungle beats until it is time for the braves to fly at each other again. They fight until one brave goes down and cannot rise up, or until the elder says it is enough. Then, if the braves have fought well, the people cheer them, and the maidens usher the next set of braves forward to fight. In this festival, the fighting continues deep into the night.

The natives I've described aren't from some faraway land. They are West Virginians competing in an amateur boxing tournament known as Toughman. Entering the minor-league hockey arena where the fights were being held, I bought myself a hot dog, a beer, and a black T-shirt with the Toughman code scrawled across the back: TOUGHMAN: NO CRYING, NO BITING, NO KICKING . . . *bleeding allowed.* The last two words dripped down the back of the shirt in a blood-red font. On the way to my seat I paused at a trash can, took one greedy bite of my hot dog, and dropped the rest in the bin before I could change my mind. I took one long pull at the beer, then used the rest to slowly wash the ketchup off my hot dog in the bin.

I had come to Toughman out of a mix of curiosity and desperation. Coach Shrader and I had been trying to line up a fight for me for months, only to watch them fall through one after the next, over injuries or licensing or because the state commission rejected a proposed matchup (usually after reasonably concluding that my much younger and more experienced opponent might actually kill me). Once, I went through all the prefight anxiety and all the misery of the final weight cut, only to be told at the weigh-in that my opponent, dreading the legendary fistic prowess of English professors, had chickened out.

This was an unhappy phase of my life, combining all the miseries of the writing life and the fighting life: the dread, the drudgery, and the isolation. Writers get isolated because the job makes you weird and introverted: as you get deeper and deeper into a project, you live more and more inside your own skull, and you can almost feel your already puny social skills (which probably led you to writing in the first place) shriveling down to nothing. Fighters get isolated, too, largely because of the food problem. An MMA fighter's relationship to food is as adversarial as a runway model's or a ballerina's. When you are struggling to stay at fighting weight, you suddenly realize that all human social life is lubricated with greasy food and intoxicating drink. And so when your hoggish, dipsomaniacal friends get together to bludgeon their livers and digestive tracts, you have to stay home chasing steamed chicken with tap water. For months I tried to line up a fight, and for the whole time I was hungry, cranky, and lonely. I was skinny, too, with my usual jowl line giving way to something like a jawline. But the magazines lie: abs don't fix everything. Or maybe that's because, even with visible abs, my belly wasn't exactly flat. A few days before my eventual fight I had cut down to a lean 176 pounds. I woke up that morning dizzy with hunger, then staggered shirtless to the kitchen. My daughter Abby watched me from the kitchen table, appraising my midsection. "I think you're pregnant," she said matter-of-factly. I turned to her little sister, who was jamming huge spoonfuls of dry Cheerios with sugar into her mouth, and asked, "Do I look pregnant to you?" Annabel came over to pat the taut curve of my belly. "Yeah, you look a little bit pregnant." Anxious to spare my feelings, she hastened to add, "I'm not saying you're fat, just that you look a little pregnant."

So I had come to West Virginia on a reconnaissance mission. If I couldn't get an MMA fight pretty soon, maybe I'd try Toughman instead. Taking my seat, I saw all the young men already lined up in fighting pairs, waiting for their turn in the ring. The sight of them in their mismatched gym shorts and tennis shoes, fidgeting nervously with their hand wraps, reminded me a little of slaughterhouse cattle working their way down the chute. As soon as one pair finished, the next pair hurried to take their place. They cycled in and out of the ring fifty times in the space of a few hours. The music was painfully loud kill-death-fuck music—the barbaric yawps of metal and punk and gangsta rap. And the rush of angry noise never stopped coming, not even when the fighting started. Thirty or forty fights into the night, the whole crowd seemed numb to it all. But then two wild men with stringy hillbilly hair, pasty skin, and meth-head arms attacked each other with spastic abandon, and the crowd rose to roar in salute.

Toughman fighters aren't pros, aspiring pros, or even talented amateurs. They are regular guys from the neighborhood: pizza delivery boys, dishwashers, maintenance men, and eighteen-year-olds who play football or baseball for local high schools. Toughman is a contest of raw toughness, not skill. And toughness is defined at least as much by the pain a man can take as by the pain he can give. Toughman fighters don't have to be fit or particularly athletic, they don't go in for fancy dancing

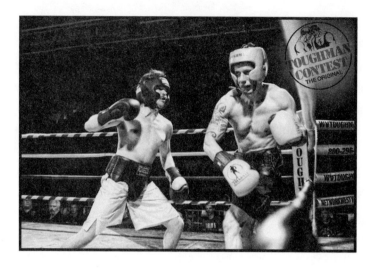

or feinting, and they certainly don't sink to sissy stuff like throwing jabs. Toughman fighters rush forward, leading with the crowns of their heads. They meet at center ring and try to decapitate each other with punches that travel in long parabolas. They throw and throw until someone falls, or until they use up their wind and lurch into the ropes, embracing fiercely, drumming each other's kidneys with their fists.

Plenty of women were on hand to cheer the boxers, but none were there to punch each other. This isn't because women are excluded. On the contrary, women are encouraged to fight, with victors in the women's division taking home bragging rights and a thousand-dollar check, just like the men. But usually only a handful of women sign up, and the night I was in attendance, there wasn't a single female fight.

Or did the women just fight differently? Between rounds, the kill-death music faded out and the dance club music faded in, and the young women took their turns in the ring—posing in their bikinis and stiletto heels, twitching their plump tails like bunnies. When it was all over, one of them was crowned "Prettiest Girl in the Ohio Valley." The rituals of Toughman may initially seem extreme or exotic while they hardly differ from what you find in football, the most mainstream of American sports. At football games from Pop Warner to the NFL, the boys and men prove their toughness by ferociously hitting each other, while the girls and women dance around, displaying their beauty and grace as cheerleaders.

All around the world, societies have invented fearful rites of passage, which, much like Toughman, qualify male adolescents as *real* men. In some cultures today as in the past, boys are whipped and branded, their skin sliced deeply enough to scar the bones. Hooks are driven into their chests, then torn out. They are banished into the wilderness without food, water, or clothing in quest of visions. They are sent out on the warpath and counted as men only if they return as killers. Through it all, they must hide every sign of fear and pain. A boy cannot cry out when an elder drives sharp reeds into his nostrils to pierce his septum or uses a sharp rock to slash his penis. (It is amazing, incidentally, how many rites of passage involve penile torture. The demented penis abuse ranges from widespread circumcision—with no anesthetic and a strong possibility of infection—to the act of subincision, in which a boy tries to lie stoically while a man splits the underside of his penis from base to tip with a stone blade, making the organ look terribly like a hot dog that has blown a seam on the grill.) Rites of passage differ around the globe, but they all test a boy's ability to handle pain and fear, and to demonstrate the toughness expected of a man.

In most societies girls have rites of passage, too. But with some gruesome exceptions, they don't rival the ordeals invented for boys. That girls will grow up to be *real* women is pretty much taken as a given. Masculinity is not. It must be won, and won at a cost. Take Toughman: the young men have to confront fear and danger to prove their masculinity. All the young women have to do to prove their femininity is reveal their bodies.

Tough, violent societies have the toughest rites of passage. Softer and less violent societies have softer rites of passage. In the modern West, the male role has gone so soft that formal rites of passage survive only in certain subcultures, such as gangs, fraternities, and elite military units. (Informal rites of passage such as Toughman or youth football are a different matter.) Western culture no longer needs most of its men to cultivate aggression and toughness. When there were bears in the woods or barbarians at the gates, everyone welcomed a certain ferocity in men. But now that our ferocious grandfathers have driven off the bears and killed the barbarians, male ferocity just complicates life in the family and the community.

Where does that leave men today? Cervantes' hero Don Quixote loved tales of knights and chivalry, but he lived in a world where there were no more dragons to battle. So the crazed Quixote invented that world in his mind, creating imaginary monsters to slay and princesses to rescue. In his book *Fighting for Life*, the scholar Walter Ong points out that there is a lot of Don Quixote in modern men. The qualities of traditional masculinity—bravery, toughness, stoicism—have less and less of a place in today's society, leading some commentators to prophesy "the end of men." But deep down men still need to feel like men, and so, like Quixote, we invent our own dragons. Taking crazy risks remains a prerequisite for manhood in most cultures, and if young men no longer take their risks in formal rites of passage, they do so on their own. YouTube offers an endless string of amateur videos from around the world, showing young men of all hues and shades accomplishing heroic feats of exuberant stupidity: Indian boys dodging hurtling trains, "urban climbers" hanging one-handed from skyscrapers high above Moscow, American boys performing Jackass stunts. This is what *Fight Club* is about: males—some of whom have literally lost their testicles and are growing breasts, others of whom were castrated only in spirit—finding a way to be men in a post-masculine world.

Those scary and spectacular YouTube videos only exaggerate the spontaneous risk taking that is typical of young men everywhere. Like many men who managed to survive their teens and early twenties, I look back on all the risks I took—in cars, in bars, and in dumb brushes with the law—and feel lucky to be alive. Not everyone is so lucky. This book is dedicated to the memory of an outstanding young man from my MMA gym named Nate Singo. I went to his wake with some guys from the gym. I saw his corpse and his dazed mother stroking his face in bewilderment. I saw his father bravely shaking hands, and a young woman

Land diver on Pentecost Island in Vanuatu. Land divers leap headfirst off a rickety wooden tower with vines tied to their ankles. Ideally the vines arrest a diver's fall just as his cranium kisses the dirt. Land diving is a rite of passage but also a duelly game of chicken. Who will leap from the greatest height? Who can resist the temptation to reach out and break his fall?

collapsing onto the floor, where she flopped and screamed with grief. It was terribly sad.

The week before Nate died, he told me he'd just passed through a screwup phase in his life—messing up at school and hassling his parents. He said he was going to straighten up, beginning with getting a job so he could pay his own MMA dues. A few nights later he went out job hunting with a friend, who for no reason at all decided to drive his SUV at over one hundred miles per hour down a two-lane road, dodging traffic. When they crashed, Nate was thrown from the car and killed. He was eighteen years old.

Young men, psychologists say, have an active "taste for risk." They like it. They seek out physical risk in a way that females and older men do not. These boys—and they are almost all boys or young men—are driven to invent situations in which they can display their masculine strength, courage, and skill in a world where formal rites of passage are fading away. They conjure dragons just so they can try to kill them. They embrace risk because safety—in the form of obeying the speed limit or wearing headgear during MMA sparring (which the guys in my gym are too tough to do)*—is kind of wussy. They may be heading toward careers at Crate and Barrel, but they want to prove that they have inherited the legacy of their grandfathers, the pure stuff of manhood: courage and strength.

WHY DON'T WOMEN FIGHT?

Two years ago I was called to the living room by my girls to deal with a bug sighting, which had turned into a highly distressing double bug

---

* In fact, headgear probably doesn't make boxing any safer and, by allowing fighters to accumulate more shots to the head before they go down, actually might make it more dangerous. That is one of the reasons headgear was recently banned from Olympic boxing. But the guys at my gym generally don't know this. They think headgear makes you safer, and that's why they won't wear it.

sighting. My six-year-old, Annabel, was standing stiff-legged and big-eyed on the couch, pointing at a daddy longlegs and a stinkbug that were converging on the far wall. Before I could save the day, the stinkbug scuttled into the spider, and a scene from *Mutual of Omaha's Wild Kingdom* erupted before us—a furious life-and-death battle. This caused Annabel to scream. Which caused my nine-year-old, Abby, to giggle. Which caused Annabel to instantly transform into thirty-nine pounds of front-tooth-less rage, charging with a war shriek down the length of the couch to slap Abby in the head. Which caused Abby to shriek from the shock and slap Annabel in the head. Which caused Annabel to extend her claws and deliberately rake them down Abby's slapping arm. Which caused me to pull them apart so they could both have a good cry.

Although my daughters peck at each other nonstop, this was the first and only time things have turned physical between them. It's not only that my girls don't physically fight; it's also that they don't play fight. There is no *boom-boom* of make-believe gunplay in our home, no soldiers gurgling in their death throes. Even their roughhousing is restrained. There are no massive wrestling matches in the bedrooms and no back-yard games of "smear the queer" with the neighborhood girls. ("Smear the queer" was part of the standard gay-bashing training of my boyhood. Before any of us even knew what being queer meant, we took turns playing the queer, who had to run for his life from a gang-tackling mob looking to smear him into the turf. The game teaches two life lessons: [1] don't be queer, and [2] if you see a queer, smear it.)

Which isn't to say that my daughters are inert. They love to run and jump and play. They love to swim and practice gymnastics. They love tickle fights and jumping on beds and climbing trees. They even love to wrestle. But to them wrestling means roughhousing with Dad. It means I lift them and twirl them and slam them into the couch cushions and tickle them to breathless tears. And then they tackle me and rough me up and jump on me from the armrest of the couch. In other words, wrestling is, for my girls, an exuberant form of play using Dad as a combination tackle dummy and amusement park ride.

On the relatively rare occasions when my girls wrestle with each other or their friends, it's not something that a boy would actually recognize as wrestling, because it's noncompetitive. They don't struggle for dominant position. They just whirl and roll and squeal, with no thought of winning or losing. The same thing holds for girls in general. Studies show that boys wrestle in school yards and playgrounds far more often than girls do (and the disparity would be far greater if parents and playground monitors weren't constantly roaring at the boys—spittle flying—to knock it off). But boys don't just wrestle a lot more than girls; they wrestle a lot differently. What I've observed about my own daughters applies to girls as a rule: their wrestling is much more likely to emerge as a frolic than as a contest. According to the psychologist Owen Aldis, children engage in two types of wrestling. "Positional wrestling" involves protracted attempts to throw, tackle, and secure a dominant "top" position on the ground. "Fragmentary wrestling" is less vigorous, less protracted (most bouts last just a second or two), and basically noncompetitive. Participants do not "attempt to achieve a clear-cut superiority but . . . merely grapple or push and pull in various directions." According to Aldis, although both sexes engage in the frolics of fragmentary wrestling, positional wrestling occurs almost exclusively among boys.

This is consistent with the anthropological record: wrestling is a nearly universal sport, but competitors are overwhelmingly, and usually exclusively, boys and men. And this even applies to the pretend violence of professional wrestling. Recently I attended a big professional wrestling show in Pittsburgh. There were many brawls between male performers: title defenses, tag-team melees, and battles royal. There was also a single tag-team match between female performers. Unlike the steroid-puffed men, the women, known as "divas," had trim, feminine builds and sported outfits that looked more like lingerie than wrestling singlets. Like most pro wrestling matches, this one was a conflict between pure good (the faces) and pure evil (the heels). The match was a wild catfight mixing gymnastic attacks with a lot of screeching, clawing, and hair pulling. The faces prevailed, with a blonde face putting a humiliating exclamation point on the win by licking her palm and smacking a defeated heel's ass. But then, as the winners took their bows, the dastardly heels climbed back into the ring to launch a sneak attack on the faces, really working them over with their boots. Things seemed dire until a furious dwarf flew to the rescue, clambering up into the ring to help the faces beat the snot out of the heels. Afterward the two faces joined the dwarf, who was bearded and dressed like a leprechaun, in some kind of Irish jig. The whole arena vibrated with laughter and cheers.

For professional wrestling, this was par for the course. As the wrestling historian Scott Beekman puts it, women have traditionally appeared "only as comedic or sexualized interludes on wrestling cards." The same thing goes for women's fighting throughout history. Going back to medieval village carnivals and zooming forward to pro wrestling and foxy boxing, women's fights have almost always been treated as salacious slapstick. For example, the ancient Japanese had *onna-zumo* (women's wrestling), but as the sports historian Allen Guttmann writes, "The debased motivation for this activity is suggested by the names of the wrestlers: 'Big Boobs,' 'Deep Crevice,' and 'Holder of the Balls.'" In medieval Europe women sometimes jousted alongside knights at tournaments, but they always did so as comic relief, tilting at each other with sewing spindles as they jostled along on the backs of goats. What the dueling historian Barbara Holland says of the few examples of European women fighting proper duels applies pretty much to women's fighting across history: "Women were always respectable objects for duels, but as players they were always a bit of a joke, like a monkey riding a bicycle."

And think back to that Toughman contest. Why were the only women in the ring sporting skimpy bikinis and manicured nails instead of boxing gloves and fight shorts? Why do so few females aspire to be known as "Toughwomen"? To fully answer the question "Why do men fight?" we must also ask "Why *don't* women?"

People usually leap to the wrong conclusion: it must be because women are smaller and weaker than men. But this explains only why

women are wise to avoid tangling with men, not why they should avoid fighting each other. And actually women are surprisingly brave when it comes to fighting men: in the context of relationship violence, women are actually more likely to attack a male partner than vice versa (though they are less likely to do serious harm). The interesting thing about women's violence isn't that they don't hit; it's that they are so much less likely to hit *each other*. This goes for the least serious forms of aggression, such as children's play, and extends all the way to homicide. For centuries women have committed an amazingly stable proportion of the world's murders: about 10 percent. But historically the largest category of homicides by females has been infanticide, which usually amounts to a desperate form of family planning by women who feel they can't support their infants. When infanticides are factored out, women commit only a tiny fraction of same-sex homicides. This illustrates the radical differences between male and female forms of rivalry. Men have disputes with each other that sometimes escalate—step by fatal step—to homicide. Women do, too—but about thirty to forty times less frequently.

When it comes to physical forms of aggression, women really are the much gentler sex. But that doesn't mean women are innocent of aggression. Women compete intensely with each other, and often over the same matters of honor that motivate men. Women prize their honor for much the same reason men do: because it's a main determinant of their value in the mate market. As one British high school girl put it, "A girl that's been called a slag is the same as a boy that's been called a chicken." Even in modern, reasonably enlightened societies, few men desire a slag for a wife, and few women find chickenhearted men sexy. In Anne Campbell's studies of aggression in female adolescents, physical fights were very rare, but they usually began with girls calling each other sluts, slags, or whores. (This is an old story. In legal records from medieval France, one woman shouts at a rival, "Whore, doubly a whore, her house is a brothel, slut bitch!" Another woman spits at her enemy, "Whore, doubly a whore, she rents out her arse!")

But usually the wars of women and girls are indirect—more like the jailhouse aggression of *Orange Is the New Black* than *Oz*. When men and boys have a dispute, they are more likely to declare open battle. Women prefer guerrilla tactics. When they wish to hurt each other, women and girls rarely choose to punch, slap, or kick. Instead, they gouge each other with words. But the harming words are less likely to be spoken to the face than behind the back. Through gossip, women and girls alienate, ostracize, and defame. But just because women battle with words rather than sticks and stones doesn't make their aggressive styles less cruel or Machiavellian.

Why is female aggression so much less likely to be expressed physically? The dueling expert Paul Kircher gives part of the answer: "Perhaps the real reason [women didn't duel] is that women throughout history have been burdened with a different concept of honor from men. A woman's honor was defined in terms of chastity, fidelity, and modesty rather than physical courage, so it could not be enhanced by a duel." In short, courage can be proved in a gunfight, chastity cannot.

But women's avoidance of physical fights also goes back to those sex differences in "taste for risk." Men take more risks when it comes to big things such as fighting wars, throwing punches, or committing robberies; and they take more routine risks in managing their stock portfolios, neglecting to go to the doctor, and jaywalking on busy streets. (Because many men treat street crossing as a kind of extreme sport, they are not only hit by cars more often than women, but they are also more than twice as likely to die as a result.) Sex differences in risk tolerance are massive, and they've been replicated in scores of studies across decades and cultures. In large part thanks to this risky behavior, human males, like the males of most other species, live shorter lives than females. Currently in America, the average woman lives five years longer than the average man.

But the life expectancy gap isn't mainly the result of old women outliving old men. It is mainly the result of young women outliving young men. Men have a higher probability of death at every stage of the life cycle, from conception (when male embryos spontaneously abort more frequently) to old age. But the differences between male and female death rates is most impressive in the late teens and early twenties. This is not mainly because young men are dying of diseases or wars. Even with the carnage of two world wars, warfare was a surprisingly small source of total male mortality over the last century. It's more accurate to say that they are dying of stupidity. The journalist Sebastian Junger sums it up this way: "[Young men] are killed in accidents and homicides at . . . roughly five times the rate of young women. Statistically, it is six times as dangerous to spend a year as a young man in America than as a cop or a fireman, and vastly more dangerous than a one-year deployment at a big military base in Afghanistan [during the height of America's war in Afghanistan]." Men are also five times more likely to die by lightning, not because they make better conductors, but because they are too "brave" to take shelter during storms.

Women are woods wary and spider shy. They fear just about everything more than men do: crime, public speaking, accidents, darkness, cancer, heights, high-risk mutual funds. Women self-report greater fear, and these reports are backed up by lab studies showing that women have a stronger reflex reaction to fearful scenes (for instance,

The Darwin Awards "commemorate individuals who protect our gene pool by making the ultimate sacrifice of their own lives. Darwin Award winners eliminate themselves in an extraordinarily idiotic manner, thereby improving our species' chances of long-term survival." Darwin Awards organizer Wendy Northcutt points out that "Lady Darwin Winners" are rare. If a person is removed from the gene pool after challenging a zoo tiger to a kung fu fight or playing a drinking game that involves stomping a land mine beneath a table (or by taking up cage fighting at age forty), the smart money says you are dealing with the male version of *Homo sapiens*.

in a scary movie): they startle more violently, their hearts race faster, and they sweat more freely. Where do these sex differences in fearfulness (or should I say prudence?) come from? The feminist theory about men conspiring to keep women weak through fear isn't too convincing. Females are more fearful than males beginning in infancy and across all different kinds of cultures. We'd do well to recall the basic biology from earlier in this chapter: compared with men, women are at a lower risk of reproductive failure, but they also have much lower hopes of spectacular reproductive success. So the potential reproductive benefits of risk taking are much lower for women. *But the costs are higher.*

The ecologists Rebecca Sear and Ruth Mace published a 2008 paper called "Who Keeps Children Alive?" Across twenty-eight traditional cultures, the answer was pretty simple: mainly mothers do. Of course, for a child to lose his or her father is bad. But across the twenty-eight cultures, a mother's death was invariably more likely to lead to a child's death, especially among nursing infants. Reviewing these results, the psychologists Catharine Cross and Anne Campbell conclude: "Women's lives are precious commodities. When an ancestral mother risked her life, she risked the lives of her descendants, in each of whom she had invested more than any father."

So if men treat their lives more cheaply, it's partly because they can better afford to. From a biological point of view, the female role is primary. As the myth scholar Joseph Campbell said of beliefs among the !Kung San people of southern Africa, "The woman is life, and the man is the servant of life." Men have a role in creating life, but throughout the history of the species (and arguably up to the present day), it's been a secondary role, indeed a servant's role. Men have assisted women as hunters and bodyguards, as women do the biologically fundamental work of bearing and rearing children. (The inherent biological preciousness of the female also explains why most of the meat on your plate comes from bulls and boars, not cows and sows.)

I have a home video of my two daughters frolicking in the backyard—

swinging, sliding, tagging. At some point my wife called the girls inside to bake cookies. The camera swung around to follow them into the house. As two-year-old Annabel crossed the threshold, she stopped the camera dead with an upraised hand: "You stay out, Daddy." And then she used both hands to slam the door in my face and laboriously twist the locks. I continued to film through the window as my womenfolk measured and mixed ingredients. Watching this little scene makes my throat ache. It seems an apt metaphor for the role most men play—even in egalitarian modern marriages—as quasi-outsiders in their own families. Of course, men have always contributed importantly to the family, and our wives and children would miss us if we were gone. But there's also a tacit understanding that we are the expendable ones: if something evil comes through the front door, everyone knows whose job it is to die guarding the family's retreat out the back. Men are a little on the periphery of family life, cut off from the biologically precious mother and children as though by an invisible pane of glass.

"A REAL MAN AFTER ALL"

My verbal duel with the poet over masculinity (which I have now spent several years laboring to win) made me think of the famous Charles Atlas ad that started running in the 1940s and that can still be seen, in one version or another, in the back pages of my childhood comic books. This ad was so effective, and ran for so long, because it touched universal anxieties of young men. In the ad, the bully insults, threatens, and physically manhandles Mac. And Mac, as a ninety-eight-pound weakling, has no choice but to silently take it, thanks to that primordial law of nature I mentioned earlier: *The big get their way, while the small give way.*

Magnifying his humiliation, Mac's girl sees the whole thing. She tries to soothe him afterward, saying, "Don't let it bother you," but Mac's meekness and weakness obviously bother her: turning her back to him,

she calls him "little boy." So Mac, "tired of being a scarecrow," commits to the Atlas system, swells himself into a full-fledged muscle head, and vanquishes the bully. Afterward Mac's girlfriend physically melts into him, cooing, "Oh, Mac! You *are* a real man after all!" The other men in the ad look upon Mac's splendor with envy, and the other girls take notice, too. (In a different version of the ad, three nubile bikini-clad girls look on dreamily and say with a sigh, "What a man!") Mac's girlfriend makes things perfectly clear: to win the respect of men and the desire of women, a man must be able to handle himself in competition with his peers. If he can't, he's just a little boy.

The young men heaving metal at my college's gym understand this. They know what Mac learned on the beach: being weak—even at a leafy private college—can mean getting a lot of sand kicked in your face, while the cool kids laugh and the girls turn cold. Being strong means deterring aggression, winning the girl, and never being laughed at.

I learned this lesson well when I was younger. Like Mac, I was an undersize weakling. Like Mac, I got pushed around and humiliated. Like Mac, this treatment was painful for what it cost me with the boys, but perhaps even more painful for what it cost me with the girls. (I don't mean to imply that girls weren't attracted to me in high school. But they were attracted to me in the same way they were attracted to all tiny things with smooth, fat cheeks. They didn't want to date me or go to the prom with me; they wanted to swaddle me up and tickle my chin.)

So when I arrived at college, I followed the lead of Mac and countless other young men: I hit the weights. I did so in fits and starts at first. But by my junior and senior years, I was hitting them hard. And it worked. The more my muscles grew, the fewer guys bothered me. After college I tried to get scientific about it, guzzling down protein shakes and supplements, and learning routines from Arnold Schwarzenegger's *Encyclopedia of Modern Bodybuilding*. By the time I was twenty-three or twenty-four, I'd built myself up from a lightweight into a 210-pound heavyweight who could bench-press more than 300 pounds. I was saved from becoming a Schwarzenegger-style mutant only by creaky shoulder joints and not being quite sick enough to eat steroids. But I did Mac one better.

Take a look at Mac's punching form in the next-to-last frame of the ad. Disgraceful. He's striking with his weak front hand rather than his power hand at the rear. There's no snap in that punch. And as he lashes out with his right, he drops his left uselessly to his waist, leaving his head exposed. Mac grew strong, but he didn't know how to use his strength. He managed to KO the bully, but that's because the bully was just a cartoon. Any flesh-and-blood bully worth his salt would have waded right through Mac, big muscles or no.

Like Mac, I had no idea how to fight. I had no idea how to throw a good punch or how to dodge one. I had built up my muscles as a deterrent against aggression, but if anyone ever put my deterrent to the test, I'd be screwed. Unlike Mac, I knew it was one thing to be powerful and another thing to know how to project that power effectively.

So I took up karate.

FOUR

SLAYING GOLIATH

Fear no man! Render any bully twice your size absolutely helpless in seconds! Become a terrifying, destructive, self-defense fighting machine—in just twelve short lessons!

Advertisement for *Joseph Weider's Destructive Self-Defense Course*

I punched my friend Nobu at a faculty party on a warm spring evening, in a leafy yard in full suburban bloom. The poet and his wife were throwing a housewarming party, and they'd invited various college people to celebrate: professors, assistant deans, librarians, and the entire English Department. It was a prim affair: the college people snacked on hummus and organic corn chips, tasted chilled white wines and microbrews, and traded campus gossip. I presented the poet with a $6.99 bottle of Old Crow Kentucky bourbon, because that's what we used to drink before he man-dumped me. The poet laughed when he drew the plastic bottle out of its brown paper sheath, but he didn't drink with me like he used to. So I went off to mingle, sipping from a red Solo cup of Crow and ice, and noting hopefully that the Muppet-headed horn blower was nowhere to be seen.

I was feeling glum and bored. I really liked these people, but hanging out with them always reminded me that I wasn't actually one of them—I was just a lowly adjunct, the academic equivalent of cheap migrant labor. Sixteen months had passed since I'd first hit on MMA as a career suicide strategy, and I still hadn't managed to get myself fired.

You may be thinking, *What a dumb plan.* I know it was. And part of me always knew it was, even when I was dreaming it up. But a different part of me thought it could work. I was already on thinning ice at the college, largely because of my failure to keep regular office hours. I avoided office hours because students never showed up. Ever. If a student needed to meet with me, he or she did so after class or by appointment. Sitting pointlessly in the dreary adjuncts' cubicle, waiting for students who never materialized—getting sympathetic glances from colleagues who passed by—forced me to confront my predicament too squarely. I'd striven hard in the academic race, I'd given it everything I had, and still I'd failed. And the cubicle was both the symbol and the proof of my failure.

In *Fight Club* the never-named first-person narrator (the tame Jekyll to Tyler Durden's uncontrollable Hyde) is so fed up with his soulless, emasculated life as a combination road warrior/cubicle slave/consumerist dupe that he creates an underground fight club. I never wanted to be like Tyler Durden, who is, for all his fearless charisma, a murderous, testicle-chopping psychopath bent on a terroristic plan of planetary destruction. But like the narrator of *Fight Club*, I thought I could use fighting to explode life as I knew it. I had this perverse idea that MMA would push me so far beyond the pale of academic respectability that there'd be no coming back from it. I knew my academic career was probably over. So why go out with a whimper? Why not go down in a hail of fists?

After all, for whatever else MMA is, it's part of the dark history of blood sport—one of the many creative ways people have invented to get a thrill from pain. As a rule, English professors don't approve of blood sport. And they also don't approve much of the kind of raw masculinity that's on display in a cage fight. In higher education generally, and literary study specifically, masculinity is associated with everything oafish, bullying, and oppressive. Masculinity is a problem. It's not something that should really be tolerated, much less celebrated. On the contrary, it should be relentlessly dissected, suppressed, and ultimately transformed into something better—something gentler, more egalitarian, more cooperative. Something closer to femininity. It's probably not wrong to say that masculinity is the real villain in the average literary theory course—the great root of all the other evils. (I don't entirely disagree. There's a case to be made that wayward masculinity is the great problem of history. But there's also an upside to masculine energy, which is why societies have always tried to harness it rather than snuff it out.)

Quick. Don't think about it. Imagine an English professor in your head. No, a *male* English professor. What do you see? Tweeds? Elbow patches? A high pale forehead with thinning hair combed over? Eyeglasses with designer frames? Oh God, do you see a cravat? His fingernails are clean and white. His palms are silky and uncalloused. If you grip him by his upper arm, your fingers plunge to the bone. He prefers wine to beer. But when he drinks beer, he favors pretentious microbrews that he sniffs and swirls, while waxing on about oaky hints and lemony essences.

You are imagining a man, yes, but one whose masculinity is so refined, so sanded down and smoothed away, that it's hard to see how it differs from femininity. It has been said that the humanities have been feminized. In English departments, where the demographics of professors and students now skew strongly female, this is literally so. But English departments have also been feminized in spirit. There's a sense in which if you are a guy who wants to be a literature professor, it's wise to actively suppress all of the offensive cues that you are actually a guy. Or at least that's how it has always seemed to me. And I think that's how it seems to most people. In the public mind, teaching English is about as manly as styling hair.

So by taking up cage fighting, and by writing a book about it that was not a fire-breathing tirade or a bleeding-heart bromide, I thought I'd be seen as embracing masculinity in its most troubling—its most violent and scary—aspects. I probably couldn't be fired for this. It might even be illegal to fire a guy over his choice of sports. But as an adjunct—as a teacher with no more protection or power than a migrant worker—I could be fired for anything. No one has to give a reason.

BUT I WAS TELLING YOU about punching Nobu. Of all my colleagues at the college, the one who took the most interest in my project was an associate chemistry professor named Nobu Matsuno. When Nobu came through the door of the poet's party, I instantly perked up. I saw him. He saw me. And I engaged him in a friendly bout of competitive disputation. We went toe-to-toe with drinks and words, and ended up throwing punches for the reason men usually do: because they drink too much, then argue too much, and then reach a point where there's just nothing else for it. Like proper duelists, we argued with civility and restraint, but when we reached our usual impasse, it seemed like a good idea to settle things as men of science should: by experiment.

"The fundamental problem of the martial arts," the jiu-jitsu masters Renzo and Royler Gracie explain, is "How can one successfully defend oneself against attack by a bigger, stronger, and more aggressive opponent?" In other words, how can David slay Goliath? All martial arts claim to teach the science and art of Goliath slaying. But I'd long ago concluded that they were mostly teaching bunk. The most popular martial arts— karate, kung fu, tae kwon do, aikido, and so on—were fatally flawed. They were not sciences of Goliath slaying; they were pseudosciences. Nobu strongly disagreed. He'd been studying karate and tae kwon do since boyhood, and he knew they worked. More than that, for Nobu the martial arts were near-sacred monuments to human creativity, ingenuity, and perseverance—just like music, literature, or science itself.

Nobu and I were sitting on the poet's patio wall, with the party burble flowing around us. I asked him if he'd like to step out into the yard and put our positions to the test. And then we were on our feet, moving excitedly onto the grass. It was what we both had wanted all along. We chose a spot on one side of the house where the lawn looked flat and soft. We

David and Goliath by Osmar Schindler. One way a David can beat a Goliath is through the use of projectile weapons. But what if David has to fight Goliath bare-handed?

emptied our pockets of wallets and keys and phones, and stuffed them in our shoes. We carefully tipped our drinks against the house so they wouldn't spill.

We squared off, barefoot in the damp grass. Nobu's stance—his feet close together, his hands hanging low and loose—screamed *kicker*. I faced him with a wide wrestler's stance, hands held high to guard my head, elbows tucked to shield my ribs. We were about the same age, but I had forty pounds on him, and as a veteran martial arts instructor and second-degree black belt, he had about twenty-five years' worth of martial arts training on me. We wanted to know what counted for more, my size or his experience.

A few college people had gathered at the corner of the poet's house to watch us, blinking in confusion over the rims of their wine goblets. Seeing them standing there made me feel ridiculous, and I thought of calling it off. But then I reconsidered. My old hopes rekindled. If repeatedly punching a tenured chemistry professor in the face in front of faculty witnesses didn't get me fired, nothing would.

DUELISTS IN THE DOJO

The Asian martial arts are as much a part of modern America as Chinese takeout. In my small, working-class town in Pennsylvania, I count seven dojos. And the martial arts business isn't limited to the dojos. It consists of movies and action figures, how-to books and magazines, gis, heavy bags, nunchakus, throwing stars, mouthpieces, shin guards, and so on. The martial arts industry seems to push a lot of different products. But it really pushes just one. The business next door to your local strip-mall dojo may sell payday loans or manicures; the dojo sells physical confidence and the serenity that goes with it. The martial arts reach out to the world's dorks, wimps, and weirdos—to the frightened fatties, victims, and bully bait—and they offer a solution. If we train hard, if we obey our masters, if we buy certain equipment and read certain books, we will be the banes of bullies, the slayers of Goliaths.

When we think of the martial arts, we think of Asian guys in pajamas moving like fearsome dancers through a complex choreography of gymnastic kicks and punches. But the martial arts are not limited to the East. In fact, it's hard to find a culture where martial arts are not celebrated and practiced in some form. In tribal societies, wrestling is often a main form of competition among men, and wherever you find "civilization," you find more elaborate forms of martial arts. In the West, for example, boxing and wrestling are highly developed martial arts with histories stretching back to the ancient Greeks and almost certainly beyond.

We also think of the martial arts as being about self-defense. And to some extent they are, especially for women, who in my experience train mainly for exercise and assault defense. But throughout history and up to the present day, martial arts training has mainly attracted men. And for men their main draw is not assault defense. If it were, the curriculum would focus much more on eye gouging and nut crunching, and much less on spinning crescent kicks. In fact, if the martial arts were primarily about self-defense, they'd probably dispense with most of the eye gouging and nut crunching, too. They'd train people to back down faster and flee smarter, and they'd hone quick-draw techniques for Tasers, handguns, and pepper spray. In a self-defense situation, weapons are far more effective than any empty-hand technique (armed with a $99 .22 from Walmart I'm instantly tougher than any UFC heavyweight).

Instead, the martial arts focus overwhelmingly on the kinds of techniques that are appropriate in a fair fight—a duel, in other words. The worldwide proliferation of martial arts systems show that men have always been anxious about their ability to win duels. The martial arts are about teaching men methods that will give them the confidence to accept and win a duel if it is offered. They are about keeping men from being exposed, as Mac was on the beach, as a non-man—a coward, a weakling. Because whatever the various ideals of manhood are around the world, a man is always someone who can bravely and competently stand up for himself.

MYTH BUSTED

In my teens I marveled at the superhero powers of Bruce Lee, Jean-Claude Van Damme, and Steven Seagal. Wanting some of that power for myself, I joined a karate school in my early twenties. I became a skeptic of traditional forms of the martial arts when I started watching those UFC tapes. In the early years, cage fighting was not about mixing the martial arts at all. To the contrary, it was developed to settle old barroom arguments: Which single, unadulterated martial arts style was superior? Who would win a fight between a good boxer and a good wrestler? Between a kung fu artist and a mean barroom brawler? And could superior skill actually overcome a massive deficit in size and strength? For example, could a two-hundred-pound karate man like Gerard Gordeau overcome an athletic sumo wrestler who was more than twice his size?

All martial artists claimed to have the best style. The UFC was about putting up or shutting up. It was about testing claims in the most rigorous way possible: by having talented representatives of each martial art square off in real, no-holds-barred fights. For the experiment to be valid, the UFC organizers felt that the clashes could have none of the restrictions of sport fights. So there would be no weight classes or padded gloves, because street fights don't have them. And there'd be no rounds, because there are no breaks in street fights. And since real fights have no fouls or scorecards, the UFC wouldn't have them either. Anything that could happen in a street fight—head stomps, knee strikes, strangulation, head butts, hair ripping, finger mangling—was kosher in the cage.

The UFC organizers did discourage biting and eye gouging, but these were matters of warrior etiquette, not hard-and-fast rules. You couldn't actually be disqualified—or even penalized—for gouging an eye (or for biting one, for that matter). As UFC cofounder Rorion Gracie put it, "We never had rules. What we had was two restrictions: no eye gouging and no biting. But neither of those were forbidden. I knew from the beginning that we could not stop the fight. Once the fighters went in, you could not stop the fight, no matter what . . . Everything was permitted. The consequences if you eye gouged the other guy or bit him would be a fine of one thousand dollars, and the money would go to the guy who got bit or gouged." (An illustration: In the finals of the first UFC, the sumo-slaying Gerard Gordeau lost by choke to Royce Gracie, but not before gasping "Fuck your mother" in Gracie's ear, then trying to bite off said ear. In a subsequent MMA fight in Japan, Gordeau severely gouged the eye of a Japanese fighter. I interviewed Gordeau on Skype and asked him whether the story about the Japanese fighter was true. Gordeau cheerfully told me, "I put his eye out. He is blind now." I asked him if he felt guilty about this, and Gordeau—who speaks intermediate English spiced with expert profanity—flared up a little: "There's no rules! What the fuck you talking?")

For a dedicated karate student like me, who had been told by movies and senseis that he was learning the universe's most brutally effective combat science, the UFC was a bitter pill. Early UFC fights were preceded by brief video segments introducing the fighters and their styles. Usually karate men would leap and whirl, giving fearsome Bruce Lee–style demonstrations of their prowess. Then the fight would start, and all of that fearsome technique would simply evaporate. The most common outcome was that the karate man would hop around with his guard held low, getting off a few ineffectual punches or kicks before being tackled to the ground and pounded half to death.

The UFC exposed a gaping hole in the martial arts. After centuries of polishing and honing, the most popular Asian styles (with the exceptions of judo and jiu-jitsu) had never developed strong methods of ground fighting. So when karate, tae kwon do, or kung fu fighters ended up on the ground—which was often—they were like fish thrown on the beach to flop and gasp. They flailed around eating knuckles and kneecaps until it was over. Black belts in the Asian striking styles didn't just lose their fights; they were, on the whole, massacred and humiliated—by boxers, wrestlers, and garden-variety street toughs. On the relatively rare occasions when they won, it wasn't thanks to the fancy stuff taught in their dojos. They usually just reverted to basic bar fighting—clenching up and throwing power hand punches. (Even Gerard Gordeau's destruction of Teila Tuli mainly came down to kicking a fat guy who'd fallen on his face.)

After studying UFC tapes for a while, I had a pretty good sense of what worked in a fight. Things that worked: being bigger than the other guy, being in better shape, head butting, face punching, expert grappling. Things that didn't work: most of the leaping, twirling stuff I'd seen in kung fu films, anything ninjas do, sumo moves. Overall, big, strong, and simple beats small, weak, and fancy.

So I continued to attend my karate classes. But now I was questioning everything. At my dojo we were constantly assured that "everything we do is for fighting." But did katas—the beautiful war dances consisting of a fixed series moves—actually make you a better fighter? Did *kihon*—the highly stylized strikes and parries we practiced endlessly in front of mirrors—actually improve our ability to hit and defend? What we were learning was obviously artistic, but was it martial?

One day I worked up the courage to express my growing doubts to my sensei. I told him about the UFC and how fighters like us were getting slaughtered, mainly because they couldn't fight on the ground. Sensei Bill, a fifth-degree black belt in Kyokushin karate who has since risen to the ninth degree, didn't see my point. He asked, not unkindly, "So what?"

"So," I replied, "what do we do if we are taken down in a fight?"

Bill smiled. "Just don't get taken down."

It hit me like a punch: *Sensei Bill doesn't know anything about fighting.* He doesn't know how often fights end up on the ground, and he certainly doesn't understand that keeping a fight standing *is* a martial art. You can't just decide not to get taken down. If you haven't practiced the techniques—sprawls, whizzers, underhooks—for avoiding a takedown, a good grappler will take you down (and if you haven't drilled techniques for standing back up, he will keep you there). It just seemed crazy to me: we were spending so much time practicing the most arcane and unlikely strikes—prancing our way through our katas and going

Overall is the key word, because the winner of three of the first four UFCs was a small, relatively weak, ultrafancy Brazilian jiu-jitsu fighter named Royce Gracie (above). At 170 pounds, Gracie was almost always the smaller man in his fights, but he still needed only a minute or two to take a big opponent to the ground and then make him quit with a choke or a joint lock. Gracie's dominance ended as soon as all the other fighters started learning Brazilian jiu-jitsu as well, after which MMA passed into a decade of domination by American wrestlers, who are still the strongest force in the sport. So what's the preeminent martial art for an unarmed mano a mano fight? What the ongoing UFC experiment seems to have proven beyond doubt is this: when a pure striker faces a pure grappler, the grappler reliably wins. At my gym, good college wrestlers—strong, skilled, and tireless—dominate all but the top guys on day one.

through the endless wax on, wax off maneuvers of *kihon*—yet we couldn't do the simplest grappling techniques.

I realized I'd made no real progress. I was no more a fighter now than when I'd first joined the dojo. I was still Mac on the beach, with the big muscles and the feeble technique. Disillusioned, I quit karate soon after, wondering how the martial arts could have gone so wrong.

THE GODHAND

As a karate student, I never asked anyone what *Kyokushin* meant. If I had, my whole experience in karate would have made a lot more sense. *Kyokushin* is short for *Kyokushinkai*, which means "Society of the Ultimate Truth" in Japanese. I was in a cult, in other words, and the charismatic, infallible founder was Mas Oyama, also known as "the Godhand." We had a framed photograph of Oyama hanging high on our dojo wall. He was a chubby, middle-aged Asian with slicked-back hair and a face that radiated a stern yet benevolent power. Oyama received his nickname, the legend goes, after he killed a Japanese gangster with a single punch. Like God, Oyama could kill with a touch.

Oyama's goal in creating Kyokushin was not simply to teach karate skills, but to forge a path to the ultimate truth. As this implies, Oyama had a misplaced sense of his own importance. Believing he was responsible for a worldwide martial arts boom, he resented the way people gave credit to Bruce Lee. And he had a megalomaniacal notion that he might somehow bring about world peace through karate. At this Oyama failed, but in producing a kind of religion with himself at the center, he succeeded beautifully. As one of his biographers has written, although Oyama is now dead, his legacy lives in his followers: "These people, in the spirit of karate, found peace and harmony through the omnipotence of Kyokushin karate and one man—Mas Oyama."

To perfect his karate Oyama, like many prophets and sages before him, went into the wilderness and lived for three years in an isolated mountain refuge. On Mount Minobu his life consisted of one long *Rocky IV* training session. To toughen his spirit he practiced techniques in the frigid rush of winter streams. To toughen the bones of his fists he pulverized stones with punches. To strengthen his legs he karate-kicked trees to death. To deepen his lungs he ran the ragged slopes. To strengthen his muscles he did three hundred push-ups at a clip. To sharpen his moves and quiet his mind he did at least one hundred katas per day.

When he came down from the mountain, his karate was superhuman. He spent a year touring America, taking on all comers in challenge matches and racking up a 270–0 record against boxers, wrestlers, and assorted toughs. Although this feat might seem impressive, beating up men without karate training was too easy. So back in Japan, Oyama fought three hundred karate experts in the course of just three days. He defeated them all, usually with a single punch. (It's important to stress that Oyama stopped beating people up because he ran out of victims, not because his "godhand" was sore.) Outclassing human males by too wide a margin, Oyama sought challenging opponents in the animal kingdom. He didn't find them. He fought about fifty ferocious bulls in his career, sometimes smashing them dead with his slaughterhouse fist, but more often sparing them, mercifully sidestepping their charges and razoring off their horns with karate chops. As one Web site celebrating Oyama puts it, "[Oyama's] fighting principle was simple—if he got through to you, that was it. If he hit you, you broke. If you blocked a rib punch, your arm was broken or dislocated. If you didn't block, your rib was broken. He became known as *the Godhand*, a living manifestation of the Japanese warriors' maxim *Ichigeki hissatsu* or 'One strike, certain death.'"

Many of Oyama's friends and associates, along with skeptics inside the martial arts community, have cast serious doubt on almost every aspect of the Mas Oyama legend—from his monkish sojourn on the mountain to his bullfights, one of which can be seen on YouTube and is laughably bogus. (There's also video on the Internet of Oyama demonstrating his prowess against mere humans, and his technique looks suspect. He hangs his hands to his waist and throws sloppy haymakers.)

Oyama's friend and protégé Jon Bluming went so far as to claim that far from winning hundreds of fights, Oyama had never been in an actual fight in his whole life. And in Bluming's support, the notion that it would be physically possible for a human being to have 300 fights in just three days—or even 270 fights in a year—reveals a deep naïveté about what fights are actually like. It seems that the spinners of the Mas Oyama myth—who certainly included Oyama himself—didn't know enough about fighting to construct plausible stories.

But Oyama may have believed his own myth. Compare him with Yanagi Ryuken, an aging master of aikido who can be seen in YouTube videos waving his hands at dozens of hard-charging student attackers and dropping them to the mat in agony—without actually touching them. At first a skeptical viewer is tempted to label Ryuken a con artist, but if so, he's also conned himself. The way Ryuken's students "cooperated" with his demonstrations for decades on end—obediently sprawling on the mat when Ryuken waved at them—gave him the authentic belief that he really was a martial arts demigod. If he was a faker, he surely wouldn't have agreed to a challenge match—on camera, in front of a large crowd, with a violently uncooperative fighter from a different dojo. When Ryuken waved his hands at his opponent, the challenger, instead of falling over, kicked and punched Ryuken's face until he lay squirming in his own blood.

Whether Oyama believed his legend or not, Kyokushin is far from alone in venerating the miraculous deeds of a semimythical founder. Take tai chi, the slow, vaguely martial dances that elderly people do in parks. Tai chi is good for exercise and meditation, but can it also be, as advocates insist, a devastating martial art? The main evidence for this claim comes from stories about the founder of tai chi, "Yang the Invincible." Yang was a martial arts superhero with ESP, a thirty-foot vertical leap, and the ability to fry people from across a room with a technique called "issuing energy like shooting an arrow." After informing us on these points, a book on tai chi warns the reader against skepticism: Yang's feats are "a record of fact, and the student should not regard it as a false story purporting to history." Similarly, even though Bruce Lee railed against the religious tendencies of the martial arts, he couldn't stop his followers from constructing a church of jeet kune do based on myths about him, its founding hero, and his God-like powers. The most balanced of the Lee biographies describes his apotheosis this way: "Bruce Lee was able to channel the archetypal energies that exist beyond the energy bound up in our own personality structure. He accessed the levels of extraordinary, supernatural energy." (The idea that Lee, who weighed about 130 pounds, was one of the world's baddest asses is based entirely on dubious anecdotes and his highly choreographed film work.)

The Asian martial arts traditions function like quasi-religions: rooted in Zen Buddhism or Taoism, based on the legendary exploits of founding demigods, and usually tied to ancient beliefs about a magical universal energy called chi, which pervades everything but is beyond physical detection. (To get a good grip on chi, just think of "the force" in the Star Wars movies. Kung fu and Jedi masters are formidable not because of their muscles, but because they learned to channel the universal energy—to "use the force.") Religions are great at doing some things, such as assuaging our fears and unifying believers around shared values. But religions are bad at other things, such as nimbly adapting to new realities. Religions demand faith. Believers must believe.

So how did the traditional martial arts go so wrong? They turned into combat faiths—complete with creation myths, violent sectarianism, and unwavering faith in spooky Jedi powers—rather than combat sciences. Science is about skeptically asking questions. Religion is about accepting answers on faith. So never questioning a senior, or a rule, or a technique, or a tradition—no matter how wasteful or illogical—is widely celebrated in the martial arts as a positive virtue. This is nicely illustrated in *The Karate Kid* (1984), when Mr. Miyagi teaches Daniel-san the value of mindless obedience by making him wax on and wax off for many painful hours.

MMA works because it is a science and not a religion. It works because many people in the martial arts community received the same shock that I did upon witnessing my first UFC event. They lost their faith in their martial religions, and they decided to throw off all received wisdom, all the authority of tradition, all the small-mindedness of sectarianism. They would design fighting anew, taking the best aspects from all the different traditions, while constantly evolving solutions to new problems. An MMA gym really is a kind of lab devoted to constant testing and refinement of martial arts hypotheses. In other words, MMA brought the Enlightenment—the one that swept away much of the superstition from the Western world and enshrined science and reason as the culturally dominant "way of knowing"—to the martial arts.

When Nobu and I first spoke about MMA, he told me that he, too, had considered training at Shrader's gym. He'd decided against it, he said, "because I wanted to improve my philosophy, and it [Shrader's MMA] does not seem philosophical." Truer words have never been spoken. There are no warrior-philosophers in Shrader's gym. There are no Zen masters dispensing wisdom. Shrader's gym is a lot like the evil dojo of the Cobra Kai in *The Karate Kid* (except for the evil part). In an MMA class, any philosophical or spiritual element is, at best, a side effect of the physical training. Shrader's MMA sells a product, and the product is butt kicking, not spirituality. The motto of the Cobra Kai—STRIKE FIRST! STRIKE HARD! NO MERCY!—would look just about right emblazoned on the wall at Shrader's.

I agree that something valuable is lost when a combat religion gives way to a combat science. You lose some of the artistic and spiritual dimensions, the serene and churchy feel of a dojo, with its background myths and legendary heroes. And in exchange you get the horrors of the octagon, with its stench of aggression and fear. In MMA the point is always and only to win fights—no matter how ugly winning has to be. So you lose something as you move from a fight church to a fight lab, but you gain something, too: a higher probability of actually winning a fight. In real life, the Cobra Kai guys would have kicked Daniel-san's ass, and Mr. Miyagi's, too.

MMA training gives you a higher probability of winning a fight, but that's all. Most guys come into the MMA gym hoping to fulfill a fantasy of warrior prowess that they've built up by watching UFC matches. But few MMA guys are able to maintain that fantasy for very long, because every day the fantasy is brought into bruising contact with reality. MMA training increases your physical confidence, but it also increases your realism and your humility. You learn painful truths at an MMA gym. Perhaps foremost among them is this: it's very hard for even a well-trained David to defeat a Goliath. The laws of physics—of strength and weight and muscular drive—cannot be denied. Unlike in sports such as tennis or golf, where small advantages in skill overwhelm large advantages in strength and size, the situation in fighting is very much the opposite. It takes a large skill advantage to overcome deficits in strength, size, athleticism, and ferocity. That's why fighting sports are among the very few with weight classes. Without weight classes, sports such as MMA, wrestling, and boxing would be as much "get big" contests as "get skilled" contests.

HOW-TO NINJA

In the fifteen years since I quit karate and took up MMA, I've watched the UFC blossom from a maligned, small-time carny spectacle into a big and increasingly mainstream sport. Going into this book, I felt sure that the rise of MMA must have shaken the faith of the traditional martial arts and forced them to modernize. The culture as a whole, I thought, had certainly turned against the notion of the martial arts superman. When I was in my teens and early twenties, you could still watch movies starring Jean-Claude Van Damme, Steven Seagal, or Chuck Norris without irony. But by the late 1990s those guys had been transformed into a cultural joke. Seagal especially was widely seen as a clown, and Norris's tough guy persona had become a jokey meme that swept the Internet. You still see martial arts superheroes in films, but the whole genre is in decline. The top-grossing martial arts films of the UFC era have been Jackie Chan comedies or unrealistic movies such as *Hero* (2002) or *Crouching Tiger, Hidden Dragon* (2000), in which kung fu masters float and fly through a fairy-tale world where the laws of physics have been suspended.

But I found, to my surprise, that the emergence of MMA hasn't changed the traditional martial arts very much. For instance, when I visited a local kung fu studio, the master told me that MMA is bullshit. He defined himself as a "militant traditionalist." If kung fu had failed in the UFC, it was because kung fu—following the lead of that hated heretic Bruce Lee—had tried to innovate. If kung fu fighters lost in the UFC, the solution wasn't to "mix" the martial arts, but to return to the true faith—to "unmix" kung fu and return to the pure and invincible kung fu of the ancient Shaolin monks.

I saw similar attitudes in the other dojos I visited, in online forums, and in the martial arts magazines and books I compulsively read. At my local big-box bookstore, the gun nut, muscle head, and martial arts magazines are all shelved together in what I call the "masculine anxiety" section. These are magazines for men who are worried about being big enough, skilled enough, and well armed enough to survive in a competitive world. Directly opposite the masculine anxiety magazines are the corresponding masculine anxiety books. Titles such as *Shooter's Bible*, *Modern Shotgunning*, *Mastering Jujitsu*, and *How to Kick Someone's Ass* are all mixed together on the same shelves. Books in the popular "how-to ninja" category promise readers the most. For instance, on the back cover of *Shadow Warrior*, the ninja wordsmith Jōtarō promises that "reading this book and adhering to its precepts will allow you to:

"**DISAPPEAR:** Become undetectable in any environment
"**READ MINDS:** Know your enemies' thoughts and intentions before they do
"**SEE THE FUTURE:** Ensure that your 'educated guesses' are never wrong

"**CONTROL MINDS:** From gentle suggestion to irresistible manipulation, bend others to your will
"**BECOME INVINCIBLE:** Guarantee that you *never* lose a fight."

Ninja Mind Control, by Ashida Kim, mainly consists of helpful tips
for ambushing and murdering unsuspecting foes. One of Kim's moves,
"Monkey Steals the Peach," stands out for the way it allows a ninja to effectively double-kill his target. Here's what you do: As your enemy throws
a punch, deflect it with your left hand while dropping to one knee. At
the same time uppercut the groin with an open-handed strike, while di-
recting your chi energy "up the Ch'ueng Mo channel of the body to stop
the heart." It's only then that you pluck your warm, ripe peach: "Clench
your fist tightly, with a crushing grip, and jerk the hand sharply back to
the near hip, effectively ripping away the genitals. Massive blood loss
causes death." (Note: It seems to me that this technique is most practical
against assailants who aren't wearing pants.) Of course, the "how-to
ninja" genre is easy to satirize, but it just exaggerates the big promises
you find in virtually all other martial arts magazines and books.

It was at this time, when I was moving through bookstores and dojos
exploring the views of traditional martial artists, that I went to visit
my friend Nobu at the gleaming new science building at Washington &
Jefferson College. I was particularly interested in interviewing Nobu
because he happened to be a dedicated martial artist as well as a practicing scientist. And the essence of science is ruthlessly testing and eliminating weak ideas. The biologist Thomas Huxley defined scientific
tragedy as "the slaying of a beautiful hypothesis by an ugly fact." The
ugly facts of cage fighting had, in my mind, slain the beautiful hypotheses of the traditional martial arts. If any martial artist would agree with
me, surely it would be my scientist friend Nobu.

I sat in his office while Nobu—trim and graceful and just starting to
show his forty years in the lines around his mouth—padded around in
his socks, brewing tea. As Nobu fetched cups and heated water, I told
him my story. I'd trained in karate but given it up after watching the UFC

massacres. Nobu was familiar with the UFC, but he hadn't followed it closely, so I filled him in on my whole argument: the UFC was a laboratory, and it had shown in repeated tests that the traditional martial arts were fatally flawed. True, I allowed, recent evidence from the ongoing UFC experiment had shown that many of the most dazzling karate and kung fu techniques, which had fared miserably in the first fifteen years of MMA, could be put to devastating use in a fight. I had been very wrong about this, having long ago reached the conclusion that breathtaking techniques such as spinning heel kicks and whirling elbows worked only on movie sets.

But, I went on, just because many aspects of the traditional martial arts turned out to work didn't validate the martial arts' whole system of katas, *kihons*, and hidebound traditionalism. Modern cage fighters could pull off these fancy techniques not because they stuck religiously to a traditional system, but because they mixed it into a regimen that also included intense training in takedowns, takedown defense, ground fighting, and brain-bruising sparring. (Most martial arts have retreated into very light or noncontact sparring.) It's a paradox, I said. The traditional techniques can work, but only when a fighter rejects tradition in favor of an open-minded, eclectic approach.

Nobu leaned back in his swivel chair, running his hands through his hair and murmuring, "Interesting . . . interesting." He took a sip of tea and asked, "In the early UFC, how do you know the karate guys were good?" I had to admit that I didn't, not really. "So maybe they were not good," Nobu continued. "And the rules of an MMA fight might favor grapplers. After all, it is against the rules to attack the eyes, and in karate you train to attack the eyes." Nobu was asking questions like a good scientist, pointing to potential flaws in the UFC experiment that might have queered the results.

Then Nobu, being an experimentalist, suggested the logical thing. He proposed a new test. "I'd like to try something," he said. "Can you get me a fight with one of those cage guys?"

Dopamine sluiced into my brain. It would make such a great scene for my book—Nobu squaring off against a cage fighter to try to replicate (or not) the original UFC experiment. Of course, I knew something that Nobu didn't. I'd trained at karate schools and observed them. And I'd trained at MMA schools and observed them. And I knew that unless Nobu's MMA opponent slipped catastrophically in Nobu's gushing blood—or drowned in it—Nobu was doomed.

"Nobu," I said, "no disrespect, but those guys will kill you."

"Maybe, but we can see, right?"

"Most of them are bigger than you."

"That's okay. I train to fight bigger guys. I am not big. I have no muscles. I am toned, but I'm not . . . [He growled and hulked out his arms like a bodybuilder.] Martial arts are *for* fighting big guys."

I left the building with a smile on my face, thinking of Nobu's fight and how I'd work it into my book. But I was thinking, too, of how a writer would stomp across a carpet of live puppies to get a better story.

I made some inquiries at the gym. I wanted one of the guys just to take Nobu down and submit him, so Nobu would know what it felt like. Mike Nesto was the idol of my gym. He had an awkward personal style: his conversation consisted mainly of welding together punch lines from the scores of dumb movies he'd memorized. But in the cage Mike was a virtuoso, and all of us desperately wanted to be like him when we grew up. I had around thirty pounds on Mike, but when we grappled, he dominated me as easily as I dominated my six-year-old daughter in our roughhousing. I knew Mike could subdue Nobu without even mussing his hair.

When I told Mike what I wanted, he flashed a wolfish smile and unconsciously fondled his dangerous left fist in his right palm. "I'll fight your friend," he said. I held both palms up at him and said, "No, no. No, Mike. Not fight. Just submit." Mike walked away, still fondling his fist. Worried that Nobu could really get hurt, I decided to let it go. In the end, I wasn't willing to stomp those puppies after all.

Mike Nesto (right) and me. Note the swelling mouse that Mike has just punched to life under my eye. I was a few months into my training when Mike hooked himself to my back on the ground and then looped punches into my face from behind. I could feel one of the punches split a vein—could feel the heat and weight of the blood as it spewed into the hollow under my eye. Afterward Mike came over to me as I admired myself in the mirror. "Looking good," he said. "Yeah," I replied with a smile, "it's actually the coolest thing that's ever happened to me." Mike laughed, because he knew it was half-true. I stood there fingering the swelling in the mirror—a thirty-eight-year-old boy proud of his first shiner. Mike eventually moved on to a top gym in Vegas, chasing the UFC dream. But like so many minor-league phenoms, Mike was achingly close to good enough—but not quite good enough.

BUT THEN NOBU and I happened to meet up at the poet's party. And that's when I decided I really did want to stomp some puppies—or at least try.

Nobu stood across from me, barefoot in the grass.

"You ready?" I called to him.

"Yes."

"Okay, but let's not kick each other in the nuts."

"Okay."

"Or poke each other's eyes out."

"Okay."

"Ready?"

"Okay."

"Okay, then—"

"But wait," Nobu said. "When you punch me, is it okay if I punch your fist in order to break your pinkie?"

"That's okay."

"Ready?"

"Okay."

Nobu sprang forward, snapping a front kick at my belly. The kick was very pretty and very fast.

FIVE

SURVIVAL OF THE SPORTIEST

Gentlemen, you are now going out to play football against Harvard. Never again in your whole life will you do anything so important.

Yale football coach Tad Jones

I know there will be violence, because he has promised, and he's a man who keeps his word. For a week he's been threatening to greet me at the airport. "Be ready," he drunkenly slurred in a voice mail message. "When you step offa the plane, BOOM! I'll hit ya and keep on hittin' ya till they drag me off your bones." The latest taunt came as I walked up the Jetway. It was a text message: "I can c u. U r dead!"

I walked out into the terminal and pressed my back to a wall so I could scan the crowd. I couldn't see him. I slung my carry-on over one shoulder so that if he showed, I could shrug it off quickly and have both hands free. I paused at the entrance to the baggage claim for a full minute. Not seeing him, I moved—head swiveling, eyes darting—through a blur of people going everywhere at once, dodging and weaving with their suitcases, milling around the gleaming steel carousels. And I felt afraid, but excited, too. When he showed his stupid, fat face, I was going to hit it, and not for the first time.

I stood and waited for the carousel to bring my bag, darting glances back and forth between the circling suitcases and the crowd. The phone buzzed with a text: "I c u. U r so fat. Prepare to die!" Before I could look up from my phone, I heard a noise at my back and knew he was there without having to turn around: a big, graceless oaf trying to move fast and stealthily over squeaky tile. The adrenaline hit my heart, and I wheeled to face him—a man in his late twenties, creep-running with a maniacal smile on his face, his rag of a T-shirt just containing the thickness of his upper arms and huge barrel chest. *My God*, I thought in a flash. *I'm outclassed.*

And then I felt my feet leave the floor, felt myself rising in his arms and crashing to the tile. We rolled and strained. I could hear him gasping. I could smell the beer and corn nuts from his long stakeout in the airport bar. I tried to get up, to get away, but his weight was too much. I saw the other people standing back in shocked silence as he furiously humped my leg, oinking in ecstasy. Why was no one pulling him off me? Why was no one calling the police?

Maybe it was because they were too stunned or afraid. Or maybe it was because we were both laughing so hard. Laughing like little boys. Like long-lost brothers.

WHY DO MEN FIGHT? A hard question. Why do men play fight? A harder question still.

In his landmark study *Homo Ludens* (Latin for "man the player"), the Dutch historian Johan Huizinga describes how play infiltrates just about everything people do—from card games and jokes to the frolics of small children and the wordplay of poets. For all his self-seriousness, Huizinga argues, man is a uniquely playful animal. But why? In biological terms, what is play for?

Perhaps the most mysterious form of human play is sport. But it's a mystery that hides in plain sight. Sport is so ubiquitous, so natural to us, that we rarely pause to ask why. Why do people care so much about sport when it seems to matter so little? Even most scholars pay scant attention to sport, consigning it to the toy department of human affairs.

More than that, many academics express a patrician disdain for the lout-ishness of individuals and societies that set so much more value—in prestige and pay—on the ability to throw a tight spiral or dunk a basket-ball than on the ability to write a poem, operate on a heart, or teach students to write a grammatical sentence. For many intellectuals, this makes sport worse than pointless; it makes sport a massive, parasitic suck on our culture's lifeblood.

But I'm starting from a different perspective. Around the world ordi-nary people rarely treat sport as pointless or wasteful. Players and spec-tators often approach sport in a spirit of high seriousness, and they treat victory and defeat almost like matters of life and death. In 1916 the Yale football coach Tad Jones told his team that nothing in their lives would ever rival the importance of a football game against Harvard, and there's nothing in the historical record to suggest that Jones was kidding or that his players rolled their eyes. For the Yale players, as for other athletes before and since, football was not just a game. Throughout human his-tory people have treated sport as very important, because, in fact, it ac-tually has been.

MARKS OF CAIN

Let's begin our discussion of sport at the MMA gym, on the day I first sparred with Nick Talarico (the National Guardsman who signed up for MMA after losing a fight to his girlfriend's ex). I'd been training at the gym for about four months, and my wrestling was progressing smoothly—the payoff, I suppose, from all that boyhood roughhousing. But the kickboxing was a different matter. First, after four decades of doing everything humanly possible to avoid being smashed in the face, I wasn't remotely prepared for the violence of it. Second, although wres-tling and punching come fairly naturally to most men, the intricate foot-work and slick combinations of kickboxing aren't natural at all. Coach Shrader goes further: "Kickboxing is a war against instinct. Your instinct screams at you to get away from this guy who's gonna knock you out. But don't back up! He'll just catch you and *fuck you up*! You've got to circle away. Or drive *into* the punch to stuff its power."

At first kickboxing cowed and confused me, but lately I'd felt that I was getting the hang of it. I'd been sparring with some of the weaker guys and pretty much holding my own. And the heavy bags were telling me the same sweet lies they tell everyone else: *Man, you hit* hard. *You must really have a knack for this thing.* So I went into the cage with Nick feeling something like confidence, not just because I thought I was improving, but because I underestimated Nick.

Nick is a handsome guy, but with his big frame, square jaw, and dark flattop, he bears at least a passing resemblance to Frankenstein's rectangle-headed monster. And in the cage Nick moves a little like the monster, staggering forward slowly and stiffly, and seemingly impervious to pain. No matter how hard you hit him, Nick keeps coming—moaning a little, relentlessly churning out punches, and occasionally throwing a spasmodic kick that makes him look, according to one of my gym mates, "like a retarded horse." I'd wrestled Nick before and come away with a draw. And I'd seen him sparring with other guys and smacking bags. I wasn't too impressed. Yes, he was bigger than me. And yes, he'd been training at the gym longer. But he moved and hit so awkwardly that I thought I'd do okay.

Nick and I stepped into the cage, touched gloves, and then tried not to look at each other in the slightly awkward moments before the bell. When we engaged, my nervous excitement turned quickly to disorientation. Something wasn't right. Nick is powerful, but he's not what you would call a graceful mover or a sophisticated striker. Nick plows forward: *jab, cross; jab, cross.* Nick plows forward: *jab, cross; jab, cross, hook.* Nick doesn't bob. Nick doesn't weave. Nick plows forward.

So why couldn't I hit him? Why were my gloves grazing harmlessly past his temples or glancing off his belly? I tracked him through the blur of our hands, and all the angles looked wrong, the planes of his face and body askew. There was nothing solid to hit. And all the while he was hammering me with punches I sensed too late—slow, heavy blows, but maddeningly oblique. Feeling woozy, I tried to take Nick down, but when I dove for his legs, the angles were again cockeyed, and I made an ugly botch of it. Nick stood back affably as I peeled myself off the mat, and then he hammered me some more.

When the bell finally saved me, we embraced. (It's a paradox: nothing makes men love each other more than a good-natured fistfight.) I sagged into one of the folding chairs, with my brain throbbing and the sweat rolling down my face, and thought, *That seals it. The Faurie-Raymond hypothesis has to be true.*

Nick is a type that most fighters fear and despise on first sight. Nick is a lefty, which is, according to Coach Shrader, "an abomination" and "a birth defect." Here, my professor joins other righty authorities in the sweet science who don't seem to be kidding when they say, "All southpaws should be drowned at birth."

But why does left-handedness exist at all? Left-handedness is unlikely to be a neutral trait in evolutionary terms (like the ability to curl the tongue, say). If left-handedness had no advantages or disadvantages, we'd expect the percentage of lefties to vary randomly in different places. In Africa you might find mostly righties, and in South America you might find mostly lefties. But that's not the case. Everywhere researchers have looked—across every culture and historical period, in the wear marks on ancient artifacts and the thumb sucking of fetuses—left-handers have been a clear minority.

Why? We don't know for sure, but Shrader's claim that lefties are defective may contain a grain of truth. In a world of scissors and school desks shaped for righties, being a lefty isn't just annoying; it may actually be bad for you. Scientists have been arguing the data for decades, but left-handedness has been associated with a variety of health problems, including low birth weight, lower life expectancy, higher risk of some diseases, and delayed maturation.

Which brings me to Charlotte Faurie and Michel Raymond, a pair of French researchers who study the biological mystery of southpaws. If left-handedness is partly heritable and carries health risks, why, the scientists wondered, hasn't evolution trimmed it away? Are the costs of left-handedness canceled out by hidden benefits?

Faurie and Raymond note that southpaws have advantages in interactive sports such as baseball and fencing, in which the competition is head-to-head, but not in noninteractive sports such as gymnastics, bowling, and swimming. Lefties make up one-tenth of the population as a whole, but around one-third (or more) of high-level competitors in interactive sports such as cricket, boxing, wrestling, tennis, and baseball. Might lefties just be more athletic? No; they are not more successful than righties in noninteractive sports. The lefty advantage in interactive sports seems to mainly come down to something simple: they confuse righties. Because 90 percent of the world's population is right-handed, righties usually compete against each other. When they confront lefties—who do everything backward—their brains reel, and the result can be as lopsided as my mauling by Nick. (Lefties are also more used to facing righties, but when two lefties face off, any confusion is canceled out.)

Faurie and Raymond made a mental leap. It's now well established that, myths of noble savages aside, the lives of our ancestors were typically much more violent than our own. Wouldn't the lefty advantage in sport—including combat sports such as fencing, boxing, wrestling, and judo—have extended to actual fighting, whether with clubs, knives, or spears? Could the survival advantages of battling left-handed have offset the health costs? In 1995 Faurie and Raymond published a paper showing a strong correlation between violence and handedness in tribal societies: the more violent the society, the more lefties it had. The most violent society they sampled, the Eipo people of New Guinea, was almost 30 percent southpaw. The second most violent society, the Yanomamö, was about 25 percent lefty. The least violent societies, such as the Dioula of Burkina Faso, were only about 3 percent lefty.

For a recent book, I was asked to contribute an essay on a scientific explanation I found beautiful. Passing on obvious candidates such as evolution, I chose Faurie and Raymond's explanation of left-handedness. I chose it partly because it was an almost recklessly creative idea, and yet the data seemed to fit. But mainly I chose it because my friend Nick had pounded the undoubtable truth of it into my brain.

But remember Thomas Huxley's definition of scientific tragedy: "the slaying of a beautiful hypothesis by an ugly fact." Many studies have examined the Faurie-Raymond hypothesis. The results have been mixed, but facts have surfaced that are, to my taste, quite decidedly ugly. For example, a recent and impressive inquiry found no evidence that lefties are actually overrepresented among the Eipo of New Guinea.

It hurts to surrender a cherished idea—one you just *knew* had to be true because it had been stamped into your brain by lived experience, not statistics. And I'm not yet ready to consign this idea to the boneyard of beautiful but dead science. Faurie and Raymond brought in sports data to shore up their main story about fighting, but I think those data may actually *be* the main story. Lefty genes may have survived more through southpaw success in the play fights of ritual combat than through success in actual violence—a possibility the researchers explored in later papers. Historically, sport has been an overwhelmingly male-dominated preserve, and winners—from captains of football teams to traditional African wrestlers to Native American lacrosse players—have gained more than mere laurels. They have elevated their cultural status; they have won the admiration of men and the desire of women.

In the Bible story, Cain killed his brother Abel, and so God "set a mark upon Cain" and thrust him into exile (Gen. 4:15). Men's bodies and minds are still marked by Cain's sin—by incontrovertible evidence of an (evolutionary) history of violence. There is a reason that most men are so much bigger and stronger than most women, that they can run so much faster and throw so much harder. Reproductive organs aside, all the things that most set men apart from women are marks of Cain, shaped over deep time by a near male monopoly on violence—between man and man, between man and beast, and between warring groups. But as with the evolution of left-handedness, a trait that appears to persist because it gives an edge in combat may actually have been selected more for its advantages in ritual combat—in sport, in other words.

WHY SPORTS?

Imagine me during the worst part of my day—the hour before my MMA class. I'm at home with my womenfolk after dinner. There is the sound of female foot patter, of laughter and chatter. Everything is nice. My TV, my bourbon, and my couch beckon. But resisting it all, I prepare glumly for the gym: brush my teeth, change my clothes, gather my armor (shin pads, boxing and MMA gloves, hand wraps, mouthpiece, cup). How hard it is to leave this warm and cozy girl world, where all the edges are soft and round, and no one ever splits me open or blackens my eye or knees me viciously (if inadvertently) in the groin. How hard it is to drive off to the big-boy world of the MMA gym, where I'll have to push myself to the point of collapse as I get battered by Coach Shrader, pretzeled by Mike Nesto, or smashed to roadkill by one of the heavyweights.

To do MMA is to hurt. The sport is one-on-one tackle football—with the addition of punching, kneeing, choking, and cranking. It leaves you so sore, bruised, and chafed that sleeping hurts. Training at the gym, I've suffered many black eyes, blood-puffed ears, pulled muscles, charley horses, jammed fingers, and swollen joints—all stuff I could work through. But there was also at least one concussion, way too many woozy "dings," a flash knockout (I charged forward and attacked my opponent's jab with my chin, then collapsed bonelessly to the mat—just like Forrest Griffin against Anderson Silva in 2009), and a chronic case of turf toe (which is so much worse than it sounds). There was also a deep hematoma that swelled my calf to twice its normal size and put me on crutches for a week. And then there was the time a heavyweight named Clark Young crucified me from a standing position, flipped me

Daddy at Resling, by Abigail Gottschall, eight years old. To keep my daughters from worrying, I told them that I was taking wrestling classes, not fighting classes. Abby's portrait of me at class—with a swollen black eye, a bloody right toe (indicating my chronic turf toe), and an expression of half-weepy resignation—captures my mood during much of this project. At other times, however, I experienced a resurgence of youth and confidence that made me feel elated. The MMA journal I wrote in most nights after class veers crazily between happiness and despairing self-reproach—like the ravings of an acute manic-depressive.

over, and drove his gorilla bulk down on the back of my neck until I squealed. It hurt so much that I crawled off the floor expecting the paralysis to set in at any moment. (The MRI showed no breaks, but the vertebrae were pushed a bit out of true, and my neck hasn't been the same since.) Over the same period I've seen guys choked to sleep, sparring with toilet paper tampons up their bloody noses, vomiting from exhaustion or blows to the gut, and writhing on the mat holding their testicles or their blown-out knees. And then there's the sickness. The biggest danger in MMA, especially in the winter, may be the microbes. To understand why, just imagine the gym on a typical boxing night. We cycle through opponents in a round-robin fashion, smearing each other's snot and slobber across the surface of our gloves, then stamping the germs into the next guy's nose and lips.

Coach Shrader sums things up this way: "Being a fighter is about getting comfortable with pain, inside the cage and out. Getting punched in the head sucks. Running sucks. Cutting weight sucks. It all just sucks." This invites an obvious question: if it hurts so bad and sucks so much, why do we do it? The same question applies to other sports. MMA is among the most extreme of all the extreme sports, but other sports are also difficult, time-consuming, and dangerous. So why do we play? And by "we" I mean *Homo sapiens*. Contrary to common beliefs, sport wasn't invented by modern, leisure societies as a way to fritter away excess time. Sports are the most common type of game across societies. And everywhere sports are played, people seem to care way more about the ability to kick a grass-stuffed kangaroo scrotum (Australian Aborigines) or throw an inflated seal stomach (the Yaghan of Tierra del Fuego) than they should.

For most of human history, sport had very steep costs. Time spent playing was time *not* spent courting mates, hunting, or patrolling against raiders. All the calories a person blew through in wrestling, running, and jumping had to be replaced by working harder to get food. And pity the injured man. For a hunter, blowing out an ACL while booting a kangaroo scrotum didn't mean relaxing for a few months while a transplanted ca-daver ligament took root. It meant the man was over as a hunter and a warrior—effectively, as a man.

Evolution is a miser. We expect costly traits to be pruned away unless they have offsetting benefits. In the modern world, elite professional ath-letes can achieve astounding wealth and fame. But the phenomenon of people making their living—forget a big living—playing sports is less than a century old and still applies only to an infinitesimally small per-centage of athletes. Most people play sports with no thought of fame or fortune. They play in slow-pitch softball leagues. They play pickup bas-ketball or club rugby with their friends. Or they are, like I was, mediocre college athletes with zero professional prospects who still treat their sport (tennis, in my case) like their whole raison d'être. So given the high costs and low apparent benefits, why is our species so obsessed with sports?

An obvious answer begins with my miserable nightly preparation for MMA class. The very last thing I feel like doing most nights after dinner is getting in a series of fistfights with a bunch of twenty-year-olds—is doing *anything* requiring strapping armor to my genitals. But since I began work on this book, trading punches with twenty-year-olds has kind of been my job, and so I drag myself to the gym like a shift worker drag-ging himself to the factory. I limp onto the mat feeling tired and old, and after I warm up and get going . . . I have so much fun. The blubbery, con-gested sensation of incipient middle age gives way, and I feel young again, and strong. When I've competed well, and especially when I've held my own in the sparring, I leave the gym feeling so *awake*, my whole system revving with something purer than a runner's high. I drive home knowing that I've been going through life half asleep, and I feel a euphoric grati-tude for my living muscle and bone and blood.

So humans play sports because they can be a source of intense joy. But the fact that sports are intrinsically rewarding, though true, is not a solution to the evolutionary mystery. It just forces us to restate the question: why do people like playing sports when the costs can be catastrophic and the practical payoffs seem so low?

Is it because sports keep us fit? Probably not. As the exercise scientists Loren Cordain and Joe Friel put it, "No adult hunter-gatherer in their right mind would have ever set off on a run or repeatedly lifted a heavy stone simply to expend energy and 'get exercise.'" In order to eat, our ancestors had no choice but to exercise intensively, every day of their lives. They had to run food down, then run it through. They had to hike out and gather it up. They had to plow, plant, harvest, and process. Obesity is a problem in modern societies, Cordain and Friel point out, mainly because supermarkets and restaurants have "totally and completely obliterated the ancient evolutionary link between energy expenditure and food intake."

So why do people play sports? Maybe it will help to ask a different question first: why were those two grown boys play fighting on the airport floor?

THE DUELS OF BOYHOOD

My poor mother had a daughter when she was twenty, and then, always hoping for another girl, she ran off four sons in a row. We boys loved her, of course, and she loved us back, but we also tormented her. Our play was rough, messy, and chaotic—always competitive and always laced with the threat that playful tussles would erupt into something more serious. Like all mothers of boys, ours understood the nature of the beast. Boys' raucous forms of play are something to be suffered, perhaps suppressed (she periodically confiscated our toy guns), but not really changed (we always stole the guns back or MacGyvered new ones out of tape and sticks). What really bothers my mother, even now, is how we never stopped acting like boys. Reaching our late teens and twenties, we moved, one by one, away from home and spread across the country. But at reunions the Gottschall boys always revert to their old play styles.

Imagine us in our mother's kitchen—four grown men hurling insults, securing headlocks, crashing against the refrigerator to apply mutual noogies, all while our father looks on proudly and our mother tries to drive us from the room with pleas and screeches.

When I was in my twenties, my brothers and I would camp in the Adirondacks, usually with my grad school friends. We went for all the good camping reasons: the majesty of the mountains, the speed of the rivers, the exercise, the tranquility. But we were also there to compete. Nothing in those woods was not a contest: Who can hike farthest and fastest with the heaviest pack? Who can build a fire using damp wood and no sissy accelerants? Who knows the best way to string edibles between trees, beyond the reach of bears? In camp we organized our leisure around "feats of strength." Sometimes a feat of strength was awarded for an actual feat of strength, such as lifting a boulder or hanging the longest from the lean-to roof. But feats of strength were more often awarded for nonmuscular proofs of manhood. Who's man enough to jump into that snowy pond? Who will eat that slug? Who will sit on that river boulder, while the blackflies swarm like piranhas, and not swat or twitch for a full minute? Is it possible for a determined man to eat a whole watermelon in one sitting? Just barely.

We usually found our inspiration for these idiot contests at the bottom of beer cans. And come to think of it, drinking was never just an opportunity to relax and chat. Drinking was a sport, too, always paired with chance-based games that were tests not of skill or smarts, but of the liver's ability to break down alcohol. With the flow of alchohol came an endless stream of insulting banter. Falling behind in your cups meant fielding mock-solicitous inquiries about your diaper or your purse or some other item that women or babies need. The competitive banter often combusted into full-fledged disputes that still stand out today as the longest and dumbest arguments I've suffered in a life that has been rich to overflowing with long, dumb arguments.

In this we were typical of young and youngish men everywhere. As boys become men, they wrestle less, but they never really give up rough-

Battle rappers having an insult contest. Men and boys compete in ritualized insult wars all around the world. Earlier we saw how the instinctive choreography of a standard human fight has been elaborated into the world's various formal dueling systems. The same goes for the monkey dance of the banter fight, which always involves the same basic moves and rules. Two men take turns hurling boasts and insults. The contests draw spectators, who laugh and hoot as the men derogate each other's masculinity, while also leveling hilariously vile attacks on relatives (especially mothers). All around the world, the verbal duel is a pure monkey dance for the mind, in which men compete in verbal artistry, wit, and the ability to take a rhetorical punch. Like other forms of the monkey dance, scholars have wondered why boys and men are drawn to verbal duels, and girls and women generally aren't. This strikes me as a very male sort of question to ask. It's sort of like a dung beetle wondering why humans don't find feces delicious. Women avoid verbal duels not because they've been told it's unladylike, but because trading the vilest attacks conceivable while vying in braggadocio just isn't most women's idea of a good time. Why don't people eat feces? Because coprophagy isn't in our nature. Why don't women like to duel verbally? Because it's not in theirs.

housing. Whenever guys gather in friendly circumstances, their conversations run to verbal monkey dances—to duelly exchanges spiced with playful insults and one-upmanship. When my MMA friend Nick calls me on the phone, he never says, "Hello, Jonathan, how are you?" Instead, he cheerfully booms, "What's up bitch/cocksucker/fuck face?" And every now and then he tags me with an unprovoked sucker punch of a text message, like this concise masterpiece from the spring of 2012: "I hope you choke on your pencil shavings, Professor Buttlick!" For men, these sorts of insults—volleyed rapidly back and forth like tennis balls—can not only be nonaggressive but downright affectionate. By a kind of lovely, pathetic alchemy, men transform harsh fighting words—and rough arm punches and shoves—into a language of endearment. Here's what my brother Robert was saying when he abused me between the baggage carousels: *I love you, but I hardly see you. And that makes me sad. And that's why I'm so happy now. Happy enough to slap your face.*

I'm aware that I've made the Gottschall brothers and our friends sound like a pack of macho jerks reveling in mindless locker room antics. But aside from my brother Rob—the one who assaulted me at the baggage claim—none of us ever qualified as particularly macho. We were dorks. Grad students in economics or English literature, and ex–Dungeons & Dragons fanatics to a man. We all suffered on the wrong end of schoolboy wedgies. What I'm describing here is pretty typical of boys and young men everywhere: they bond through contests, no matter how frivolous the form. While these contests can be silly, risky, and crass, they actually serve a vital function. Through constant monkey dancing, men form their alliances and compete inside them. And in little-league versions of the monkey dance, boys train themselves, body and mind, for the contests of manhood.

HERE IS THE DIFFERENCE between what girls and boys do for fun: girls play; boys play fight.

True, boys are more violent than girls. By the age of seventeen months, five times as many baby boys as baby girls frequently hit, claw, and bite. But boys really outstrip girls not in fondness for fighting, but in fondness for *play* fighting. As the child psychologist Eleanor Maccoby puts it, "Boys are *not* aggressive, in the sense of possessing a consistent personality disposition that involves frequent fighting . . . Among most groups of boys, fighting does not occur frequently, and most of their rough play occurs more in the spirit of fun than of anger." Similar sex differences apply to other forms of play. The sex difference in affinity for competitive games, for example, is enormous: in one study, boys were fifty times more likely than girls to engage in games involving direct head-to-head competition, while girls were twenty-one times more likely to engage in turn-taking games. Boy games are straightforward dominance contests; girl games are close to the opposite. Girls tend to prefer games that promote cohesion and allow them to accomplish something cooperatively.

This is the big reason that close opposite-sex friendships are so rare, even in adulthood. It's not mainly because—as Harry theorized to Sally in the eponymous 1981 movie—romantic yearning on one side or the other eventually queers the friendship. The reason is a clanging incompatibility in preferred social styles, connected especially to male preferences for playfully competitive forms of friendship. The phenomenon of mainly gender-segregated friendships starts very young, at the age of about two, when little girls start avoiding rambunctious boys as playmates. I asked my daughter Annabel about this when she was in kindergarten.

"Do the boys and girls play together at your school?" I inquired.

"Not too much," she replied.

"How come?"

"Because the boys are badder. They are so crazy in games like Star Wars and robbers. The girls don't wanna be around noisy boys."

"What do you mean by 'crazy'?"

"They're loud. They like to wrestle."

"How about the girls?"

"The girls are quiet and calm in the [play] kitchen. Girls just talk to each other in there, playing."

Annabel's experience is typical. Preschoolers play with members of their own sex three times as often as members of the opposite sex. By the time they are six, they engage in same-sex play eleven times as often. These patterns, which have been documented all around the world—and even in apes—are not results of adult efforts to segregate children for the purpose of gender indoctrination. To the contrary, over the past few decades educators have desperately tried to break down sex segregation in hopes of reshaping traditional gender roles. As I documented in my previous book, these attempts have resulted in spectacular and illuminating failures. Girls and boys self-segregate simply because their play styles clash. Scientists have identified higher levels of male rough-and-tumble play not only across human societies but also across scores of different species, including our close primate relatives. Young male monkeys and apes group together and engage in more pretend and real aggression, while young females—just like their human counterparts—enjoy gentler modes of play, seek to build intimate relationships, and show far more fascination with infants.

In his 1898 book *The Play of Animals*, Karl Groos wrote, "Perhaps the very existence of youth is due in part to the necessity for play; the animal does not play because he is young, he has a period of youth because he must play." More than a century later, most experts share Groos's point of view: for humans and other animals, play is vital. We enjoy play for the same reason we enjoy food or sex: because it is good for us. And for most boys nothing is as deliriously, maniacally fun as rough and exuberant play. Nature has designed boys to delight in rough play because it is important. It literally trains boys in combative arts. It teaches them how to wrestle each other for dominant position, both physically and verbally. It teaches them how to flee, chase, and tackle, how to hurl missiles and dodge them. It teaches them how to be brave and tough—how to flirt with danger and tolerate pain.

But boys are also beginning a lifelong male process of forging and maintaining their status arrangements through contests. They are engaging in kiddie ritual combat that hashes out dominance without the danger of fighting for real. In early childhood boys start setting up clear-cut dominance hierarchies that are largely based on strength, toughness, and athletic ability. And status matters, even among kids. Among young children, high-status kids get preferred access to toys, play areas, and food. Among twelve-year-old boys, successful play fighters are more dominant and more attractive to girls. Of course, status matters in the immediate sense that popular kids usually enjoy good quality of life, while unpopular kids may feel that they have no lives at all. But the perquisites of high status in childhood extend into later life. The social status of six-year-olds is a good predictor of their social status in young adulthood.

But at some point boys have to grow up and become men. When I meet my friends for a beer, we don't take breaks from our discussions of campus politics or movies for a little impromptu wrestling. If it seems a little sad to think of this boyish exuberance fading out of male life, it shouldn't. As the neuroscientist Jaak Panskepp suggests, boys like play "with a strong competitive edge," and as they grow up, they just graduate into more formal types of exuberant play. They take up sports.

"GETTING AHEAD WHILE GETTING ALONG"

Sport is another form of the monkey dance—a form of ritual combat that is equivalent to animal contests. To equate complicated human sports— cricket, Afghan buzkashi (a rough mock cavalry war fought over a dead goat), Australian rules football, chess boxing—with the way rattlesnakes or gazelles battle for females may seem absurd, but bear with me. Biologists habitually compare animal ritual combat to sports, duels, or tournaments. For example, the biologists Amotz and Avishag Zahavi note that male gazelles don't try to sneak up and gore each other when they compete for does. Instead, they lock horns and have a contest of strength, balance, and stamina—pushing and pounding and wrestling from side to side. "It would be a mistake," the Zahavis write, "to call such a struggle a fight. It is more like a competitive sport in which contestants try to show off their superiority while following fixed rules." The biologist David Barash has the same idea. Animal ritual combat is "so stylized as to be more aptly described as tournaments rather than fights . . . Although written by evolution rather than by a human hand, the strictures appear to be no less real, and adherence is remarkably complete. Animals whose behavior is characterized by such rules are no more likely to break them than a human prizefighter is to pull out a revolver and shoot his opponent."

The big difference between human and animal sports is that the latter are purely instinctive—the rules "written by evolution" and followed with robotic regularity. Human sports, by contrast, are massively elaborated by culture. But sports are cultural only in this limited sense: different societies develop somewhat different ways for people to compete in strength, speed, endurance, fortitude, and skill. Beneath all the wild diversity of human sporting events, there is a shared underlying structure and purpose. Sports, just like gazelle wrestling, are always about finding reasonably safe, rule-bound ways for people to demonstrate their physical prowess and mental toughness to others.

Humans are defined by biologists as an "ultra-social" species. And for men (we will get to women later) forming functional male-bonded groups was once a matter of life and death. But so was a man's ability to compete inside the male-bonded group. Males needed ways to determine "the better man" without the physical danger and social chaos that come with fighting for real. Sports are one of nature's solutions to the problem. They allow men to compete—intensely and to the best of their abilities—without blowing their coalitions apart.

"GAY PORN FOR STRAIGHT MEN"?

The way sports allow men to get along while they strive furiously to get ahead is nicely illustrated at an MMA gym. MMA—with its ripped physiques and grappling positions straight out of the Kama Sutra—has been likened by *Out* magazine to "gay porn for straight men." I know MMA can look that way from outside the cage, and I admit that going into this project, I felt a little squeamish about how much time I would need to spend rolling around playing sweaty Twister with other guys. But I got over that quickly. There's nothing erotic about MMA. In competition the impulse to survive and prevail swamps any erotic feeling. The physiological reaction is the opposite of arousal. The cremaster muscle contracts, forcing the genitals to suck in self-protectively, in the reflex *Seinfeld's* George Costanza called "shrinkage."

Our tendency to see any physical contact or affection between men as latently homosexual, or at least homoerotic, represents a crushing failure to recognize that for most of human history, a man's ability to survive and thrive depended on forging strong alliances with men as much as women. To understand why, you can study male bonding in history and anthropology, or you can just watch almost any cop movie. Take the Jake Gyllenhaal film *End of Watch* (2012), which, for all its amped-up chases and shoot-outs, realistically portrays an intense platonic love affair between two young police partners and how they cultivate their relationship through physical and verbal roughhousing. The film also shows why male bonding has been so important throughout time: standing alone the police officers are weak, but bonded together they are strong.

My MMA gym is a comfortable, comradely place. There's a lot of fist tapping, shoulder chucking, and bro-hugging. We learn moves through an endless sequence of trust falls. I let a man attach himself to my back, for example, and he begins the process of murdering me. He sweeps one arm across my throat, locks it together with the other, and squeezes. The blood pressure in my head soars instantly, veins bulge at my temples, and my eyes swim with bright spots as I begin to die. But he releases me when I gently tap his arm, and the blood rushes back into my brain. Or Coach Shrader teaches a boxing technique, and I stand in front of him as he throws annihilating punches that he pulls at my jaw—like he's the circus knife thrower and I'm the girl. For the gym to work, each man must trust his partners and protect them, and this inspires warm fellow feeling. But it doesn't change the fact that the gym is a zone of fierce competition. We go there to learn how to physically dominate men in the outside world and how to compete for dominance inside the gym. We work out our hierarchy directly, by hitting, choking, and tackling. But the competition is friendly—we hope to win but not to harm. And even though sparring can occasionally escalate to very heavy contact, I have never seen a real fight—in the sense of an angry and uncontrolled exchange—break out in my three years of training.

This is partly because our contests are regulated, with clear rules about what is and isn't allowed. But it's also because our dominance hierarchy keeps things civilized. Everyone knows who is strong and who is weak. Everyone knows, to a near certainty, who would lick whom if it

Mark Shrader tapes Clark Young's hands before a fight.

came to a real fight. At the gym the dominant guys don't bully or oppress the weaker guys. This is partly because there's no glory in it and partly because the subordinates give clear signals to the dominants—sometimes in the form of terrified body language, sometimes in words—that are equivalent to animal submission displays. Clark Young, for example, is a neckless, heavily tattooed 270-pounder. In addition to being a competition MMA fighter, Clark is also a bar bouncer, a National Guardsman, a rider in a motorcycle club, an expert in the U.S. Army's Close Quarters Combat system, and a worker in the tough guy world of western Pennsylvania shale frackers. He is, in other words, much man. So the first time I faced him in the cage, I went straight up to him in that awkward moment before the bell, buried my head in his meaty cleavage, and whimpered through mock tears, "Clark, come on man, *I've got a family.*" Since I'd effectively surrendered at the start, Clark didn't exactly go easy on me, but he did let me live.

As in the ritual contests of animals, sparring starts to escalate only when guys are evenly matched and neither will send a submission signal. Nick, for example, will never do what I did with Clark: roll over like a craven dog and show his soft belly. No matter who he fights, Nick comes on hard. I admire Nick's spirit, but because he's a big guy who probably doesn't feel comfortable making a submission display, he absorbs more punishment from the gym studs than anyone else.

Most people think of dominance hierarchies as bad. They go against ideals of fairness. But without our pecking order—without our ways of establishing rank and deferring to it—the little society of my MMA gym would be a grisly bloodbath. And the same goes for the world outside the gym. Humans are inherently hierarchical animals, with pecking orders reliably emerging even among toddlers. This is especially impressive in boys, who often form stable hierarchies within one play session. (Girls do, too, but their hierarchies are more prone to coups d'état.) Once boys work out their dominance ranks, aggression tails off and dominant boys use more cooperation than coercion. Among humans and other animals, a desire to move up in the pecking order causes a lot of aggressive competition, but once a pecking order is formed, it diminishes the frequency and severity of conflict.

In real cage fights, the competition is savage, but the fights almost always end in a mutual display of authentic affection—with handshakes, hugs, and sincere expressions of consolation or congratulation. Often fighters hold long embraces, expressing the kind of mutual affection that straight men can express only after a barbaric demonstration of masculinity. In this fighters are replicating European code duellos, which specified not only that hostility should be canceled by a duel but also that duelists should part with a handshake and expressions of goodwill, even if one man had mortally wounded the other. And fighters are also replicating the code of ritual combat in social animals as varied as goats, horses, dolphins, and hyenas. After two chimps fight, for example, they usually share a bro-hug or even a kind of handshake: the loser holds his hand out in meek submission, and the winner takes it, signaling that, yes, bygones will be bygones. The same sort of postfight reconciliation— kissing, hugging, grooming, hand holding—has been observed in more than thirty other primate species.

For humans it's true that team sports can create sharp animosities and rivalries between groups, which is something I'll explore in the next chapter. But for the most part sports do their job. They serve the same dominance-sorting function for big boys and men that unstructured rough-and-tumble play serves for younger boys. While minimizing rancor, sports establish who is stronger, fitter, and abler, and broadcast this information to the community at large. Observing men take careful notice, tucking away crucial information about who is formidable and who is not. And women notice, too.

WHAT ABOUT WOMEN?

There's a famous moment in Homer's *Odyssey* when Odysseus's faithful wife, Penelope—exhausted by two decades of waiting for her husband's return from the Trojan War—finally succumbs to the pressure from her suitors and says she is ready to remarry. She has more than one hundred eager suitors—all strong, healthy, and well-bred. How's a girl to choose? Penelope has her servants set twelve axes in a row and bury the butts in the ground. She announces that she will marry the suitor who can use Odysseus's bow to zing a single arrow through the tiny gap in all twelve axe heads. Penelope sits and watches as the men try futilely to bend and string Odysseus's mighty bow. Their humiliation is magnified when a beggar who's been hanging around the house takes up the bow, strings it with ease, and almost casually fires an arrow through all the axe heads. The beggar then reveals his true identity: it's Odysseus himself who, through this sportlike display of prowess, once again proves he is a man above all others—the perfect man for the perfect woman.

Ritual combat is often seen as a process whereby active, strapping males battle it out among themselves, with the victor "taking" the passive females—who have no choice in the matter. This is ass-backward, or at least one-sided. Remember Penelope: she's the one who sets up the contest for her hand, and she does so in her own best interests. The same goes for other species. It may look like the males have the power and have set up contests for rights to the females, but try to look at things the other way around: the females have the power, and they have set up grueling, dangerous contests to eliminate fakers and reveal mates of authentic quality. In most species females could, if they chose, refuse the dominant male. An elephant seal cow could flop away from the magnificently fat alpha male and debauch to her heart's content with the losers on the bachelors' beach. Instead, she normally does the opposite: she sprawls out on the sand and bawls in protest if a low-ranking male tries to mount her—which has the effect of summoning all the males within earshot to come and fight over her. Similarly, the doe could trot safely away from the victorious buck, but she usually doesn't. Females in many species directly instigate male mating competition, or at least cooperate with the winners.

Given the high costs of sports, we should expect them to come with at least potentially high rewards. The very word *athlete* comes from the Greek *athlon*, meaning "prize" or "reward." An athlete is one who competes for a prize. At the Greek Olympics the most common prize was a laurel wreath—a crown of woven branches and leaves. According to Herodotus, the Persians were shocked that Greek athletes competed not for gold or silver but for mere foliage. But clearly the Greeks weren't competing for a handful of leaves. They were competing for the enormous social status symbolized by those leaves. And that status was so valuable partly because of its links to sex.

That athletes have more sexual success is something almost everyone who went to high school or college knows about. Anecdotes about young women flocking to high-level professional athletes are backed up by studies showing that even small-time high school and college jocks do better with the ladies. The same goes for athletes all around the world. Among the Mursi of Ethiopia, young women instigate wild stick-fighting contests among young men and lavish their attention on the winners. In the Micronesian state of Truk, the boys get drunk and fight in no small part because they know the girls are watching. Among the Sereer people of Senegal and the Mehinaku of central Brazil, winning wrestlers attract more wives and have more children than nonwrestlers. And in ancient Rome, gladiators were sex symbols despite their lowly social status.

Women's attraction to athletes is, of course, matched by an attraction to athletic physiques. Michelangelo's statue of David is a timeless ideal of male physical beauty. But David also represents a poignant paradox in the beauty of men. David is a warrior, and Michelangelo portrays him glaring across the battlefield, in the moment before he crushes Goliath's skull with a river-polished stone. The statue is a reminder that the beauty of a man's body correlates almost perfectly with its destructive potential. Everything beautiful about David's body—his broad shoulders, swollen muscles, and agile legs—is a cue of his formidability, his capacity to project physical force. Michelangelo carved

David out of marble, lovingly shaping all his contours. Similarly, over eons, our grandmothers and great-grandmothers have, through their loving, carved such features into the genes of men. Women, in their aggregate mate choices, have created men over time, sculpting better providers and protectors. In the modern world, of course, women no longer need men to provide them with meat or to protect their children from bears. But evolution works slowly, and modern women still respond to the cues of physical prowess that moved their great-grandmothers.

This is all noteworthy, because it is so *not* what men are looking for in their mates. Men generally like women's bodies to be fit and graceful, yes, but they are not looking for the heavy bones or bulging muscles advertising a woman's physical formidability. To the contrary, they are looking for bulging fat deposits, which, though they interfere with a woman's ability to do some types of work, provide good signals of her age and fertility. Men are, in other words, choosing mates based on cues of *reproduction* (fertility), while women are selecting them based on cues of *production* (ability to do work). (This is why, when entering the prime years of reproductive competition, pubescent girls naturally plump up with fat, while pubescent boys pump up with muscle.) In other words, as the biological anthropologist David Puts argues, when it comes to the mating game, men seek physical beauties, while women seek physical beasts.

WHY DO WOMEN PLAY?

Is women's evolutionary role in sports limited to cheerleading—admiring the boys from the sidelines while representing the spoils of victory? Of course not.

One day a new kid came into the MMA gym. The kid was like nothing we'd seen. The kid was an outstanding athlete, able to leap into effortless backflips and dance around the gym like an acrobat on the hands. The kid looked tough, with cornrows and a crooked nose. And the looks weren't deceiving: the kid had won that battle scar while losing a bloody brawl against one of the top-rated amateur fighters in the country. On the ground especially, the kid was an ace—more than a match for the best of us in jiu-jitsu. I asked some of the guys at the gym, "Strictly theoretically, do you think you could take the new kid?" Some hemmed and hawed. Most scoffed, "Hell, no!" The bigger guys figured they could blast through the kid with sheer power, but they knew they couldn't match the kid's technique.

The kid was a stud fighter from Pittsburgh, and she was also a woman. Jena "Jenacide" Baldwin didn't stay at the gym for long. She visited as a favor to Coach Shrader, to help teach class while he was on vacation. But she stayed long enough to earn the respect of all the guys at the gym. If any of us harbored lingering doubts about the legitimacy of women's MMA, Jena choked them out cold.

Jena is part of a new women's movement in MMA headlined by top fighters such as Ronda Rousey, Miesha Tate, and Cristiane "Cyborg" Justino. In the past few years female MMA fighters have gone from a sideshow attraction to the top of UFC cards. The rise of women's MMA mirrors a movement in women's sports participation generally. Since the enactment of Title IX in 1972, women's participation in sports at the high school and college levels has steadily moved toward parity with men's.

But if it's true that sports are a human form of ritual combat, we'd expect women to be less motivated to play. This is because, across species, ritual combat is overwhelmingly a male preserve. Yet most scholars and activist organizations insist that there is no intrinsic, natural difference in men's and women's interest in sports. That is the pious thing to say, and really the only position that can be safely expressed in polite company. But that doesn't mean it's so. Forty years after Title IX mandated equal access to sports opportunity, and however you want to measure it, the average male cares more about sports than the average female.

Men care more about sports as entertainment. Depending on the

Jena "Jenacide" Baldwin.

survey, men are between two and five times more likely to identify themselves as serious sports fans. This gap, big as it is, may be an understatement. If you asked my wife, she'd *say* she is a sports fan, and so would I, but she has invested vastly less time and energy than I have watching and discussing sports. (Put it this way: she's never had to be gentled out of a bar to keep her from strangling a childhood friend who kept stupidly arguing against a salary cap in major-league baseball.) Men spend more time and money consuming sports on TV and in person. They spend more on team-branded attire, expensive memorabilia, and sports video games. They dominate the ranks of fantasy sports leagues, and they consume massive quantities of sports information on the radio, the Internet, newspapers, and ESPN, which has been men's favorite TV network for fourteen straight years. Sports are, moreover, a crucial lubricant of male social networks. Without sports to watch, play, or debate, many male friendships would grind to an awkward halt.

The same interest gap appears in sports participation. Studies in big, modern countries always report greater male interest in participating in and excelling at sports. The same pattern seems to apply to small-scale band and tribal societies all around the world. In a 2012 study of dozens of cultures, the psychologists Robert Deaner and Brandt Smith found that 80 percent of all the sports in the cross-cultural sample were exclusively male. Of all references to sports in the sample, "males were participants in 95%, whereas females were participants in 20%." The gender gap was largest for combat sports such as wrestling, boxing, and stick fighting, in which participation was "almost exclusively male." As Deaner and his colleagues concluded in a different paper, boys and men seem to "have far greater inborn motivational predisposition to participate in and monitor sports."

Almost everyone agrees that this gender gap exists, but it's usually been attributed to universal sexism, not universal biology. Throughout time, the argument goes, women have been discouraged from playing sports. If not for the obstacles thrown up by patriarchal societies, women would be just as sports obsessed as men. The best evidence for this view comes from America in the wake of Title IX. Since passage of the amendment, which mandated equal opportunity in men's and women's scholastic sports, female participation in sports has increased 560 percent at the college level and 990 percent at the high school level.

This proves something that should never have been in doubt: many women love playing sports. But does it show that they are just as interested in sports as males? One problem with scholastic sports participation is that it is polluted—for men and women—by external incentives. High school students, for example, know that sports participation looks good on college applications, and college students may play to maintain scholarships. What does gendered sports participation look like outside a scholastic context? In other words, if you take away external academic incentives, who keeps playing?

Historically, the burdens of mammalian biology have limited women's sports participation as much as sexism. Prior to the (very recent) advent of reliable contraception, almost all sexually mature women were more or less constantly pregnant, nursing, and/or toting small children—which posed obvious problems for vigorous game play.

Mainly men do. In a 2012 study, Deaner and his colleagues found that men were three to five times more likely to compete in intramural sports in college, and three to four times more likely to keep playing strictly recreational sports after college. The researchers also conducted systematic observations of sports and exercise at forty-one public parks in four states. Females accounted for 37 percent of exercise participation, 19 percent of individual sports participation, and 10 percent of team sports participation. Finally, the researchers analyzed the Bureau of Labor Statistics' American Time Use Survey, in which 112,000 people were interviewed regarding their activities during one day. Females accounted for 51 percent of exercise participation (e.g., jogging or lifting weights), but just 24 percent of total sports participation. The takeaway: women are just as physically active as men, but when it comes to exercise, they are drawn less to competitive forms; they are just as happy getting their exercise at a Zumba class or on a jogging trail. (And what's so wrong with that?)

These percentages conceal a richer story about sports interest. Just because men and women both play sports, doesn't mean they approach them in the same way. For example, studies show that female athletes put a lower priority on competition and victory than male athletes. This difference in competitiveness has been quantified in ingeniously simple studies by Robert Deaner, which crunch tens of thousands of results from professional and recreational road races and show that male races are always more competitive than female races. Deaner writes, "In a typical local 5 K road race with equal male and female participation, for every female that finishes within 25% of the female world record, there are roughly three males that finish within 25% of the male world record. This pattern holds robustly for elite runners and recreational runners . . . Because relative running performance is an equally strong predictor of training volume (e.g., kilometers/week) in men and women, these patterns indicate that the sex difference in willingness to train is large and stable." A clear conclusion emerges from Deaner's analysis: about three times more men than women train and race in an intensely competitive spirit, while many more women than men train and race for sheer pleasure, camaraderie, and exercise. (And what's so wrong with that?)

Of course, Deaner and his colleagues, like all civilized people, believe that girls and women should have the same opportunities to play sports as boys and men do. They are not attacking Title IX, and they are not suggesting, as Homer Simpson explained to his daughter, "Lisa, if the Bible has taught us nothing else, and it hasn't, it's that girls should stick to girls' sports, such as hot-oil wrestling, foxy boxing, and such-and-such." Moreover, Deaner and his colleagues allow that culture plays a role in all of this: boys probably receive more social incentives to play sports. But they still conclude that cultural factors are bending men and women toward their native inclinations, not away from them. Women like to exercise, and most like sports as well—just not as much as men.

Now's a good time to deal with the question "What's so wrong with that?" Sports have emerged as a strangely important battlefield in the movement for women's equality. Many activists seem to feel that recognizing any intrinsic sex difference in sports motivation would be a major setback. This position has always puzzled me. How can the notion that women are less motivated to play sweaty games threaten the feminist project? Why would the world be a nicer place if women were just as stupidly obsessed with sports as men? I can't say for sure, but I've developed a theory. Men have ruled the world, I think, not because they are smarter or wiser than women (they are not), but because they have been more likely to live life as an endless string of competitive monkey dances. High-achieving men—politicians, CEOs, Wall Street wolves—experience life as an open-ended dominance contest, with all its bluster and high blood pressure and sawed-off life expectancy. Far fewer women understand how to monkey dance or are interested in learning. Far fewer women feel that a life of endless, often silly, striving represents a good model of a life well lived. For many feminists conceding that men care more about sports by nature would be too much like conceding that the average man is more competitive across the board. And if this is the case, if worldly success comes down to a fanatic willingness to live in monkey dances, then the dream of a society in which power is fairly shared between the sexes may be exactly that—a dream.

No one can read the future, but I think this concern is probably misplaced. Stunning advances in women's lives and roles over the last century show that biology is not destiny. And while skillful monkey dancing has historically been a reliable route to male power, it may not be as effective in times to come. In fact, some commentators argue that a new era is already dawning, one where traditionally feminine virtues—the ability to cooperate, to reach consensus, to steer around conflict—will allow women to outcompete men, and to bring a close to the "age of testosterone."

LOOK AT IT THIS WAY: what we find in women's sports is exactly consistent with what we find in girls' forms of play. Girls use play to establish intimate friendships and have less interest in competitive games than boys do. Given that most girls especially dislike physically rough, dominance-oriented forms of play, it's no wonder that, as girls mature, they remain less keen on the exuberant dominance contests of sports. Given that girls and women put a higher value on cooperation and cohesion than males do, it is not surprising that they are not as attracted to the sports men have invented to show off their prowess and thrash out bragging rights.

But it is also obvious that many women play sports with great avidity and fierceness. That women are motivated to play sports at all is one of the truly fascinating things about our species, because in most animal species females don't participate in ritual combat at all.

What's going on here? My explanation for men's sports applies to women as well, only more weakly. Most female animals don't compete very hard for mates because, high-quality sperm being in abundant supply, there's no point. In humans, sperm is also cheap, but a father's investment in his offspring is not. So women must compete for quality mates who are able, and willing, to share the uniquely heavy burden of rearing human young. In sports, women, like men, make a gaudy display of health and physical quality. This should be attractive to men, because a woman's athleticism—and the quality genes underlying it—are likely to be passed down to her children. But women don't invest as much in sports because, in the end, men only care so much. Women value kindness and intelligence in mates, but they also gravitate to dominance cues—including the cues exhibited by successful athletes. As the psychologist Anne Campbell argues, the attributes that allow a man to successfully compete with other men—physically, economically, socially—pretty much sum up what turns women on. But while there's something undeniably sexy about the sheer physical excellence of Jena Baldwin, studies reliably show that men don't care a whit whether a prospective mate can dominate other women, physically or otherwise. For most men, power in women is simply not an aphrodisiac. If anything, men's preference for women who are young and delicate in appearance— whose looks signal lots of estrogen, not lots of testosterone—means that men are most attracted to women who would likely *lose* fights and other physical forms of contest. I don't think this is mainly because—as many would argue—men find female power threatening (though they well may; men certainly find *male* power threatening). I think it's simple biology: men seek out fertility cues; women seek out strength cues.

So humanity's love of sports is a riddle that needs a solution based in evolutionary biology. But having come so far, there's still a way to go. The evolutionary mystery of sports extends beyond the motivations of players to those of fans. It's weird enough that people care so much about *playing* sports; it's weirder still that they care so much about *how other people play them*. Let's talk about fans.

SIX

WAR GAMES

A violent ground acquisition game such as football is,
in fact, a crypto-fascist metaphor for nuclear war.

Student activist in *Back to School* (1986)

I'm at a small-time professional wrestling event in a rusted-out steel town outside Pittsburgh. I'm sitting with about 150 fans in the sort of bland civic center where volunteer firefighters serve up pancake breakfasts. In an elevated ring, men in bright spandex are kicking, whirling, colliding—knotting each other up in Boston crabs, cobra clutches, and chicken wings. The wrestlers aren't enormously steroidal like the guys on TV, and they don't have pro-level microphone skills, but they put on a lively show. And a skilled one. If I didn't *know* the violence was fake, I'm not sure I'd know it was fake. The wrestlers prance and pose; they howl in triumph and spit in rage. (They really spit.) In short, they ham it up.

All the matches are tied together by a single narrative thread: evil has come to Pittsburgh in the form of the 216 Clique, a group of wrestlers who represent everything mean and nasty in life, and hail from Cleveland, Pittsburgh's ancient rival in sports and commerce (216 is Cleveland's area code). Rules mean nothing to the 216 Clique. Their favorite tactic is to ambush and gang-stomp a lone Pittsburgh wrestler, shrieking blasphemies against the Pittsburgh Steelers the whole time.

Blaspheming the Steelers is like burning an American flag on Veterans Day or dipping a crucifix in urine on Easter. It's a vile sacrilege that cannot be tolerated. And so we rise up and throw it back at them, chanting, "Cleveland sucks! Cleveland sucks!" One of the Pittsburgh wrestlers catches our rhythm and shouts between beats, "And swallows!" (*"CLEVELAND SUCKS! And swallows! CLEVELAND SUCKS! And swallows!"*) Then, to fortify home team morale, we start chanting Pittsburgh's area code, "412! 412! 412!" Just hearing those hated digits seems to drive the whole 216 Clique pretty much insane. "Handsome" Frank Stiletto howls back at us in agonized rage, "Oh, shut up! Shut up you stupid Yinzers!" A different 216er suggests—through skillful grunting and face making—that we are all mentally retarded.

The evening's hostilities climax in a vicious gang war between fifteen to twenty wrestlers per side. The battle begins in the ring but quickly blows through the fourth wall, with the wrestlers chasing each other between our chairs and savaging each other in the aisles. Pittsburgh's brave champions hold their own at first, but gradually, one by one, they are beaten up, knocked out, and flung—limp and lifeless—from the ring. A gloomy pall descends on the crowd as our defeated heroes rise and stagger for the exits, surrendering the sacred hall to the enemy. As the curtain closes on the night's performance, a Pittsburgh wrestler calls back a challenge to the 216 Clique (and a reminder to the fans): "This isn't over! We'll see you here next week!"

The week passes like a long intermission of a play. When I return for act two, it's the same clash of good versus evil, except that after another vicious battle royal, the Pittsburgh men hold the ring, and the Cleveland men lie in twitchy heaps all over the hall. One of the Pittsburgh wrestlers—"the Steel City Prodigy"—taunts the 216 Clique by calling them "fairies" and "bitches." Enraged, the 216ers rise up and charge the ring, but only get themselves massacred for a second time. With evil thoroughly vanquished, the night ends with the Steel City Prodigy hooking his long locks of wet blond hair behind his ears and waving a Pittsburgh Steelers flag at center ring. As the crowd mills toward the exit, some of the younger wrestlers—216 and 412 working side by side—are already disassembling the ring with socket wrenches.

IN RESEARCHING THIS BOOK, I sought insights about fighting in all of its forms. I made a careful study of the unwritten codes governing hockey fights. I marveled at the demented creativity of chess boxing. I took notes at tournaments of jiu-jitsu players, college wrestlers, and amateur boxers. I went to the library and ransacked historical archives, reading up on nineteenth-century duel forms such as purring (two men lace on iron-tipped boots, lock arms, and have a shin-kicking war) and rough-and-tumble (a brutal duel form in which American frontiersmen tried to blind each other with a technique called "feeling for a feller's eye strings"). I read up on horse fighting, cockfighting, dogfighting, and insect fighting. I discovered ferret legging—a manly game of endurance invented by English coal miners. Ferret leggers square off, stuff angry ferrets into their pants (no underwear allowed, naturally), and see who can bear it the longest. (As one competitor explains, to become a ferret legging champion "you just got to be able to have your tool bitten and not care.") I read about the inventive ways men have killed each other in formal duels—by trading shots from hot air balloons, taking turns hurling billiard balls at each other's faces, and drawing straws (with the man holding the short straw committing suicide by dawn). I also watched video of XArm, or Extreme Arm Wrestling—the single dumbest monkey dance ever dreamed up by a human. (That it's vastly dumber than chess boxing and ferret legging says a lot.) XArm is just like arm wrestling, except the competitors are chained to the table, and while they strain for a pin, they are also free to slug and kick each other in the face. In most of the contests I saw, the competitors ignored the arm wrestling component in favor of brutal one-fisted slugfests. Because the men were chained up and strapped together by one hand, they couldn't dodge blows or block them. One contest I watched ended in just a few seconds, with the loser dangling unconscious at the end of his chain.

In addition to real forms of fighting, I became fascinated with the fake fights of professional wrestling—reading books about its present and past, watching tons of stuff on TV (you can stream old WrestleMania events on Netflix), and attending a handful of live shows in the Pittsburgh region. I was hoping that pro wrestling—with its shameless exaggeration of everything—might give me a concentrated insight into the nature of men's duels. After all, pro wrestling doesn't put on fake sport fights so much as fake duels. One wrestler has dissed another, or betrayed him, or seduced his wife, and the furious men make an appointment to settle things in the ring. Wrestling is blue-collar theater, and its formula is just like so many other forms of storytelling: men have a conflict that builds and builds until it explodes in a climactic mano a mano fight (think Darth versus Luke, Harry versus Voldemort, Hector versus Achilles, or the final showdown in just about any thriller or action film).

So I turned to pro wrestling for insights into the duel, but I ended up being way more fascinated by the *fans'* performances than the wrestlers'. Attending live events, I realized that for the show to really work, we fans had to act as well. We had to play the parts of yokels who actually believed that the stories were true and the violence was real. Some fans sank so deeply into their roles—they got so method about it—that they seemed to lose track of the fantasy-reality line. For act one of 412 versus 216, for example, I sat next to a couple and their eight-year-old son. As the outrages of the 216 Clique mounted, the wife became more and more dismayed, wringing her purse in her hands and launching f-bombs into the ring. Following some particularly gruesome instance of 216 depravity, she looked at me over her son's head and said plaintively: "They're such fucking cheaters—how is it even fair?"

FANDEMONIUM

Sports fandom is a strange, strange bird—and an old bird, too. Wild devotion to spectator sports isn't some quirk of modern industrial culture.

The sports historian Allen Guttmann has found clear evidence of avid sports spectators in Greek, Egyptian, Minoan, Etruscan, and Aztec artifacts, including a vase from the sixth century BC showing Greek fans "quite obviously screaming their heads off." In Roman times some men were so wild for chariot racing that they hung out at the stables fingering and sniffing the dung to make sure the horses were being fed properly. Chariot racing was a team sport in which drivers on one team would cooperate to defeat drivers on the others. The teams, or "factions," were divided into reds, whites, greens, and blues, and the fans lived and died with them. Like modern football (soccer) hooligans, or ultras, supporters wore team colors and were segregated at different ends of the stadium. But they still warred with each other in the stands and the city streets, with men of one color running riot—smashing, burning, killing—in enemy neighborhoods. Taking this all in, one Roman wrote that chariot-racing fans appeared to be "under the influence of some maniacal drug."

And here's the impressive part. It wasn't as though the blues represented the rich and the greens the poor, or that the reds represented the native-born citizens and the whites noncitizens. There were no real divisions between factions—not ethnic, economic, or political. Just like modern Pittsburgh Steelers and Cleveland Browns fans, the factions were demographically indistinguishable. This reminds me of Jerry Seinfeld's bit about the irrationality of sport fandom: "Loyalty to any one sports team is pretty hard to justify. Because the players are always changing, the team can move to another city. You're actually rooting for the clothes when you get right down to it. You are standing and yelling and cheering for your clothes to beat the clothes from another city."

Seinfeld raises a good question. Why do so many people root so hard for clothes? How can we care so much about things that seem to matter so little?

UFC president Dana White predicts that MMA will one day be the world's most popular spectator sport. Bet the farm that he's wrong. By far the world's most popular sports are vigorous team-based contests

About a quarter of a million people could cram into the Circus Maximus to watch chariot races, cheer for their colors, and cast hexes on the opposition. This was done by scratching hideous curses on tablets or amulets, then burying the curses in the earth or, better yet, tossing them like Frisbees at enemy drivers. One excavated curse tablet read "I adjure you, demon whoever you are, and I demand of you from this hour, from this day, from this moment . . . that you torture and kill the horses of the Greens and Whites, and that you kill in a crash their drivers Clarus, Felix, Primulus and Romanus, and leave . . . not a breath in their bodies."

such as football, soccer, and cricket. Individual sports, such as tennis or swimming, draw audiences, but their fans are less fanatical: they almost never riot in stadiums or city streets. Singles play never rivals the leading team sports, because it doesn't rouse tribal passions—the love of "us," the hate of "them." This helps explain why, contrary to common

belief, the fans at an MMA show are markedly tame and quiescent compared with their rabid counterparts at big-time football, soccer, or
hockey games. It explains why the crowds at Roman gladiator fights
were so much better behaved than the fans at chariot races. And it helps
explain why boxing, which was once a leading spectator sport, is not
anymore. In the bad old days, boxing matches were frequently—even
usually—promoted as clashes between tribal champions: Irish versus
Italian, Puerto Rican versus Dominican, black versus white. Boxing
started going out of style exactly when naked race-baiting did.

Tribalism also explains much of pro wrestling's appeal. Pro wrestling
is a fake sport, but its storytellers, known as bookers, understand that
the strongest energies are tribal energies. That's what the Pittsburgh
bookers were going for when they unleashed the 216 Clique, whipping
the crowd into an ecstasy of hometown patriotism. In this they were
following a classic playbook. Going back to pro wrestling's origins in
nineteenth-century carnival sideshows, promoters realized they could
generate more "heat" (audience emotion, especially anger) by pitting
native-born good guys against "terrible Turks." When I was a boy, for
example, the WWF got us all chanting "USA! USA!" as Sgt. Slaughter or a
flag-draped Hulk Hogan battled the villainous Iron Sheik or the USSR's
Nikolai Volkoff.

So team sports activate our tribal psychology. They intoxicate us
with love for "our" guys and something near hate for "theirs." But why
should this be? After all, we don't get swept up in maniacal enthusiasm
for the local symphony orchestra. And liking our city's orchestra certainly doesn't require hating another city's. It's impossible to overstate
how bizarre this is. Tens of millions of Americans care deeply about how
Alabama is doing in the college football rankings. Yet hardly anyone,
even in Tuscaloosa, follows the rankings for the university's engineering
department or medical school, even though the quality of its surgeons
and bridge builders should matter a billion times more than the quality
of its pass throwers and catchers. Why do we get fanatical about team
sports but not about other collective endeavors that would seem so much

more important? Why is it that almost nothing in human life reliably calls forth tribal fervor—orgies of love and hate, storms of passionate emotion—like team sports?

Nothing, that is, except war.

"A FREENDLY KINDE OF FIGHT"

As a teenager I watched the Rodney Dangerfield comedy *Back to School* (1986), and I remember a student activist, played by Robert Downey Jr., condemning football as a "violent ground acquisition game" and "a crypto-fascist metaphor for nuclear war." We were supposed to laugh at the pseudo-intellectual activist, and most current sports pundits would still be laughing—if they weren't so offended by the shallowness and insensitivity of analogies between war and sports. But I think the student activist was onto something. Just think back to the origins of organized Western athletics in the ancient Greek Olympics. Every event had a purpose as combat training: wrestling, boxing, *pankration* (basically, Greek MMA), footraces in full armor, chariot racing (chariots being an ancient weapon of war), long jump, javelin, and discus (flung rocks made brutally effective weapons in ancient battles). And the Greeks weren't alone in this. What the third-century philosopher Philostratus said of the ancient Greeks—"War was an exercise for sport and sport was an exercise for war"—could be just as aptly applied to many other societies. Among peoples as far-flung as the Maori, the Zulu, the ancient Chinese, and various tribes of Native Americans, sports had a clear function in enhancing warrior skill and toughness.

Anthropologists estimate that roughly a third of the world's tribal societies practiced "sham warfare," which refers not merely to rough sports—or rough team sports—but to sports that were directly based on the typical activities of war. In sham warfare there was no score keeping. As in real war, the winners simply inflicted more damage than they absorbed. For example, in the Marquesas Islands men played a violent game of team dodgeball, hurling coconuts or stones, until one side or the other was so depleted that it had to give up. (Similar stone-fighting games occurred in Italy, Kurdistan, and Korea.) In the Amazon, Aché tribesmen from different villages converged every year or two for brutal club fights. In Australia shield-bearing mobs of Aborigines from different villages used to gather to fire ritualized taunts and curses at each other, followed by spears and boomerangs. The Dani of highland New Guinea played similarly at war. In a boisterous atmosphere, Dani men ran about trying to hit each other with arrows and spears (nearby, Dani boys squared off in the little-league version, warring with small "grass arrows"). Believe it or not, in all these societies war games were seen as tremendously good, if dangerous, fun.

So in my view, *Back to School*'s student activist was mistaken not in seeing a connection between sports and war, but in seeing the connection as merely metaphorical. I think the actual relationship is deep and literal, not shallow and metaphorical. This goes especially for team sports, which amount to ritualized warfare between groups. These team-based monkey dances serve the same function for groups as head-to-head monkey dances serve for individuals: they allow groups of men—from different communities or from cliques within a community—to gauge one another's strength and establish a stable hierarchal relationship in ways that fall short of all-out battle.

Sham warfare isn't just a "them" thing, limited to ancient history or the far-flung societies studied by anthropologists. It's an "us" thing, too, strongly represented in Western history. For example, from at least the 1300s to the 1700s, large mobs of Italian workingmen routinely squared off in helmets and shields to war for fun, pounding and poking each other with sharpened sticks in front of screaming crowds. Similarly, medieval knights competed in tournaments, which in the twelfth and thirteenth centuries were barely ritualized forms of warfare. Aside from a roped-off safe zone and a gentleman's agreement not to fight with bows (fighting at a distance was for cowards), there were no rules, and battles between teams of knights, wearing full armor and swinging unblunted steel, raged across the countryside and through towns. In one tournament in Neuss in 1240, sixty knights were killed.

Still, these examples may seem so exotic and remote, so foreign and savage, that they can't have much to do with us. All these tribal people running around braining each other with clubs or piercing each other with arrows seems very far from our idea of sport. Even Europe in the heyday of the medieval tournament was a strange and savage land, where people blew their noses on tablecloths and farted freely in polite society. So what do the war-sports hybrids of our ancestors have to do with the modern experience of sport?

Quite a lot. Take football. The game began in England at least a thousand years ago. Football was highly adaptable, and villagers and townsmen across England (and stretching into other countries) played endless variations on the basic football theme: two groups of young men formed teams based on logical rivalries. The men of one church parish would challenge a neighboring parish, the city's fishmongers would play the city's skinners, or the east-enders would play the west-enders. The goal of the game was simply to gain control of the ball—usually a fresh pig bladder that had been blown up, tied off, and laced up in protective leather ("a ball full of wynde" as one early source puts it)—and drive it through or around defenders to a goal. The goal could be just about anything: you might toss the ball into the other village's well or touch the ball down (the origin of our word *touchdown*) on the front porch of the opposing parish's church.

In some versions of football, players were allowed to carry the ball in their hands (the forebear of rugby); in others they could dribble only with their feet (the forebear of soccer). Sometimes games were limited entirely to water play, and this is the game we now call water polo (essentially, aquatic rugby). English football is, in fact, the grandfather of the world's most popular sports. There are the obvious ones: American football, soccer, rugby, Australian-rules football. But it is also the grandfather of other games that involve penetrating into defended territory to score goals—games such as ice hockey, which began in Europe

Civil war soldiers in hand-to-hand combat? No, just Winslow Homer's drawing of Union troops playing a holiday game of "foot-ball."

as football on an icy pond. History credits James Naismith with inventing basketball in 1891. But Naismith's only real innovation was constructing an elevated goal made out of a peach basket. Otherwise the game was entirely derived from the standard pattern of football-like games. Basketball is just football adapted to a small Massachusetts gymnasium.

For centuries English football had few rules. Tackling and tripping were common, and so were punching, kicking, gouging, throttling, and brawling. Teams might consist of a handful of boys per side, or they could swell, for big festival games, to many hundreds of players. There were no referees to keep the peace or call fouls, and there were usually no boundaries—the "field" could stretch out over miles, with players following the ball wherever it bounced, over hills and into water, where they swam and splashed and half drowned each other. (It was perfectly kosher to hold an opponent underwater until he coughed up the ball.) Football was, in those days, more like a running gang fight than the tightly controlled versions of the game we know today. But they were usually good-natured affairs. As the Englishman Franklin Stubbes wrote in 1583, football may have been a "bloody and murthering practice," but it was essentially "a freendly kinde of fight."

In America football has evolved, over about 140 years, as a highly mutated form of rugby. The early decades of American football were the era of so-called massed play. The rules allowed the offense to arrange almost all its players in the backfield, then sprint ten or fifteen yards and explode into the defensive line with the snap of the ball. Massed play was very dangerous. Sometimes the offense would choose a single man on the defensive line and stampede over him again and again, often attacking the defensive line with wedge formations ripped directly from books of military strategy. Massed play also encouraged other dangerous maneuvers, such as hurdling (the offense would pick up a small ball carrier and heave his body over the scrum) and ramming (offensive players would lift the ball carrier and use him like a battering ram against the defensive wall). The defense might resort to similarly extreme tactics, such as flying dropkicks. For example, when Princeton was trying to run a wedge play against Yale, a Yalie named Heffelfinger "got a running start and vaulted the line, hitting the man at the apex of the wedge in the chest feet first."

Early American football wasn't just violent; it was dirty violent. The nature of massed play made it very difficult for the referee to spot fouls. And even when he did, players had three strikes before they were out. So each player was allowed to commit two free outrages, such as one punch and one crotch stomp. It was only on the third outrage—say, trying to drown an opponent in a mud puddle (as in the Harvard-Yale game of

At first glance lacrosse looks like an obvious member of the football family of games, but it was actually a war game played avidly by Native Americans before European contact. The Indians called lacrosse "little brother of war." The game, sometimes played in war paint, could be extraordinarily violent, with teams of men ranging from six to more than one thousand players—all of them tackling, spearing, and even strangling. Like modern ice hockey players, pairs of Indians would sometimes drop their sticks to duke it out. As with rough sports in all other times and places, men played lacrosse to have a good time, to show off for the women and girls, and to advertise their courage and ferocity. But sham warfare, like other forms of ritual combat, is inherently unstable and always threatens to boil over into plain old warfare. In 1790, for example, the Creeks beat the Choctaws in a game of lacrosse. The Choctaws took the loss hard and attacked the Creeks for real. By the next day, five hundred people were dead.

1880)—that he would be ejected. Owing to lax, hard-to-enforce rules, line play in early college football was a rumble, with plenty of slugging and choking. Here's a newspaper description of Yale versus Princeton in 1886: "A person standing two-thirds of the length of the ground away from the players could hear the spat, spat, of fists on faces constantly. One Princeton man on the rush line threw down the man opposite him and deliberately tried to kick him in the head."

As all this suggests, early American football was a real threat to life and limb. In 1905, 18 young men died playing football, and 159 were severely injured. In 1909, 30 players died, and 216 were severely injured. Attempts to make the game safer by modifying the rules and strapping players into heavy armor have backfired. (Exactly like boxing gloves, the football helmet was well intended, but by encouraging players to lead with their heads, it has been a neurological disaster for athletes.) According to the National Center for Catastrophic Sport Injury Research, from 1982 to 2009 there were 295 fatalities—direct and indirect—in high school football alone. In football at all levels, the same period saw about 300 spine injuries and 138 cases of serious brain damage (not garden-variety concussions). And, of course, this leaves out all the routine broken bones, blown knees, and accumulated brain trauma caused not only by huge hits but also by small, jostling dings.

It may be hard to look at men playing soccer today and see any meaningful connection to warfare, but Western culture has had a long time to elaborate sports into forms that are farther and farther removed from their warlike roots. We can see this evolution in the contrast between the ancient Olympics, with their laser focus on training and rewarding obviously war-relevant skills, and the modern Olympics, in which many of the sports have no war relevance at all (e.g., table tennis and rhythmic gymnastics). We can see the same process in lacrosse, which has steadily evolved from a sport with clear connections to warfare into a sport in which the connections are so veiled and indirect that most of us don't see them at all. The same change has been at work in American football, which has evolved from chaotic village gang fights into an almost sti-flingly structured, rule-bound, strategy-based game.

But these changes haven't changed football's essential character as a game of war. One team wins a football game by scoring more points than the other, but scoring means pounding the other side into submission. As the former Auburn football coach Gene Chizik has put it, football is a battle where you either "whoop or get whooped." Football continues to be a (somewhat) "freendly kinde of fight" between gangs representing different communities. The vocabulary of modern American football is infamously thick with borrowings from the vocabulary of war (bullets, bombs, trenches, blitzes, sacks) and martial metaphors (the players are armored "warriors"; the contest is a "battle"; the quarterback is a "field general"; a lopsided game is a "massacre"). These linguistic parallels are not superficial; they give the game away. Football is now, and always was, a game of war—exactly equivalent to the sham battles of ancient knights and tribal warriors all around the world.

THE WARRIOR ETHOS

I was in my middle twenties, lounging with some grad school friends on a couch that stank of must and beer, watching the Penn State football team play some hated rival. A defender crushed the Penn State quarter-back a little late, and my friend Bob—an econ grad student and a Happy Valley alumnus—leapt up to stomp and flap and tell the guy off. At the same moment, the fans filling the open bowl of Beaver Stadium did ex-actly the same thing: 100,000 people rising in unison to give themselves up to the thrilling ecstasy of hate. I didn't care about the teams or the game. I was fascinated by the warlike intensity of the fans and the play-ers, and by this question: could Bob get mad enough to spray blood out of his eyes?

As Bob ranted about crooked referees and angrily sucked beers, I started drawing connections between football and war. Before long I had a pretty good list going in my head, and I nudged Bob's elbow. "Bob, isn't this just like a war? Like a mini war between two different colleges—two different tribes? I mean, look at the military-style marching band. Look at how the people are all dressed in their tribal colors, roaring out fight songs. And some teams blast cannons when they score. And think how the whole game comes down to bands of brothers coordinating their violence to control territory—but with graybeards drawing up the battle plans, just like generals. And the terminology is so martial. I mean, the trenches, the blitzes . . . And look at you. You've got war fever. You've completely lost your—"

Bob wasn't about to put up with this. He cut me off: "Can we please not be graduate students today? Drink your fucking beer."

And so I dropped this line of inquiry for a good fifteen years. When I came back to it for this book, I learned that I'm not alone in seeing a kinship between sports and war. Many scholars see it. They just can't agree on whether it's good or bad. As the sociologists Norbert Elias and Eric Dunning explain, scholars group up in "diametrically opposed" camps. The first camp argues that rough sports train men for war by toughening them up and, in the case of team sports, teaching them to sacrifice for the good of the group. The second camp argues for the opposite: sports bind men together with ties of mutual respect while allowing them to safely burn off aggression. For the first camp, sports are more likely to be a cause of real violence. For the second camp, including the organizers of the modern Olympics, sports are a big part of the solution to violence. Let's consider these two perspectives in turn, keeping in mind something most previous scholars haven't: both ideas may capture part of the truth.

In our age of push-button war, it's easy to forget that throughout the history of our war-besotted species, the very survival of tribes and nations has depended on the physical strength and valor of young men. As the Duke of Wellington (allegedly) put it, "The battle of Waterloo was won on the playing fields of Eton." At Eton schoolboys were addicted to rough games that cultivated the warlike stamina, courage, teamwork, and loyalty that ultimately defeated Napoleon. Although the Wellington quote is probably a fabrication, people have endlessly attributed it to him because they think he should have said it. And in any case, similar claims were very common in the nineteenth century and well into the twentieth. For example, Wellington actually did write this: "I regret to observe the decay of the good old English practice of boxing, as I believe that it tends to produce and keep up that national spirit of undaunted bravery and intrepidity which has enabled our armies to conquer in many a hard-fought battle." And one French writer argued that developing an intense sporting culture was a pressing national security issue, opining, "Whoever learns not to shrink from a football scrimmage will not retreat from the mouth of a Prussian cannon."

Today this may seem pretty naive. Does a culture of fisticuffs actually contribute to national defense? Do players of macho sports really make more willing cannon fodder? But this idea may not be as naive as it sounds.

For some men bravery probably comes naturally. But for most of us bravery is a habit that we acquire—if we acquire it at all—by practice. In the early weeks and months of my MMA training, the gym was a frightening place. I didn't know the guys. I didn't know the moves. And I didn't know the codes that governed how we would compete. Monday nights were by far the worst. Monday became known in my house as "punch-in-the-face night." Of course, you can get punched in the face any night of the week at an MMA gym, but sometimes we'd focus on wrestling or jiu-jitsu, and no glove leather would fly. But Monday nights were always devoted to boxing and kickboxing, and you knew you were going to get punched in the face dozens and dozens of times. So I looked to Mondays with dread, knowing I'd spend the night backpedaling as guys chased me around trying to club my brain.

Week by week, however, my dread waned. It wasn't just that I gradually improved and stopped being such a helpless victim. I also grew acclimated to the pain and the fear. Most people think fight training is about building your muscles and your arsenal of techniques. That's part of it. But it's not the main part. Ask any boxer or MMA competitor to define the word *fighter*, and he'll speak more about toughness of mind than of body. A fighter masters a set of physical tools, yes, but above all he develops a warrior disposition consisting of mental toughness and a stoic attitude toward pain and risk. (An anecdote to illustrate: One day I interviewed the head coach at a local wrestling academy. The coach had been an elite college wrestler, but his battles had taken their toll. He constantly fondled his cauliflowered ears as he described his injuries, including a trick knee that was in need of an MRI. One of his pupils, a cheeky high school kid, overheard him from across the room and called out helpfully, "Why don't you get an MRI on your vagina?" The coach grinned, and his wrestlers rolled on the mat laughing, but the message was clear: Real men don't hurt their knees, and if they do, they ought not to whine about it.)

So MMA fighters go to the gym to learn a slew of different strikes, throws, locks, and chokes. But above all we go to the gym to try to acquire the habit of bravery. We hone our bravery in the same way we hone our technique—by putting it to the test night after night. And it works. Take Max, a sixteen-year-old high school kid who trains at my gym. One of the first times Max stepped into the cage to spar, an older guy named Dave lit him up. Dave wasn't swinging to hurt Max, but he was coming too hard, smothering Max with punches and kicks, making him feel helpless. Toward the end of the round, Max was on the verge of tears. I called out to him from cageside: "Doing good, Max. Forty seconds! Hold on Max! Forty seconds left!" And Max did hold on. He did not cry. His eyes brimmed and his lips quaked, but we all did him the favor of not noticing.

I knew what Max was going through because I'd seen it happen to a couple of other new guys, me included. In one of my first sparring sessions, I felt suffocated by the punches and pressure, and something shameful began to well up in my throat. At the end of the round, I hurried to get my face to a wall so I could—half-panicked and totally confused—swallow the shameful thing down with gulps of water. My gym is a pretty forgiving place, but it would be hard to show your face again after boo-hooing on the floor.

A few new guys come into the gym tough. But for most beginners, sparring is scarily intense. Sparring is not a fight, or at least it shouldn't be. But it takes your brain a while to figure this out. There's a dangerous man in front of you, battering your face with his fists. And your brain processes it as a real assault, dumping fight-or-flight chemicals into your blood. But you learn to discipline your emotional response. In the three years since I joined the gym, I've never come close to tearing up again. And neither has Max. Now you cannot hit Max hard enough to make him cry, and I've seen people try. He didn't cry during the frenzied sparring wars he had at least once a week with his buddy Jake. He didn't even cry the night his kneecap slipped out of joint and bulged out of the side of his leg. Max just stared at the ceiling until the paramedics took him away.

An MMA gym is a man factory. It's where men go to hammer the soft-ness, weakness, and timidity out of each other. Yes, fighting is danger-ous and scary, but a fighter walks forward into fear with his gloves up and his chin down.

Can such training produce a better soldier? The U.S. military appar-ently thinks so: hand-to-hand combat training—increasingly based on MMA techniques—is part of its basic training curriculum. This training is partly about practical battlefield self-defense, but according to the U.S. Army Combatives School, it is just as much about instilling "the Warrior Ethos."

DO WAR GAMES CAUSE WAR?

But there's another way of looking at the relationship between sports and war. Maybe if the British and French could have just battled *each other* on the playing fields of Eton, they wouldn't have needed to bother with Waterloo. For thinkers like Freud and the influential zoologist Konrad Lorenz, the whole point of sports is to safely channel aggression. As Lorenz wrote, "The main function of sport today lies in the cathartic discharge of the aggressive urge, especially the purging of collective militant enthusiasm." This basic idea motivated the founding of the modern Olympic movement in 1896, and it has since become conventional wisdom. It's what we mean when we say that sports help people—especially boys and young men—blow off steam.

But the notion that sports purge stored-up aggression isn't holding up so well. First there's history: it's a myth that the ancient Olympics put a halt to Greek fighting, and in the century after the modern Olympics were inaugurated, humanity fought its goriest wars. And then there's anthropology, which shows that societies with a lot of rough, combative sports generally have a lot *more* warfare and homicide, not less. The anthropologist Bruce Knauft writes that wherever you find warlike societies, you nearly always find "ritualized non-lethal combat as a kind of competitive military sport."

At first blush this seems sharply at odds with my argument that ritualized forms of fighting—including the play fights of sports—blunt real violence. But a closer look shows that anthropologists may have leapt to a false conclusion: *since fierce sports are found with fierce wars, the sports must be the cause of the wars; war games cause wars.* But because the anthropological data is strictly correlational, it's just as logical to interpret the data the other way around: *the sports aren't causing the fierceness of the wars; the wars are causing the fierceness of the sports.*

I think the latter interpretation—fierce wars breed fierce sports—is closer to the truth. The most warlike societies engage most intensely in warlike sports because they need ritual combat to help them manage conflicts. It is undeniable that rough sports frequently escalate to unrestrained violence and even, as George Orwell wrote in 1945, to "orgies of hatred." As we learned earlier in this book, with ritual conflict there is always danger of escalation. But overall, ritualization restrains violence. Some male rattlesnakes may be injured in ritualized wrestling for females, but countless would die if the males fought without their rituals, killing each other with venom. The same goes for the team-based duels of human males. If the Creeks vanquished the Choctaws with lacrosse sticks, the Choctaws might feel tempted to vanquish the Creeks with war clubs. But more typically, native tribes would meet for fierce but restrained contests and in this way exchange high-quality informa-

On Christmas day in 1914, soldiers all along the trench lines of World War I spontaneously enacted an informal truce. British and German soldiers serenaded each other with Christmas carols and walked out into no-man's-land to talk and exchange gifts. Numerous games of football broke out. This so-called football truce symbolizes the beautiful hope that sport can be used as a tool to reduce male aggression. Through sport, the soldiers affirmed their common humanity: whatever divided their nations, at bottom the soldiers were all just boys who loved playing football. But the beautiful hope was empty. The truce occurred early in the war, and soon football players on both sides were slaughtering each other on an epic scale. By 1916, when this photo was taken, British soldiers were playing ball only among themselves and taking proper defensive precautions.

tion about each other's strengths and weaknesses. As in individual forms of ritual combat, both sides benefited from this means of establishing dominance without having to fight it out for real.

OF ANTS AND MEN

Let's see if we can get some clarity through comparisons with other animals. Ritual combat is extremely common across species, but it's usually limited to individual contests. Animals rarely engage in team-based contests, as is so common in humans. But some animals do. Ants, for example, are very different from humans. But in the sophistication of their teamwork and their penchant for war, they are more like us than any other species. If two ant colonies are relatively evenly matched, a war can be a disaster for both sides. So some species of ants have developed ways of achieving the ends of war—territorial expansion—without the steep costs. For example, honeypot ants are constantly on guard against intruders into their territory. When a scout ant encounters a trespasser on the border between two colonies, both ants rush back to their anthills to summon soldiers. Within a short time battalions of soldiers, with their big bodies, tough armor, and scissor jaws, will be squaring off along the borderline.

But the ants don't fight. They don't clip each other to pieces with their jagged mandibles or kill each other with squirts of formic acid. Instead, they engage in what entomologists call a "tournament." The soldiers prance around, drumming each other with their antennae, pushing on each other's bodies. To make themselves seem bigger, they flex out their legs, pose on top of pebbles, and poof out their abdomens. One scientist compares these displays to "competing military parades." Based on the information exchanged in the display, both ant colonies modify their behavior: the stronger group asserts itself, pressing farther and farther into the weaker group's territory, while the weaker group gives way. This system of ritualized conflict resolution works because both sides get what they want: the stronger colony gets territorial expansion without the price of war; the weaker side gives up ground but doesn't get annihilated. As with contests between individual animals, both ant colonies would be worse off if they went without the ritual and just warred from the start.

What does this have to do with human sports? Bert Hölldobler and E. O. Wilson, world authorities on ants, draw a clear line of parallel: "The entire bloodless performance [of the honeypot ants] resembles the 'nothing fights' of the Maring tribe of New Guinea, in which combatants line up on either side of the territorial boundary to display their ceremonial dress, facial adornment, numerical strength, and weapons. Dances are performed and threats shouted back and forth across the field. The warriors fire arrows until someone on one side or the other is injured or killed, whereupon both parties return home. The desired result is the communication of fighting ability. All-out war is rare."

Rare, but not unknown. Among the tribes of highland New Guinea, if one side in a "nothing fight" sends a message of weakness—too few men behaving too timidly—things can turn very ugly. The stronger side may be emboldened to attack in dead earnest—massacring enemy men, raping women, burning huts and crops. The same is true of the ants. If one anthill can't send a robust signal of strength in a tournament, the other side will invade for real—overwhelming defenders, killing the queen, enslaving the young.

So which of the diametrically opposed ideas about sports wins? Are sports a way of preparing for war or a way of avoiding it? I think the answer is both. For most of human history, sports played a clear role in honing armed and unarmed combat skills—in building strength, stamina, teamwork, and warrior toughness. But it's a paradox: sports were a preparation for war, which made real war less likely. Like the honeypot ants, tribes around the world worked out their dominance relationships in sham-war "tournaments" to make it less likely that they'd have to fight real wars.

RATIONAL FANATICS

Imagine that you are living long, long ago in a jungle far, far away. Your village has fought endless, nasty wars against its neighbors. But now there is a shaky peace—a peace that must be carefully cultivated through rituals of gift giving and mutual feasting. At such feasts, the men play a peculiar sport. Individuals from each village form lines opposite each other. Two men come forward from each group and stand face-to-face. One man poses with his arms behind his back, while the other man rears back like a baseball pitcher, steps in, and throws a violent punch into his opponent's chest. The blow thwacks like a fastball in a catcher's mitt, sometimes dropping the recipient to his knees. The puncher may be allowed several blows before receiving an equal number from his opponent. Then the next pair of men come forward.

The hitting goes on for a long time, with each man taking multiple turns hitting and being hit. At first the pain is bearable. But after a few punches, most men's pectorals are welted and swollen, and some men are wheezing or coughing up blood. At some point one side may dare the other to raise the stakes, and the hitting will escalate from chest punches to slaps with the flat side of an axe. Gradually, injured men start dropping out of the contest until one team is whittled down to just a few stalwarts taking all of the other team's blows. As a group, they decide it's time to give up.

The contest I've described is not a figment of my imagination. It's a description of team-based hitting duels among an Amazonian tribe called the Yanomamö. The hitting duels are violent, but according to the anthropologist Napoleon Chagnon, they may "be considered as the antithesis of war, for they provide an alternative to killing. Duels are formal and are regulated by stringent rules about the proper ways to deliver and receive blows. Much of Yanomamö fighting is kept innocuous by these rules . . . Thus Yanomamö culture calls forth aggressive behavior, but at the same time provides a somewhat regulated system in which the expression of violence can be controlled."

When one Yanomamö group finally taps out of the duel, they are acknowledging something awful: the men of their village are weaker, softer, and probably fewer than their rivals. If it came to a real war, their side would likely lose. And so the winning men walk away with more than bragging rights. Having proved they are stronger, they may be able to intrude into the losers' hunting grounds or muscle them into handing over some women. The prizes in this game are not symbolic. They are food and sex, life and death.

Now imagine you were a villager watching the men of your tribe competing for a victory that could bring bounty or loss, pride or shame, to your whole group. How hard would you root for your team? How high would you get with victory and how low with defeat? How irrational would it be to cheer for your guys, to idolize them a little, and to wish ill on the other team? Would it be bizarre if you saw your own prospects wrapped up with the fortunes of the team?

Go to a local high school football game, and it will feel very far away from those jungles where men teamed up to play fight on behalf of their tribes. It no longer matters that much whether Trinity High beats neighboring Peters Township. But the old stuff of human nature hasn't really changed. As fans, we still cheer and rage as if the games matter a great deal, because for our ancestors, they actually did.

SEVEN

BLOODLUST

After the kill, there is the feast.
And toward the end, when the dancing subsides
and the young have sneaked off somewhere,
the hounds, drunk on the blood of the hares,
begin to talk of how soft
were their pelts, how graceful their leaps,
how lovely their scared, gentle eyes.

Lisel Mueller, "Small Poem About
the Hounds and the Hares"

I'm in my early twenties, and I'm back home in Plattsburgh, New York, visiting my family for the holidays. I'm crouching in our basement laundry room, which is dark save for the glow of a small television. Cheery voices and kitchen clatter filter through the ceiling above my head, but I hardly notice. What I'm watching on the small TV goes against everything my parents raised me to believe, and yet I can't look away—and I don't want to. Between scenes the frenzied action slows to a crawl, and so—as men do when viewing such tapes—I thumb the VCR remote, and the machine whines, whirring forward through the lame attempts at plot weaving and scene setting. A black man and a white man, both handsome, fit, and strong, zip into the frame. I back the tape up just a little and give myself up to it.

The door swings open, and the lights flash on. I'm so flustered that I fumble the remote and can't find the Stop button until it's too late. My father is standing in the doorway with a basket of dirty laundry in his hands, goggling at the TV screen. My father, a gentle and open-minded guy, watches for only a little while before he starts bellowing from the doorway: "What? What is this? What is this shit?" Ashamed, I mumble that it isn't what he thinks. But he has eyes, and he stalks to the VCR, confiscates my tape, and leaves the room without another word.

FIFTEEN YEARS LATER, in preparation for writing this book, I purchased a used copy of that tape on Amazon. I wanted to know if it was as obscene as I remembered. Sitting in the basement of my own house, I watched it from beginning to end, even the lame attempts at plot weaving and scene setting.

My father couldn't have appeared in my childhood laundry room at a worse time. He was socked in the nose by one of the most infamously brutal fights in the history of the UFC. The contest, from UFC 2, pitted a long, strong kickboxer named Pat Smith against a ninja named Scott Morris. Back in that laundry room, I trembled for Smith. He looked like a good kickboxer, but he was just a sportsman playing a violent game. Morris, by contrast, was *not* a sportsman. He was a ninja assassin, and he wasn't playing at all. It was the mid-1990s, and some of us still took ninjas pretty seriously. (An announcer for the broadcast said of Morris, with a straight face, "We don't know much about him [slight pause] because he is a ninja.") In the 1980s I had, like many boys, been swept up in the ninja craze—watching ninja movies and turtle ninja TV shows, and tiptoeing around in black pajamas with fake nunchakus and very real mail-order throwing stars. So I was programmed to expect Morris to enter the cage, do the usual prancing and backflipping, and then scythe off Smith's head with the blade of his hand.

Here's what actually happened. Morris, wearing black pajama pants but no gi and no ninja mask, dispensed with the usual tiptoeing and cartwheeling. Instead, he charged across the cage and drove the kickboxer into the fence. Then the ninja tried a judo throw. He lifted the kickboxer off the ground while falling backward. If the move had been executed properly, Morris would have twisted on the way down, pinning the kickboxer beneath him. But it didn't work. Morris lifted and fell, but Smith resisted the twist and rode him straight to the mat. Just a few seconds into the fight, the ninja was in terrible danger, with the big kickboxer straddling his waist.

In the movies, ninjas have plenty of options from this position, but most involve a smoke bomb or grappling hook. Having neither, Morris desperately tried to hug Smith while the latter landed a flurry of punches, followed by seven crushing elbows to the top of Morris's head. The elbows jackhammered Morris with brutal speed and power. It looked like the kickboxer was trying to gore through Morris's skull with the sharpest bone on his body.

MMA enthusiasts wax indignant about the era of persecution, when pussies and know-nothings slandered their sport as "human cockfighting" and nearly succeeded in getting it banned. But the early UFC was very different from the current product. With its near-total absence of rules and its reckless disregard for fighter safety, that UFC *was* human cockfighting, and it richly earned its flak. After Smith landed his first ten or fifteen unanswered blows, it was pretty clear that Morris was concussed and had lost the ability to "intelligently" defend himself. In the modern UFC this is when the referee would stop the fight, usually by hurling himself into the fray, shielding the vulnerable fighter's body with his own. But the early UFC explicitly barred referees from intervening to protect a fighter and even toyed with the idea of removing the referee from the cage entirely. (When the referee for UFC 1 instinctively leapt in to save Teila Tuli from Gerard Gordeau, he was criticized for breaking the rules.) The UFC was serious about putting on *real* fights, and in real fights there are no referee stoppages. Fights could end three ways: by knockout, by tap out, or when a fighter's corner literally threw in the towel. So although referee "Big" John McCarthy could see that Morris was in serious danger, he wasn't supposed to do anything about it. And even if Morris had wanted to tap out, he couldn't because Smith's punches were annihilating his ability to think.

Yet even after absorbing all those punches and elbows, Morris remained stubbornly conscious. So Smith rose up and landed a dozen more shots to Morris's face, as the latter blindly waved his arms in the air. One of the punches finally put Morris out. And he lay there limp and serene as Smith, in a frenzy, rose up and dropped three more elbows—heavy as anvils—on Morris's skull. In the end, Morris's mouthpiece went flying, and the blood spattered with the strikes, as though Smith were splashing in a puddle of it. The whole fight lasted twenty seconds.

Afterward, Morris looked like a car crash victim. Streaming blood, he tried to stand a couple of times, listed to one side, and fell. When the producers cut away from Morris, it wasn't out of shame or decency—it was because the carnage had happened so fast that there'd been no time to savor it. So they played and replayed slow-motion footage of what looks like a man being murdered, the announcers showering Smith with compliments for his prowess in bludgeoning. I think it was the most ghastly thing I had ever seen—a brutally skillful attempt by one human being to destroy another.

By the time my father started hollering at me, he was speaking in the voice of my own conscience. I felt nauseated. I didn't need him to point out that this cage fighting stuff was vile and dehumanizing. In renting the tape, I'd given in to some deeply carnivorous part of myself and become as complicit as the UFC organizers in the damage done to Morris and the other fighters. I swore off cage fighting for good.

I swore it off with as much passionate sincerity, and as much success, as I've sworn off other vices in my life. My resolve weakened with time, and before too long I was back at the video store, staring guiltily at the gleaming silver UFC tapes. When I first started renting the tapes, I could plausibly tell myself that I was doing so for educational purposes: I wanted to be a real martial artist, and the UFC was a master's class in what worked in a fight and what didn't. I could plausibly claim that I was watching in spite of the damage to fighters, not because of it. But I kept watching the fights long after I stopped training in the martial arts. Watching the tapes still made me feel nauseated, especially during bloody fights. (I've always been squeamish about blood.) But the fights also aroused me at a deeply physiological level, engorging my veins, tightening my chest, and moistening my palms. I watched because the violence and pain, being real, gouged down through all my calluses. In time I admitted to myself that I was watching, at least in part, *because* of the damage, not in spite of it.

I set out to write this book not only to try to understand why men fight but also to find out why seemingly decent people like to watch. I've gradually arrived at a disturbing conclusion. Most of us greedily slurp up violent entertainment while still assuring ourselves that we personally hate violence, that it makes us sick. But we're kidding ourselves. In truth, whereas some forms of violence do sicken us, other forms delight us. Even people who'd rather go blind than watch a cage fight revel in the brutality of football or gore-spattered crime novels, or even in the silly mayhem of *The Three Stooges*. For a century social scientists optimistically argued that our attraction to violent spectacles was good for us. If we fed our hunger for aggression vicariously, we'd be less likely to behave aggressively ourselves. But there's no evidence that this is true. I will argue for a more pessimistic position: we are drawn to violent entertainment simply because we like it. We are not nearly as good or as civilized as we think.

RUDE AND NASTY PLEASURES

Our ancestors have, everywhere and always, had an appetite for carnivals of suffering and bloodshed. The best-known example is the gladiatorial contests of ancient Rome. But movies portraying ruthless men battling for raving crowds give us the wrong idea about gladiators. Gladiators were valuable, trained men, and their lives were not treated cheaply. If a gladiator fought strongly and bravely, he could expect his life to be spared in the end, even in defeat. Most of the blood was spilled not by gladiators, but in the wanton slaughter of many hundreds or thousands of animals, criminals, and prisoners of war. Imagine it: the smell of fresh meat and feces and so much sunbaked blood; the sounds of screaming and snarling and blades on bone; the people laughing and shouting as they ate their lunches.

The Roman games are infamous, but Europeans from the Dark Ages up until the past couple of centuries were also fond of creative butchery. Being poorer than the Romans, however, they had to settle for carnage on a smaller scale. Still, they developed a great variety of animal torture sports that were usually played for crowds of spectators, who hooted and guffawed as the beasts hilariously screamed out their lives.

Take bullbaiting, which the famous diarist Samuel Pepys called "a very rude and nasty pleasure." In bullbaiting, which lasted in England for at least seven hundred years, a bull was tethered to a stake so dogs could run at him, clamping onto his face and neck while he tried madly to shake them off. Sometimes a good bullbaiting was drawn out over many days, in which case it was necessary to constantly rouse the exhausted animal to new fury. Methods of reinvigorating a half-dead bull included stabbing him in the haunches, blowing pepper up his nose, lighting his straw bed on fire, grinding salt into his wounds, and dumping boiling water into his ears. When the bull was just about licked, men would take turns working on him with a cudgel. Whoever dropped him for good went home with the lion's share of meat. And, oh, the succulence of that meat! The bull's ordeal left a special tang in the beef. It was as if the animal's flesh had been marinated in its own terror and agony— and the flavor was exquisite. People loved a good bullbaiting so much that they rioted when authorities tried to ban the sport. They loved it so much that in some places it was illegal to butcher a bull without baiting him first.

In addition to bullbaiting, there was also cock throwing (pegging a tethered rooster to death), goose quailing (same thing, except using a goose), duck in a hole (same thing, except using a duck stuffed neck-deep in a hole), cock thrashing (blindfolded thrashers attempted to smash a rooster with sticks), pig clubbing (laughing men chased a squealing pig around a pen, trying to kill it with clubs), pig sickling (laughing men hurled sharp sickles at the pig instead), cat bashing (head butting a tethered cat to death as it tried to defend itself with teeth and claws), and cat burning (in one variant, a bag of yowling cats was set aflame, and men beat on it like a flaming piñata). People also liked to drive animals across a kind of sling lying on the ground. When the animal crossed the sling, strong men yanked hard at the corners, pulling the sling suddenly taut, launching the shocked animal twenty or thirty feet into the air, and then watching it pinwheel down toward a splintering of bones. In a single eighteenth-century tossing event in Dresden, 647 foxes were killed, along with 533 hares, 34 badgers, and 21 wildcats. A Swedish envoy witnessed a tossing in Vienna in March 1672 and noted that Emperor Leopold I personally helped the boys and court dwarves finish off the tossed animals with clubs.

The Europeans enjoyed human suffering, too. They liked to watch murderers and cabbage thieves dancing on the gallows. They liked to observe the whipping of vagrants, the branding of whores, and the burning of witches and heretics. They liked to witness the state's enemies being buried alive, deep-fried in bubbling oil, or deprived of their rebel tongues. They liked to see men broken on the wheel, which was just what it sounds like: "The executioner tied the victim to a wagon wheel, smashed his or her bones with a club, braided the shattered but living body through the spokes, and hoisted it on a pole for birds to peck while the victim died slowly of hemorrhage or shock." An eyewitness account from 1607 describes how a man on the wheel was transformed "into a sort of huge screaming puppet writhing in rivulets of blood, a puppet with four tentacles, like a sea monster of raw, slimy and shapeless flesh, mixed with splinters of smashed bones."

Seeing these sights didn't bother people. In fact, witnessing such spectacles was viewed as good wholesome fun. And since it was morally instructive fun, children were released from school to learn the wages of sin. Thousands of people would flock to London from the countryside to attend executions, buying expensive tickets for seats in hastily built bleachers, drinking beer, and gorging themselves on carnival foods. On October 13, 1660, Samuel Pepys watched the execution of Major General Thomas Harrison for treason. Harrison was hanged first, but only half to death. Then, still alive, he was dragged to the quartering table, where he was gutted and castrated. Harrison was made to watch his own genitals being roasted on the fire before he was carved up into pieces. Finally, the executioners lifted Harrison's head and heart high above their heads so the whole crowd could see and cheer. Pepys wrote in his diary that he watched the whole show and then took his friends "Captain Cuttance and Mr. Sheply to the Sun Tavern, and did give them some oysters." Later that night Pepys felt uneasy not because of Harrison, but because when he came home a bit tipsy from the tavern, "I was angry with my wife for her things lying about, and in my passion kicked the little fine basket, which I bought her in Holland, and broke it, which troubled me after I had done it."

It would be easy to provide multiple examples of the sadistic torture of people and animals from around the world and from almost every historical epoch. Granted, the best-documented examples come from Western societies, but this isn't because, as many self-flagellating cultural historians might like to believe, there is something uniquely depraved about Western culture. The West just happens to be where the most records have been kept and the most historians have lived. Bloodlust seems to be something that boils up from human DNA and not from human culture. The best evidence *against* this view comes from modern societies that see the gratuitous killing and torture of humans or animals as evil. For modern people, it's hard to think of all the pointless agony described here without feeling some outrage. How could it be, we wonder, that our ancestors—men, women, and children; rich and poor; learned and ignorant—could sink so low? How could they be so different from us? But we aren't as different as we'd like to think.

Members of a lynch mob proudly immortalizing their role in the killing, mutilation, and burning of Will Brown, an African American, for the alleged rape of a white teenager in 1919. The expressions on their faces give a good sense of the pleasure people can get from killing, especially when they believe they are doing so morally. As Donald Horowitz writes in his distressingly massive book *The Deadly Ethnic Riot*, the general atmosphere of a genocidal mob is one of "sadistic gaiety."

SNUFF

Imagine that you find a magical device that allows you to pass into an alternate universe as an invisible observer. Before entering, you know you will witness brutal, scarring things: women and children will be raped and murdered; bodies will be tortured, defiled, and dismembered.

Seemingly decent men will reveal themselves as evil Nazis and sick maniacs. Watching, you will grow angry, tense, and scared; your heart will beat harder, and your breath and sweat will come faster. When it's over, the bad men may torture you in nightmares.

Will you use your magical device? If you answer "Not a chance!" think again. The device is a novel, and the fictional scenario I'm describing is from Stieg Larsson's *The Girl with the Dragon Tattoo.*

The 1970s and 1980s saw periodic panics about snuff films, which were supposedly crafted for porn viewers who'd grown bored of the tame outrages of XXX and needed an extra jolt to get the raw thrill they once got from garden-variety sexual degradation. Snuff films did the job. They were just like ordinary porn, except for one thing: the film's real climax wasn't the money shot, but the on-screen murder of the actress.

The snuff film phenomenon turned out to be an urban legend. Except for true monsters, men don't find it arousing to see women murdered on-screen. But men do like seeing pretend women murdered on-screen—and women do, too. Many tens of millions of people, mainly women, have read Larsson's Millennium trilogy or seen the film adaptations. This trilogy, with its computer-hacking, man-bludgeoning, man-raping, man-slaughtering heroine, Lisbeth Salander, presents itself as a high-minded critique of violence by men against women. (The original Swedish title of *Dragon Tattoo* translates as *Men Who Hate Women.*) The way Larsson pays lip service to feminism while still showing us tons of sexual ultra-violence helps explain the wild popularity of such staggeringly pokey and bloated books. (The novels devote as much attention to coffee brewing, Internet browsing, and the painstaking construction of disgusting Scandinavian sandwiches as they do to typical thriller material.)

Larsson's novels delight audiences with their pornographic violence, but they are hardly alone in this. One night in October 2010, I went to the movie theater to watch a double feature. The first film was *Jackass 3D.* *Jackass,* a very high form of very low art, appeals irresistibly to the eleven-year-old boy in me. I laughed myself sweaty as I watched the now middle-aged jackasses doing the same old stunts and pranks and nut punching and corn holing. When the film ended, I moved over to the adjoining theater to watch the latest installment in the horror franchise *Saw*, this one also in 3-D. The film opened with a man being cut in half with a buzz saw—with the 3-D chunks and globules spattering out into the crowd, and with his guts falling to the floor with a warm, wet plop. There was hardly any characterization in the film, and very little plot. For ninety minutes the film scraped up just enough story to disguise what it actually was: an excuse to watch insanely clever torture devices destroy human bodies. When you buy a ticket to a *Saw* film, you are really buying a front-row seat to the Spanish Inquisition. The gore looks real; the 3-D geysers of arterial blood look real; the characters shriek and beg and drool and weep, and it all seems real. And on that October night in a movie theater in Washington, Pennsylvania, we voyeurs reclined in our cushy seats and watched in rapt silence—except for the dry rustle of popcorn in buckets and the slurp of soda dregs.

Jackass and *Saw* clearly aren't for everyone (but they are for an awful lot of us—the ultra-low-budget *Saw* films have grossed close to a billion dollars in worldwide sales). Still, one way or another, almost all of us consume a rich diet of violent entertainment. Violence is, perhaps even more than sex, the great and eternal staple of our entertainment diets. This includes Shakespeare, Homer, and Tolstoy, as well as modern action flicks, video games, and cop shows. Great works such as the *Iliad* and *War and Peace* may be profoundly moving artistic explorations of the human condition, but they are also thrilling and mesmerizing descriptions of homicide on an epic scale.

Not that our fascination with violence is limited to fantasy forms. We watch sports, in which the most exciting moments—the moments looped endlessly on *SportsCenter*—are the bench-clearing brawls, the hockey duels, the NASCAR crashes, the big hit that KOs a football player or snaps his leg in half. We tune in to shows such as *Tosh.0* or *America's Funniest Home Videos* to giggle at real pain. And how about the news? It's a huge, for-profit business that exists, in the end, to bring eyeballs to advertising. And news organizations know that nothing draws eyeballs like mayhem ("If it bleeds, it leads"). What the historian Robert Muchembled has said of the origins of the newspaper industry in Europe is just as true of news today: "Blood and gore sold ink and paper."

In his great book *The Civilizing Process*, Norbert Elias argues that society is, on the whole, becoming much softer and safer, and much subsequent research has proved him right. But as Harold Schechter points out in *Savage Pastimes*, when it comes to the consumption of violent entertainment, what civilized us wasn't a moral epiphany, so much as simple technological advancement. Movies, special effects, and literature let us consume vast amounts of suffering without the goop or guilt of using real humans. And we consume far more of this realistic, if pretend, carnage in a given month than our ancestors accumulated in a lifetime.

Perhaps it appears that I'm missing the point: there's a big difference between thrilling to real gladiators killing each other and thrilling to a Russell Crowe flick. True enough, but our moral edge is thin. We can feel superior to our ancestors in exactly the same way a pedophile can feel superior to his pedophile brethren if he limits himself to animated kiddie porn. Our ancestors consumed real violence; we mostly consume pretend violence. They ate honey and meat; we eat aspartame and Tofurky. Yet our taste for suffering seems as real as our taste for sweet or meat, though much harder to explain. Why is blood and pain such a great staple of our entertainment diets?

Could it be because we need it? Maybe an MMA show or a violent film such as *Goodfellas* gives us a healthy catharsis, allowing us to vent aggressive impulses in a harmless way. Indeed, that is how the director of *Goodfellas*, Martin Scorsese, defends the violence of his films: "Maybe we need the catharsis of blood-letting and decapitation, like the Ancient Romans needed it, as ritual, but not real like the Roman Circus." Stephen King has the same idea. A horror author, King believes, is like a premodern physician who cuts the patient, bleeds away dangerous toxins, and rebalances the humors.

Baseball's TV ratings have been slipping for years. So I have a modest proposal. Major League Baseball should establish a roster spot for a designated
fighter (DF) on each team. Every time a pitcher plays some chin music or
someone slides spikes-up into second, the DFs would charge out onto the
infield to brawl, while the umpires stand back and watch. Absurd? Well, just
look at hockey. Professional hockey is the world's premier fighting sport by
far. In the 2000s the National Hockey League (NHL) averaged more than
seven hundred regular season fights per year, far more than the UFC. Each
hockey team has a de facto DF or two, who mainly fight the other teams'
DFs over and over again in duels regulated by unwritten rules that players
call "the code" (e.g., no gloves in a fight; no sticks; no hair pulling; no using
the top of the helmet as a shield; no challenging a much smaller man, or an
injured man, or an exhausted man at the end of his shift). While apologists
argue that fighting plays a vital game function by policing dirty play, everyone knows the real reason the NHL hasn't abolished it. The hockey announcer Don Cherry puts it simply: "When [legendary tough guy Bob]
Probert was fighting, did you ever see anyone get out of their seat and go for
coffee?"

But the catharsis theory of entertainment violence—flattering as it is to men like Scorsese and King—has been universally discredited, not only because of its theoretical deficiencies (modern scientists no longer think of aggression as a drive that can be purged), but because of the utter absence of confirming laboratory evidence. The sociologist Dolf Zillmann sums up the results of decades of research: "The evidence concerning cathartic effects of exposure to violence, fictional as well as nonfictional, is entirely non-supportive." (The evidence for the alternative notion—that consuming fake violence leads to more real violence— is also pretty shaky.)

So if the cathartic theory of entertainment violence can't explain our attraction to bloody spectacle, what can? Maybe it's time to question our premises, which are as follows: (1) violence is bad, and (2) therefore good people despise it. Both premises are wrong. Violence is not inherently bad, and good people do not always despise it. In fact, under the right conditions, most of us love violence very much.

WAR JOY

Both women and men like violent entertainment, but men seem to like it more. Males make up most of the audience for combat sports, professional wrestling, shoot-'em-up video games and action flicks, and just about anything having to do with war. Check out the browsers in the military history section of your bookstore; it's a sausage party. Men's delight in aggressive spectacles begins early in childhood. Despite a determined, decades-long effort by parents, educators, and gender activists to de-masculinize boy play, boys still like nothing better than fantasy violence. In a fascinating 2008 study by Joyce Benenson, Hassina Carder, and Sarah Geib-Cole, boys and girls ages four to nine were asked whether they'd prefer to make believe they were (1) gun-toting heroes such as soldiers or police officers, (2) heroic, nonviolent characters such as astronauts or firefighters, or (3) heroic, nonviolent helpers such as doctors. The researchers also asked questions about what sort of TV shows the children would most like to watch. The boys strongly preferred potentially violent play scenarios and TV shows. Being an astronaut or a firefighter is incredibly cool, dangerous, and physically demanding, but the lack of bad guys and gunplay made these professions much less exciting to boys as fantasy material. (And isn't it interesting that even though software moguls, scientists, and civil rights leaders have enormous cultural prestige, little boys seem never to pretend to be Steve Jobs, Albert Einstein, or Martin Luther King Jr.?) Girls expressed precisely the opposite preferences. They showed the least interest in potentially violent characters and scenarios, and the most interest in helping characters and scenarios.

Benenson and colleagues' study reminds me very much of my own childhood, which consisted of nonstop war play with my brothers and other neighborhood boys. We were Marines mowing down commies; we were Jedi slicing through storm troopers; we were bold elves hacking our way through Dungeons & Dragons fantasies. Like the good liberals and Unitarians they were, our parents did not approve. They tried to convince us that real war isn't at all like a G.I. Joe cartoon or a John Wayne film. Real war isn't about heroically vanquishing evil and going home jangling with medals. It's about catching bullets in no-man's-land, seeing your friends mangled, and coming home (if you are lucky) ruined in body and mind. But my parents had no more experience of fighting wars than their boys did, and their description of the hellishness of war, though not wrong, was only half-right.

Across time and cultures, warriors have experienced the fear and suffering of war as the closest thing to hell on earth. But many of those same men also experience war as a thing near to heaven. Warriors are confused by the experience of war because it pulls them very hard in opposite ways: it feels like the very worst, very best thing that has ever happened to them. Here's how the journalist and combat veteran William Broyles Jr. put it in his classic *Esquire* article from 1984, "Why Men Love War": "I had to admit that for all these years I also had loved it

Danish boys pretending to be Nazi fighters during World War II. We can perhaps take some comfort in the fact that all those little boys running around punching, shooting, bombing, and stabbing are fighting the bad guys. They are not training to become spree shooters; they are training to be the ones who run to confront the spree shooters. They are playing at the only kind of male aggression cultures celebrate: a self-sacrificing, prosocial heroism that has been the male ideal from time immemorial. Even today, nothing raises a man's status so much as being competent in the use of aggression, but in socially acceptable ways—for instance, as cops, soldiers, or athletes. In fiction, too, the aggression we really savor is moralistic aggression. It is the pleasure of comeuppance, of the bad guy getting his just deserts at the hands of the good guy. Across the world, in epic literature, films, and adventure novels, the great heroes—from Hector to Beowulf to James Bond—are men of violence above all else. But what's celebrated is never a wild, ungoverned aggression. Across the world, hero stories always send the same message: violence is for protecting the weak and the good from the bad and the strong.

[Vietnam], and more than I knew. I hated war, too. Ask me, ask any man who has ever been to war about his experience, and chances are we'll say we don't want to talk about it—implying that we hated it so much, it was so terrible, that we would rather leave it buried. And it is no mystery why men hate war. War is ugly, horrible, evil . . . But I believe that most men who have been to war would have to admit, if they are honest, that somewhere inside themselves they loved it too, loved it as much as anything that has happened to them before or since. And how do you explain that to your wife, your children, your parents, your friends?" And how can you tell them, Broyles goes on, that when the war ended, "something had gone out of our lives forever, and our behavior on returning was inexplicable except as the behavior of men who had lost a great—perhaps the great—love of their lives, and had no way to tell anyone about it."

Men don't love war, and they don't hate it. Men love-hate war. Take Robert E. Lee, gazing out over the Battle of Fredericksburg, with the Union soldiers charging behind streaming banners, while the Confederates bowled holes in their lines with cannonballs. Lee said, "It is well war is so terrible; we should grow too fond of it." Similarly, in his memoir of Vietnam, *A Rumor of War*, Philip Caputo makes us feel the hellishness of the war, but also admits that he was happier in that hell than he'd ever been in his life. When the writer Henri de Man scored a direct hit with his World War I artillery piece and saw the body parts wheeling through the air, he burst out crying—from the pure joy of it. And in his great war novel *Matterhorn*, the Vietnam veteran Karl Marlantes painstakingly recreates the intense fear, frustration, and sadness endured by a Marine company at war. But Marlantes also shows us young men discovering the ecstasy of defeating enemies—of learning that they have a "mad monkey" inside that loves to kill.

Soldiers frequently compare the ecstasy of battle to the ecstasy of sex. This isn't because they literally find combat arousing, but because sex is the only thing they've experienced that rivals the intense excitement of combat. My MMA friend Nick, like most guys at the gym, gets anxious when it comes to sparring (unlike most others, though, Nick is

On the subject of mad monkeys, chimpanzees *love* to kill. In 1974 eight chimps from the Gombe Stream region of Tanzania crossed into the territory of a neighboring group of chimpanzees. The Gombe chimps snuck up on a lone male named Godi, who was sitting alone in a tree, enjoying a meal of figs. When Godi tried to run, the Gombe chimps tackled and pinned him down, then pummeled his body, bit his face, and stomped his head. After ten minutes the raiding party ran screaming and howling back to their home range, leaving Godi mortally wounded. Over the next few years the Gombe chimps made repeated sorties into the neighboring range until, one by one, they killed all the males. Primatologists have since documented raids of this kind across different populations of chimpanzees. What disturbed primatologists wasn't just the systematic killing, but the clear joy the chimps took in the work, exhibiting all the behaviors associated with pleasurable excitement. The chimps hooted, barked, and danced through the assaults, then ran home yelling in exultation, slapping the trees they passed.

brave enough to cop to it). But when I asked him if he had been afraid in combat, Nick, who served as an infantryman in Iraq in 2007, replied, "Nah, that shit don't scare me." He raised and shook his dukes: "When it went down I was like, 'Yeah, get some!'"

I didn't ask what he meant by "get some," but it seems pretty clear that he meant his share of the combat, his share of the shooting and killing. For Nick "getting some" meant setting up his SAW (the light machine gun assigned to each squad) and unleashing hot squirts of bullets. Nick would take aim and squeeze the trigger long enough to say *"Die, moth-erfucker, die!"* in his head. If he held the trigger down any longer, the steel barrel might get so hot that it would wilt and just hang there, flac-cid and useless. "Getting some" has become a common way for soldiers to speak about the eager pleasures of combat. The only other times I've heard men use that phrase in quite the same hungry, excited way is when they were referring to sex.

CAGE JOY

War can be intensely pleasurable, and there can be similar pleasure in a fistfight. Guys at my gym struggle for words that are huge enough to describe the feeling of winning a fight, and like soldiers, they generally fall back on comparisons to sex or drugs. One day, in the final lead-up to my fight, Coach Shrader told us in his blunt, unapologetic way, "A fighter may be the nicest guy on the street, but once he's in a fight, he has to like it. When I fought, I wasn't trying to be your friend. I was like, 'I wanna see your blood. I'm going to fuck you up! I'm going to hurt you.' And after I'd buy him a beer. That's how I am. That's a fighter." When Mark said this, I went quiet. I know it sounds naive, but I joined the MMA gym hop-ing to get good at violence, while somehow not getting my hands red. Whenever I go into the cage to spar, I want to be my opponent's friend. Whenever Mark goes into the cage or the ring, even just to spar with a

Nick Talarico, geared up for a raid, Anbar Province, Iraq, 2007.

friend, part of him wants to see their blood. That's why Mark's a fighter and I'm not.

But could I become one? I'd certainly come a long way since first joining the gym. I came into the gym spazzy and timid, but for fifteen months I lived, sparred, and ate like a real fighter. For fifteen months I was mostly at the gym training, on the roads running, or at home watching jiu-jitsu videos on YouTube and practicing the moves on my grappling dummy. With a few exceptions, writers aren't known for being tough. But we are hard workers and famous gluttons for misery, and I brought an obsessive professional drive to fighting that was nurtured by my fear of being terribly maimed by a cage fighter.

I made steady progress. There were injuries, but my body held up to the pounding better than I'd expected. I got better and better at MMA until, about a year in, the stronger guys at the gym started picking me as a training partner, and the weaker guys started avoiding me. I still re-member how surprised I was one night when Mark told a kid named Drew to come in and wrestle me in the cage. Drew walked to the cage with his head down, and I heard him mutter "Oh, shit" under his breath. It surprised me, because Drew was a young muscly guy, and I was think-ing *Oh, shit*, too. But he was right. He was newer than me, and less ath-letic. And when he came into the cage, I trounced him, bulling him into the fence again and again—where I'd lift him, turn him, and drive him to the mat.

My skills and conditioning had improved, but I still didn't have the warrior disposition of a "real fighter." Shrader tried to instill it in me. He yelled at me when I was timid in the cage, throwing my strikes as I back-pedaled in retreat. He told me to hit harder and flat-out ordered me to quit apologizing every time I connected a little too cleanly. One night he looked right at me when he was addressing the class. He said that we all have a wild animal inside that we keep penned up in ordinary life. But a fight has nothing in common with ordinary life. In a fight you have to set the animal loose. He pointed up at the yin-yang symbol on the wall. "See that symbol? That means we all have a side that is ruled by light. And we all have a side that is ruled by dark. In a fight you let the dark side rule. We all have that dark side." We were standing in a circle around Mark, and Nick quipped from across the circle, "Even you, Jon Gottschall."

"Why did you say that?" I asked Nick later.

"Because you do have a dark side," Nick said. "But you are so nice that you probably don't know it."

I've thrown many punches in my life. I ripped bully punches into the shoulders of my little brothers. Once, I threw two short, feeble hooks into the ear of my best friend during a drunken college scuffle. We threw thousands of kicks and punches in karate class, but the sparring was light and the face was off-limits. In my rages I've punched more doors and walls and refrigerators and steering wheels than I care to admit.

But coming into the gym, I'd never thrown a punch at another person with my full heart behind it. And I quickly saw what a serious thing it is

My daughters, Abigail and Annabel, thrashing the fully articulated jiu-jitsu dummy we built together out of cable, pillows, pool worms, and pounds of duct tape. They named the dummy Uncle Robert, and I'd wrestle him as I watched TV at night, trying to master basic submissions. One night when I was triangle-choking Uncle Robert to sleep, Annabel sprinted across the living room, took flight over my face, and landed a pro wrestling move known as an atomic butt drop. Thus she illustrated one of the big knocks against jiu-jitsu as a system of self-defense: it's no good against multiple assailants.

to hit another man in the face. In MMA sparring, the goal is to throw the punch hard and fast, but to pull it at contact. Often the punch penetrates to shake the brain, but that's not really what you are going for. You punch to sting, not to concuss. But in real fighting, you don't pull the punch. In fact, some fighters try to visualize punching *through* the shield of the face, penetrating to the back of the skull—obliterating everything in between.

So when Nick called out to me, "Even you, Jon Gottschall," I doubted him. I flattered myself that I was wired differently—that I was a better person than that. But I wasn't. One night in the second year of my training, I was sparring with Will—a strong guy, about my weight, who already had a few fights under his belt. I noticed that he was holding his guard too high and leaving his middle exposed. So I feinted high with my jab, and when he flinched, I threw a front kick that he never saw. My forefoot sank into him, inches deep, pushing the air out of his mouth in a moan. He collapsed to his hands and elbows with his cheek pressed to the mat, trying to fill his lungs, while I stood over him patting his back and apologizing. I apologized with absolute sincerity; I would have taken the kick back if I could have. But I also felt tall. I drove home that night with the music up loud.

There have been a few other times when I've hit guys too hard and seen their eyes lose focus—seen them stagger to one side or plop down like babies on their butts. When I've hit someone this hard, I've felt bad and apologized. And always, secretly, I've felt a little good, too. It felt a little good that night when I opened my friend Mike's nose, then watched my gloves paint his face red. To physically dominate another man is intoxicating. It's a deeply satisfying feeling. And I can see how real fighters, who are usually nice men outside the cage, can acquire a fondness for that feeling and want to experience it again and again.

BLOOD PORN

There are two big entertainment staples: sex and violence, love and death. Why are we drawn to erotic entertainment—from romantic comedies and romance novels to museum paintings of reclining nudes? Obviously it's because sex interests us deeply in real life. The success of the pornography industry isn't mysterious. Porn feeds our appetites for real sex by giving us vicarious sex.

Could the same explanation apply to violent entertainment? Are we drawn to pretend forms of violence because given the right circumstances, we love the real thing? If you asked, "But why would we love violence?" I'd ask you a better question: "Why wouldn't we?"

In evolutionary terms, aggression is an awfully good trick. Most of us think of aggression not only as a categorically bad thing but as pathological—a behavioral defect owing to a bad upbringing or crossed wires in the brain. And some aggression—think of Jeffrey Dahmer or a rabid dog—is clearly pathological. But most aggression isn't. Aggression is part of the behavioral repertoire of virtually all animals because, in the appropriate conditions, it simply pays. It would have to. Otherwise, as the evolutionary scientist Donald Symons points out, "long ago the meek would have inherited the earth."

What are the appropriate conditions? Most obviously, situations that bring profit. Chimps enjoy killing when they gain an advantage from it. When a chimp troop overruns a neighboring troop, they kill the competitor males and absorb the females. Then they use the new territory and the new females to drive their own genetic expansion. Given humanity's history of nonstop murder and rapine, it makes no sense to assume that we should categorically dislike violence or killing. Tigers don't dislike killing. Nature has designed tigers to like hunting and killing because that is how tigers make their living. The same goes for us. For eons humans have made their living partly in the same predatory fashion—by hunting animals and men. As Mark Twain put it, "We are nothing but a ragbag of disappeared ancestors," and those ancestors could be a bloody-knuckled lot.

The truth of this smashed me in the face one night at the gym. I was wheezing and snorting through a hard round of sparring. Unable to bring in enough oxygen through my nostrils, I let my jaw hang and sucked air through my mouth. Then a roundhouse kick reminded me of why it's much better to bite down on the mouthpiece. The kick sank my teeth hard into my lower lip. I struggled on as my opponent pushed me into the fence and tried to drag me down. The flavor of the blood pulsing into my mouth was nauseatingly good, and it made everything clear: by nature, men like the salt taste of blood.

EIGHT

WHAT A FIGHT MEANS

But no. It's not as simple as that. *Anna Karenina* and *Debbie Does Dallas* are both about sex, but one is immortal art and one is a mere masturbation aid. The *Iliad* and *Saw 3D* are both about violence—about the scary fragility of the human body—but one addresses itself to the best angels of our natures and one to the worst. Here's the question: do viewers come to a cage fight more for the poetry of the *Iliad* or the pornography of *Saw*?

ON THE EVE OF MY FIGHT, I kissed my wife and daughters good-bye and pulled away in my car. I hadn't wanted my girls to know about the fight, but my keen-eared nine-year-old pieced it together from snatches of overheard conversation. Abby asked, "Are you going to fight in one of those tournaments?" And when I had to admit that I was, six-year-old Annabel held my face between her palms and said: "Please don't, Daddy. I don't want you to die."

"Yeah," Abby said, "you're gonna lose bad, you know."

"Where's the tournament?" Annabel asked.

"In a town called Johnstown. It's not too far away. At a hockey arena."

Arena is a Greek word meaning "place of sand." It goes back to the days of Greek athletics and Roman gladiatorial contests, where sandy surfaces were preferred not just for their softness but also for the way they absorbed spilled blood. The arena where the Johnstown Toma-hawks play minor-league hockey is no longer a place of sand. But we'd be fighting on mats that were partly selected for the way they interact with blood: the vinyl surface makes it easy to swab it up between rounds.

Driving down the two-lane rural highway toward Johnstown, I was worried about the blood, but I was even more worried about my hollow belly and my dry tongue, and whether I'd be able to make weight in the morning. I'd been starving myself for days without dropping many pounds. For the last twelve hours, I'd been dehydrating myself as well, trying to get the scale to read 170 (about twelve pounds under my "in-shape" weight). For many fighters, this process—of trying to cram the biggest possible body into the smallest possible weight class—is the most miserable part of MMA. They call it the "fight before the fight." They also call it "cutting weight," but that's the wrong image. It's more accurate to say that you spill the weight, since almost all of the loss comes from fluid. Right before weigh-in, fighters routinely try to spill many pounds at once—boiling in hot baths or roasting in saunas, then bundling themselves in sweats or bedclothes to keep the sweat rolling. Depending on weight class, many professional fighters routinely shed two or three gallons of fluid (sixteen to twenty-five pounds) in the lead-up to weigh-in, reducing themselves to cadaverous states. And then, in the twenty-four hours between weigh-in and fighting, they pour all that fluid back into themselves—through IV tubes and their mouths. What this means is that when MMA athletes fight at 170 pounds, they almost never actually weigh 170 pounds. In the professional ranks, they are more likely to weigh around 190 when the bell sounds.

The next morning I got up and climbed on a treadmill wearing layers of sweats under a silvery plastic outfit called a sauna suit. Looking like an extremely sweaty Russian cosmonaut, I poured out my last five pounds (a little more than half a gallon of fluid) in about thirty minutes of light jogging. I finally weighed in at an arid 168.5. A little wobbly from malnourishment and dehydration, I had, for the first and last time in my life, the sort of fat-free muscle definition that I'd always wanted. In my friend Clark's hotel room (he would also be fighting that night), I took one of those narcissistic cell phone pictures of myself in the bathroom mirror, justifying it to him by saying, "I'll never look this good again." In fact, my ripped look didn't even survive the day. Amateur fighters in Pennsylvania have about twelve hours between their morning weigh-in and the fight, and I spent those hours gorging on fajitas, potato chips, and energy bars while chugging chocolate milk, Enfamil, and Gatorade. I regained more than half a pound per hour. By fight time I weighed 176 pounds. By the end of the next day I was back up to 182.

The night of my fight, Coach Shrader wrapped my hands, helped me muscle my gloves over the tape, and then walked me through the gauntlet of spectators to the cage. Cageside, an official checked my gloves and mouthpiece and made me tap my groin to prove that I'd remembered my cup. Shrader greased my nose and brows with Vaseline so the punches would slide, not bite. Then he sent me up the steps to the elevated cage. As I waited for my opponent to make his entrance, I felt an almost painful energy building up inside me, and I tried to dance some of it away. But I no longer felt much fear.

Fear is useful going into a fight. It's your brain's way of saying, *This is so dumb—are we sure we want to do it?* My fear had faded partly because it no longer had much purpose: there's no place to hide in a cage, and cowering won't save you. But that wasn't the only reason. Fear had dogged me throughout this project because I'd always felt it would end very badly for me. Lately, however, I'd changed my mind about that.

Standing there in the cage, I was definitely nervous, but I didn't feel like a lamb awaiting slaughter. On the contrary, for the first time in my life I felt like a tough and capable guy. I was strong and my lungs were strong, and I was growing in skill and bravery. I'd proved that I could eat a big punch and keep going. I wasn't anything like cocky. There were so many guys at the gym, not to mention in the outside world, who could handle me with ease. And sometimes I still folded under attack—cringing and running, then cursing myself for a coward later. But I'd come a long way, and as I hopped and paced in the cage, it occurred to me that I might just be up to this.

As a writer, I was vaguely aware that a win was probably the worst thing that could happen to me. A win might impose a cloying hero arc on my book: *Wimpy professor grows stronger and stronger until he triumphs, Rudy-like, in the end.* But on fight night I wasn't thinking about the book. The book was still a hazy, uncertain dream; I hadn't written a word, and I didn't even have a publisher. The young man coming toward me through the crowd, however, was no dream. This cage fight was going to happen. I was about to take an elemental test of skill, character, and courage, and I didn't want to fail. And I didn't want my wife to see me fail. And I didn't want to disappoint Coach Shrader, who had worked so hard to prepare me.

When the bell finally rang, I had zero desire to beat my opponent up. But I was desperate to beat him.

CLIMAX

My drive to Johnstown took me through the rust and wreckage of Pennsylvania's industrial economy, past derelict steel mills and coalfields and a volcano-shaped smokestack breathing white clouds into the sky. I drove past farms and dejected small towns, past churches and gun shops and diners. I passed trucks dragging the big infernal machines, Seussian in their complexity, that they use to drill down and frack shale. I saw NRA and pro-life billboards, and one showing a massive gold-embossed Bible above the words INSPIRED. ABSOLUTE. FINAL. I spun through the FM dial and found hardly any Devil music. So instead I listened, fascinated, to almost two hours of Jesus radio: Christian Pop, a radio play reenacting a Bible story about Jezebel, and a preacher veering madly between sobs of pity and joy.

I had driven down these roads many times on my way to MMA shows in other small Pennsylvania towns, and it always shook me to see, in the midst of this all-American goodness and godliness, the conspicuous infrastructure of a rural sex trade. There was no population base to speak of. No big towns. Just small villages and cornfields and truckers rumbling through. And yet I drove past so many windowless roadside sex shops and shacklike strip clubs that I wondered if this might be the per capita sin epicenter of the world.

About halfway to Johnstown, I veered off the road, as I always did, to marvel at Climax Gentleman's Club, which was the world's first, and perhaps only, drive-thru strip club. Climax went out of business a few years ago when its owner died, but until then you could pull down the gravel driveway behind Climax and pass into a tin-roofed carport. There you'd find the familiar two-window drive-thru setup. After paying at window one, you'd drive up to window two, the curtains would part, and a coal miner's daughter would jiggle at you through plate glass.

As I was walking around the ruins of Climax, it struck me that even good, Christ-loving Americans could be possessed by the Devil. Who else but the Devil could make fight fans hand over between twenty and fifty dollars for the pleasure of seeing men—me and others—pitted against each other like fighting dogs, slipping and flailing in each other's sweat and blood? Who else but the Devil could compel a farmer or traveling salesman to ease behind a bar called Climax and pay five dollars per minute to ogle a girl while he wanked in the peace and privacy of his automobile?

Strip clubs, porn shops, cage fights—they mock our hopes that man's stubborn carnal streak can be washed away, that we can be better than we are. As I pulled back onto the road to Johnstown, I began to feel that I was rushing down a river of asphalt into the heart of men's darkness—through a metaphor for man's inhumanity to man, and to woman.

THE KILLING ART

On March 24, 1962, Norman Mailer sat ringside—close enough to feel of the flecks of blood and sweat—as Emile Griffith beat the life out of Benny Paret. Innuendos about Griffith's homosexuality had appeared in the tabloids, and at the weigh-in Paret had goosed Griffith's ass, cooing, "*Měricon* [faggot], I'm going to get you and your husband." When the bell rang, Griffith rushed out in a fury, and Paret sucked up punches like a man "seeking to demonstrate that he could take more punishment than any man alive." In the twelfth round Paret, bobbing and weaving under the onslaught, got his head and one arm tangled on the wrong side of the ropes. And then, in the space of a few seconds, Griffith fatally wounded Paret with twenty-five unanswered blows. (Mailer said it was like seeing a pumpkin destroyed by a baseball bat, like hearing an axe thudding into a wet log.) Mailer converted Paret's killing, which you can still watch on YouTube, into a beautiful meditation on the meaning and mystery of boxing. For Mailer there is something profoundly important but stubbornly unsayable at the heart of boxing: "[Boxing is] a religion of blood, a murderous and sensitive religion which mocks the effort of the understanding to approach it, and scores the lungs of men like D. H. Lawrence, and burns the brain of men like Ernest Hemingway when they explore out into the mystery, searching to discover some part of the secret."

In *On Boxing*, Joyce Carol Oates makes the same point as she gropes for the hidden meaning of a fight. Ultimately Oates, who is famous for the sheer tonnage of her literary output as well as its excellence, finds herself at a loss for words. At the heart of boxing, she concludes, is "a hu man experience too profound to be named." But Mailer was wrong about Hemingway. Hemingway saw combat sports clearly and plumbed them more honestly than any other writer I know. Although Hemingway, like Mailer, took pride in his skill as a recreational pugilist and occasion- ally battled friends and foes in street duels and drunken living room

Ernest Hemingway's passport photo of 1923. Hemingway used this passport to visit Pamplona, Spain, where he developed a lifelong infatuation with bullfighting.

sparring sessions, he wrote most seriously and perceptively of bullfights, not boxing. (Hemingway loved boxing, but he didn't write too much about it, aside from bragging about his prowess in letters.) But everything Hemingway wrote about the one applies to the other.

Hemingway's book on bullfighting, *Death in the Afternoon* (1932), runs to five hundred pages and is based on exhaustive research: a bibliography containing two thousand items, his presence at the killings of fifteen hundred bulls, and all the time he spent hanging out with famous matadors. For Hemingway a bullfight was art, not sport. *Death in the Afternoon* is a dissertation on the bullfight—with its magnificent bull and its posing, preening matador—as a form of flowing sculptural art, and also as a genre of staged tragedy. In the classical tragic fashion, a bullfight slowly builds pity and fear, and ends with catharsis—the "super-emotional climax" that comes with death in the afternoon, whether the bull dies or the man. Hemingway compares this climax to a "religious ecstasy" that "takes a man out of himself and makes him feel immortal."

To get this good feeling, Hemingway needed not only for the bull to die, but also for the man to recklessly risk his life. The allure of the bullfight wasn't in the killing of the bull (butchers do that daily), but in the coyness of the matador's dance with Death. Which matador will dance more bravely and more beautifully with Death? Which will slip the bull's horn and slide his sword home with the most grace and manly arrogance? Hemingway well knew that "all matadors are gored dangerously, painfully and very close to fatally, sooner or later." But he was still angrily opposed to efforts to civilize the sport by blunting the horns, breeding down the size of the bulls, or slaying them only symbolically (say, with daubs of red paint). Without grave risk to man and beast, Heming-

way couldn't feel it. When confronted with a prudent matador who preferred safety to applause, Hemingway slouched in his seat, slugging
glumly from the bottle of Spanish sherry he always carried into the arena
and ruing the fact that with the man beyond danger, he couldn't pop a
decent art boner.

Hemingway thought people demeaned bullfighting by calling it a
sport. I see Papa's point and think it also applies to boxing and MMA,
which are sports—I allow—but very strange and special sports. (Here's
how you know: you can't *play* them.) A sport fight is more like theater,
complete with spotlit performers on an elevated stage. A fight is drama
sweated to the bones—an enactment of the whole human tangle, with
everything lovely and terrible on display. Perhaps this is why so many
great writers have been so attracted to boxing. In addition to those already mentioned, add Lord Byron, John Keats, James Baldwin, George
Plimpton, Albert Camus, A. J. Liebling, Richard Wright, Colum McCann,
D. H. Lawrence, Vladimir Nabokov, William Hazlitt, William Thackeray,
and Jack London (who was the first to yearn for a "great white hope").
And the literature of boxing (it's the one sport that can truly claim a
"literature") comes down to a long, sad death song. Writers see boxing
as a metaphor for the human condition: life is lovely; men are beautiful
and brave and poetic; but life is a fight at bottom, and we are all doomed
to lose.

For Joyce Carol Oates, just as much as for Hemingway, the whole
tragic effect of blood sports depends on real, not pretend, suffering.
Boxing is about taking a splendid specimen of manly strength, spirit,
and skill and watching it get used up. "If boxing is a sport," Oates writes,
"it is the most tragic of all sports because more than any human activity it consumes the very excellence it displays—its drama is this very
consumption."

This is why Muhammad Ali is boxing's greatest tragic hero: never
has a fighter possessed more excellence, and never has that excellence
been more thoroughly consumed. A 2012 translation of Homer's *Iliad*
features the young Cassius Clay on the cover, exulting over Sonny Liston

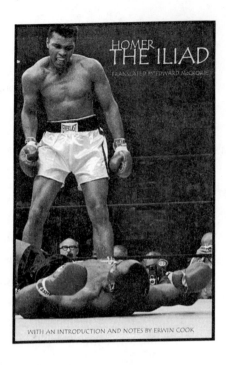

like a Homeric warrior over a fallen foe. How perfect. From an early age, Ali strove to be a larger-than-life hero. He understood that heroes need poets (what would Achilles be without Homer?), so he cultivated relationships with the most famous writers of his age. And because poets also need heroes (what would Homer be without Achilles?), the writers eagerly shaped Ali into a striving epic hero—with all the bigness and beauty and splendiferous battle boasts. And with all the flaws of a hero as well—the laxness around training, the womanizing, the cruelty and selfishness and pouting. Ali's poets followed him around the world, converting his life into art. Here's how Mailer describes the frustration of George Foreman (the decent, doomed Hector to Ali's arrogant Achilles) facing the rope-a-doping Ali during the "Rumble in the Jungle" in 1974:

> Across that embattled short space Foreman threw punches in bar-
> rages of four and six and eight and nine, heavy maniacal slamming

punches, heavy as the boom of oaken doors, bombs to the body, bolts to the head, punching until he could not breathe, backing off to breathe again and come in again, bomb again, blast again, drive and steam and slam the torso in front of him, wreck him in the arms, break through those arms, get to his ribs, dig him out, dig him out, put the dynamite in the earth, lift him, punch him, punch him up to heaven, take him out, stagger him—great earthmover he must have sobbed to himself, kill this mad and bouncing goat.

Ali survived Foreman, but he kept fighting until other men beat the beauty out of him and scarred his brain and mangled all his fine words. Ali's fate is tragic, but that's what sweetens our consumption of his life as drama.

There's a sentiment that runs through boxing literature that the savagery of fighting—its steep human toll—is redeemed by the lofty emotions it inspires. But reading Hemingway on bullfighting or Oates on boxing, I can't help but recall the Roman emperor Heliogabalus (AD 218–222), who was another connoisseur of killing arts. Here was Heliogabalus's favorite thing: slaughtering slaves on his lawn so he could thrill to the loveliness of all that red blood shimmering on all that green grass. Dumb caricatures aside, Hemingway was certainly no Heliogabalus, and Oates is even less so. But Hemingway's aesthetic response was like Heliogabalus's in that to get the real pop, he needed to see death, to watch hot blood blacken the dirt. And Oates's thrill of pity and fear depended on young men recklessly spending their life force for her artistic delectation. At times Hemingway's and Oates's books seem like attempts by masters of language to draw halos of fine, shimmering words around their bloodlust—to call sadistic voyeurism by a prettier name. Maybe we fight fans should all just admit that we are little Heliogabaluses. Better that than to compound our bloodlust with hypocrisy.

THE FIGHT

The referee yelled, "Fight!" And so we did.

The young man and I moved to the center of the octagon, extended our left arms in the laziest of jabs, and bumped fists in a show of sportsmanship. It was one of just two punches I would throw that night, and the only one that landed.

We circled away from each other, then converged again, with fists held high. Going into the fight, Coach Shrader and I knew nothing about the young man. We didn't know if he was southpaw or orthodox. We didn't know if he was a wrestler or a boxer or a jiu-jitsu player. These are very bad things not to know. But we did know a lot about me, and we knew I was better fighting on the ground than on my feet. Our game plan was simply to take the young man down and make him fight me off of his back.

So I immediately threw my second punch of the night, flicking a jab at the young man's face. When he blinked and brought his gloves up in defense, I ducked down and dove for his lead leg, hugging his thigh to my chest, driving my right ear into his navel, and twisting him to the ground. When we crashed down at the base of the fence, he had me in a headlock, but I slipped it, reached a hand out to block his legs, and swung my left leg up over his waist. I was about an inch away from securing the mount—a dominant position where the top man can throw strikes while looking for submissions.

Then came the first clue that I was out of my league. The young man shifted and wiggled and pulled me effortlessly into his guard: missionary position, me on top. He seized one of my arms and started rotating beneath me, niftily tiptoeing up the fence for leverage. Shrader told me afterward that he was trying to warn me from across the cage: "Watch out! Watch your arm! He's wall walking! He's wall walking!"

Shrader wasn't just saying this. He was roaring it. And yet I never heard him, not even faintly, because I was lost deep in the fog of war—

truly physically unable to see or hear or sense anything but the man in front of me. But feeling him constrict around my arm like a python, I realized that it was time to flee, not fight. Standing up, I yanked and yanked again, until my arm was free and I was backpedaling away, with the young man rolling lightly to his feet to give chase.

And then came the moment that would haunt me for months afterward. What if I hadn't been so stupid? What if my ears had worked and I could have heard Coach Shrader? Or what if it had simply dawned on me—from the skill of the young man's ground maneuvers—that rolling around on the mat with this guy was a bad idea? Stand-up fighting isn't really my game, but what if I'd actually felt him out as a striker? Might it have ended differently?

But I couldn't hear Shrader and my mind couldn't race as fast as the action, and changing the game plan never crossed my mind. Instead, I set a classic ground fighter's ambush. I shuffled just outside the young man's range and waited for him to move forward and throw something, anything. When a man is going to throw a punch or kick, he usually gives it away with the smallest twitch. I waited for that twitch, that small convulsion in the hips or shoulders, and when I saw it, I crouched down and drove forward. On my way in, his roundhouse kick thwacked loudly into my ribs, but then my shoulder hit his belly as I yanked at the back of his

knees, lifting him and driving him to the mat with a crash. The takedown was pure and powerful, and maybe the single coolest thing I've ever accomplished in my life.

I landed in the young man's guard (again: missionary position, me on top). I had two options: I could rise up and punch down or try to "pass guard"—to break out from between his legs and move to a more dominant position. Feeling I had matters well in hand, I took a moment to gather myself and decide. I didn't hear him, but Shrader was already roaring at me, "Posture! Posture!" He was trying to save my life. He wanted me to come up on my knees—back straight, head high. He was reminding me not to slouch down lazily and let a jiu-jitsu ace hold me chest to chest. But that's just what I was doing, and it was my undoing.

One moment I was on top and in charge—imposing my will, or so I thought. I was beginning to feel high. I was thinking, *I'm a wild boar. I'm a takedown machine. I'm a hand grenade. I'm stronger than this guy.* The next moment was deeply confusing. The ceiling was where the mat used to be, and I was about to sustain a crippling arm injury. And then it was over, and we were on our feet again, and I was hugging him as ardently as I've ever hugged another man, clapping his back as hard as he was clapping mine.

I lost by arm bar. I console myself that it wasn't the basic off-the-shelf move, which I might have seen coming. It was a sort of custom-deluxe version that I'd never seen before. He clamped my left arm tight and spun sideways beneath me while throwing his legs up in the air and sliding his free hand under my knee to help flip me like a pancake. The net effect of all these maneuvers, executed simultaneously, was to put us both on our backs, with me pinned under his legs. He had the back of one knee crooked tight to my face, and the back of the other knee snugged to my chest. My left arm was extended pipe straight between his legs. He was pulling down on my wrist while thrusting up with his pelvis against my elbow, bending the joint the wrong way. I could feel the elbow giving out, the tendons and muscles and cartilage all poised to pop. There was

The author taps out.

no fighting it, no way to squirm out or gut through. The choice was simple: have my arm ruined or beg for quarter. I tapped his leg with my free hand.

I'd trained for fifteen months for a fight that lasted forty-seven seconds.

THAT NIGHT IN JOHNSTOWN, the young men fought desperately, frantically—like living meant winning. Of the ten fights on the card, only one went to the judges; the others ended in knockouts or submissions. In one fight, a bantamweight named Andrew Daversa walked to the cage throwing wild haymakers against the air. When the bell rang, he just kept throwing those wide-arcing punches until, twenty-one seconds in, one touched Matthew Boyer's chin and put him instantly to sleep. In a heavyweight bout, my friend Clark Young tore through Lance Phillips almost as fast. Clark came out of his corner with kicks and punches, knocking Phillips down. Then Clark fell on his dazed opponent and made him quit by wrenching his arm behind his back. In a seesaw jiu-jitsu battle, Blaine Shutt and Shawn McMahon flipped and leapt like acrobats until Shutt attached himself to McMahon's back, squeezed his throat, and made him hammer the mat in outrage.

The last fight of the night was a professional contest between a striker from Virginia, D'Juan Owens, and a grappler from Texas, Brett Ewing. The fight started predictably, with Owens coming out of his corner looking to hit and Ewing shooting immediately for a takedown. Ewing wrestled Owens down and kept him there for the whole five-minute round, but he was unable to work a submission or land telling blows. When the bell rang for the second round, Ewing again tried to take the fight to the mat. He succeeded, but after a scramble Owens ended up on top. And that was the end of the competitive fight and the start of a relentless beating. Mainly working from half guard, Owens pinned Ewing's neck down with his forearm and used his free arm to batter Ewing's face with elbows, hooks, and hammer fists. Owens threw strikes in a steady, machinelike rhythm, while Ewing swiveled his head to take the blows first on one cheek and then the other.

The bell rang, ending the second round. Owens hopped to his feet and walked to his corner—mouth closed, not even breathing hard. Ewing rolled shakily to his hands and knees and staggered to his stool. The cut man swabbed away Ewing's blood and plugged his lacerations with Vaseline, while the doctor searched his pupils for signs of a concussion. In round three Owens quickly put the exhausted Ewing on the mat again and started hammering him in his unhurried, methodical way. It became the kind of fight in which people start calling out to the ref to stop it, or start praying that the dominant fighter will lock in a submission that ends the misery. By midway through the second round, it must have been as clear to the exhausted Ewing as it was to the rest of us that he could

Brett Ewing and D'Juan Owens.

not hope to win. From that point forward, for seven long minutes, Owens was fighting to win, while Ewing was just trying to show the Virginian, and all of us, how much damage he could take. I began to root for Ewing to fight through those punches. I began to hope that the ref would stand back just a little longer and let Ewing struggle through to the moral victory of the final bell. But Owens spooned up behind Ewing on the ground and finally sank a choke in deep.

At the end of the fight, the crowd broke up around me and hurried for the parking lot. Ewing was sitting on his stool with his head lolling, and with the doctors and trainers milling around. Owens couldn't force his way through the knot of men to get to Ewing, so he reached over the top to gently tousle his hair with his hand. I rose slowly to my feet and was suddenly aware of how tired I was, and how my ribs ached from the young man's kick, and that my left elbow hurt so much that it was best to just let it dangle. On my way to my car, I passed Ewing as he came out of the cage. He looked half-dead from pain, fatigue, and humiliation. His handsome young face wore a mask of risen welts, claw marks, and bloodstains. I had a powerful urge to embrace him. But instead I just patted his damp, blood-pumped shoulder as he passed and said, lamely, "Nice fight, man."

As I watched Ewing make his way to the locker room, a snatch of a poem by William Makepeace Thackeray came into my mind—a poem Thackeray wrote after attending a famously ruthless slobber-knocker between Tom Sayers and John Heenan in 1860:

> Ah, me! that I have lived to hear
> Such men as ruffians scorned,
> Such deeds of valour "brutal" called.

Exactly.

"THE STEEPS OF LIFE"

A fight twists viewers hard in opposite directions. On the one hand, a fight seems like a Hobbesian metaphor for the human condition: nasty, brutish, and short. But on the other hand, a fight displays virtues that can reveal themselves only in dire struggle. A fight confuses us because it puts the worst and the best in us on display at the very same time, while showing that you can't get the best without the worst. A fight sets up conditions of harrowing adversity that calls forth heroism. It gives men the opportunity to suffer so they can show their bigness. Without fighting, some of the poetry would go out of life. Without war—without the widows, orphans, and wasted young lives—there could have been no

Iliad. Without war, Hector would have had no proper outlet for his valor, or Odysseus his guile, or Penelope her shrewdness or steadfastness. Without war, they would have had no reason to cultivate those virtues in the first place.

Or at least that's an idea raised in William James's great antiwar essay, "The Moral Equivalent of War." The essay's greatness resides not in James's critique of war, which is conventional, but in the way he acknowledges war's terrible, irresistible grandeur. James shows us how, from a certain point of view, a world at peace would be unbearably bland. Attributing these views to defenders of militarism, James writes: "The notion of a sheep's paradise [of world peace] . . . revolts, they say, our higher imagination. Where then would be the steeps of life? . . . [War] is human nature at its highest dynamic. Its 'horrors' are a cheap price to pay for rescue from the only alternative supposed, a world of clerks and teachers, of co-education and zo-ophily, of 'consumer's leagues' and 'associated charities,' of industrialism unlimited, and feminism unabashed. No scorn, no hardness, no valor any more! Fie upon such a cattleyard of a planet!" Yes, war is a horror, but "the horror makes the thrill."

James argues against the militarists: the thrill of war is *not* worth the horror. The same argument has often been applied to fighting. Yes, it's a thrill, but it's a primitive and nasty thrill, and it is not worth the costs in blood and the deadening of empathy. When I first took up this project, I might have agreed, at least in principle. Although I watched a lot of fights, I never felt very good about it. But my time studying fights and fighters has brought me around to the opposite point of view: the thrill of a fight—for combatants and fans—*is* worth the horror.

The stereotypical fight fan is a troglodyte grunting for blood. So when I attended my first UFC event, I expected to find myself in the Roman Colosseum, with spectators hooting madly. But to my great surprise (and even greater disappointment), I found fifteen thousand fans who were extremely knowledgeable, well behaved, and even a little quiescent. The standard UFC event is *so* tame compared with the rabid hatefests of big-time football, soccer, and hockey games. This is true at the top professional level, and it's even more evident at amateur MMA shows, where the crowd's basic civility is pronounced. There is nothing that feels ugly or sadistic at an amateur MMA show, where a community gathers to cheer the skill and bravery of its young men in a highly controlled rite of passage. After all, the crowd is dominated by the families, friends, and training partners of the fighters. They want the boys to have their fun, but they don't want anyone to really get hurt. The fights are restrained by rules and unspoken codes, and they are usually quite comradely—with fighters immediately apologizing for fouls and sometimes pausing spontaneously to high-five or even embrace after a hot exchange has brought out the best in them. The atmosphere of an amateur MMA event reminds me of the mutually supportive atmosphere I've found at community road races, where people cheer for one another rather than against one another. Backstage, winning fighters console losers, and there's a sense that no one loses if he has the courage to step into the cage.

The most consistent and damning criticism of fighting sports is that they exploit the competitors. In ancient Rome, for example, the gladiators were mainly dehumanized slaves who bled to delight Roman citizens. In the bare-knuckle era, there were aristocrats in the crowd but not in the ring, where the fighters were a motley assortment of canal diggers, brick makers, chair carriers, butchers, masons, watermen, lamplighters, hack drivers, carters, draymen, hod carriers, corn porters, oilmen, fishmongers, coalers, dockers, coal-whippers, button makers, and ship caulkers. And this has been true of boxing in the gloved era as well: men from the poorer classes—along with dark-skinned men and scrounging immigrants—beat each other witless to put meat in the seats.

But I think the exploitation narrative has always been oversold, usually by people who are incapable of even *imagining* the truth: many young men, rich and poor, are magnetically attracted to the test of fighting. After all, a significant number of free Romans, even aristocrats, voluntarily entered the arena as gladiators, and well-off Brits certainly went in big for bare-knuckle boxing, even if actual prizefighting was beneath their station. When it comes to MMA, the exploitation narrative falls apart completely. Over the twenty-year history of MMA in America, mainly white, college-educated ex-wrestlers have dominated the ranks of UFC fighters. And the same thing is true at the grassroots level: there are few truly poor people in MMA—athletes who turn to fighting because it is the only way out of the ghetto or the trailer park. It comes down to money. Fighters require a tremendous amount of skilled instruction in high-quality gyms, patiently learning an endlessly evolving science. And this instruction is expensive.

The relationship between fighter and fan is not one of exploitation. It is symbiotic, not parasitic. The fighter desperately wants to be a hero, and the fan desperately wants to worship heroism—and neither can get what he needs without the other. The fan needs the fighter to put on a show, but the fighter needs the fan to cheer him on and bear witness to his courage. For fighter and fan to get what they need requires real, not counterfeit, danger. As Hemingway says, if you shear off the bull's horns, you might save the man's life, but at the cost of killing the drama and robbing the matador of his test. And if you wrapped cage fighters in bubble wrap and had them whale on each other with feather dusters, you could still have a supreme test of skill, stamina, and athleticism, but you'd rob them of their chance to test their hearts on the steeps of life.

I sympathize with those who see fighting as sheer barbarism. When watching fights, I frequently feel the same way. But some people get deep satisfaction out of fighting, and in a free society people are allowed dangerous pastimes—riding a motorcycle, rock climbing, having unsafe sex—as long as they don't bloody any bystanders. I have a hound dog named Sam—a beagle-basset mutt that lives in a world of scent. When riding in the car, he thrusts his head out the window into a rushing feast of sheer smell; his tongue goes flying, and his ears stream out like ribbons as he bawls at people and squirrels and enjoys life. But it's dangerous. If I were to crash, or even brake hard, Sam would go flying. So if I really cared about my dog, I'm told, I would buy him a special harness and run a seat belt through it. But I think strapping Sam down in a seat is what I would do if I hated him. How is a dog better off? Buckled and bored? Or unbuckled, at risk, and intensely happy?

And how is a person better off? I've decided that I like to live with my head out the window. When I began this project, I expected my involvement in MMA to last for a year and to end the very instant my fight did. But fighting has seeped into my bones, and although I don't intend to ever take an official fight again, I still go the gym to learn the science and to try to apply it in friendly bouts of face punching and limb wrenching. I don't do this in ignorance of the risks. I do it largely *because* of the risks. MMA steepens my life. It allows a dull, professorial type like me to live a headlong sort of life, if only for a few hours each week. I'm forty-one now, about twenty years older than most of the guys at my gym, so I know this can't last forever. And I have a pretty good idea of how it will end (probably with me leaving the gym for the last time on a stretcher). When that day comes, I will leave it behind sadly, feeling that my life will be smaller and drabber, and knowing that I will never again be able to run and laugh with the young men.

MMA is really, really bad for you. No one should try to deny that, and no fighter should be allowed to compete who isn't fully educated about the risks. MMA has done lasting damage to my body, and maybe even to my brain. But MMA is also really, really good for you. It's improved my self-image. It's made me stronger and fitter and more confident. It's given me a good reason to get enough sleep and not to eat like a pig or drink too much. It's given me a good reason to go out and run or do push-ups, even when I don't want to. And it gets me out of the house, forcing me, a natural introvert, to move around in a social world and make friends.

My body hurts. I keep spraining my left wrist and thumb boxing. I started this project with perfectly healthy big toes and am leaving it with arthritis in both. I've been struggling with Achilles tendinitis for about a year and a yanked tendon in my groin for half as long. And my neck injury from wrestling Clark has never fully healed, which limits me in grappling. My body is telling me something loud and clear. It's telling me

I've pushed my luck far enough. It's telling me I'm too old for this and I'm done whether I like it or not.

But I don't want to listen. Not yet. I'm not ready to slide down off the steeps of life—down, down to the long, dull flats. And I know now, in my own tiny way, why so many fighters keep at it long after they should have quit. It's because fighting is a good drug, and it's hard to kick a good drug even when you know you should. As Mike Tyson put it, in his bluntly eloquent way, "other than boxing, everything else is so boring."

SLAYING DAVID

I sat in the stands after my fight watching the boys compete and scanning the crowd for my opponent, Justin McCloskey. I looked for him in the locker rooms and the bathrooms and at the concessions stands. I couldn't find him anywhere.

I drove home at midnight, trying not to use my aching left arm, while slugging disgusting gas station coffee to stay awake and gorging my underweight body with huge quantities of disgusting gas station food: cheese popcorn, hot dogs, donuts in cellophane. I was feeling broody and sad. For months I'd been dreaming of getting this fight behind me, but I felt none of the relief I had expected and zero sense of accomplishment. I just felt shame. I had been mastered by another man who had held me down in front of the crowd—in front of my friends and my wife—and had made me say uncle. When I tapped his knee, I was communicating to him in MMA sign language. You may not know that language, so let me translate: *Please stop. I admit you are the better man. I acknowledge that you could end my life—right now—if you chose to. You'd do it first by snapping my arm at the elbow. At that point I would be helpless, and you could joint me like my mom used to joint a roast chicken—yanking and twisting until my limbs gave with a crunch. Then you could finish me at your leisure, by strangling or pounding, whichever you liked.* Referees stop fights when one man is rendered so helpless that the other man could kill him with only token resistance.

Driving home from the fight, I dictated notes into my MP3 player, trying to nail down what I'd learned in my entire MMA experience. I concluded that I'd been wrong about MMA people, fighters and fans alike. I expected the fighters to be high school bully types and the fans to be sadistic voyeurs. They weren't. And I discovered that MMA is less about feasting the worst angels of human nature than cultivating the better ones. The whole project made me think differently about masculinity, about the codes, tendencies, and rituals of manhood. It made me feel more compassion for my own sex—locked as we are, pathetically and sometimes tragically, into a lifetime of monkey dancing. Although it is perhaps regrettable that men are so competitive, so dominance obsessed, it's still a lucky thing that we have our monkey dances. Most of the time, they keep our contests civilized.

I also took stock of my own performance in the cage. Going into the fight, I'd formulated three main goals. First, I wanted to be in the best shape of my life. Check. I didn't lose on conditioning and don't think I would have if the fight had gone the distance. Second, because I was better at grappling than striking, I wanted to get the fight to the ground. Check. Third, and by far most important, I needed to fight bravely, or none of this would count. During sparring at the gym, I'd eventually learned to compete bravely. This counts for something but not a whole lot. Being brave gets pretty easy when you are just play fighting with your friends and you know they will *really* hurt you only by accident. A real cage fight demands a much higher level of bravery. You are locked in a cage, more naked and alone than you have ever been, and you have to battle your way out. Going into my fight, I didn't feel as though I needed to win to succeed. But if I lost, I had to lose bravely.

But had I lost bravely? A couple of weeks after my fight I met Clark at a bar, and over glasses of Old Crow I told him that I hadn't stopped stewing day and night over the way I'd lost. "Why did I shoot that second takedown?" I asked. "His jiu-jitsu was obviously better than mine. Why didn't I try him on his feet?"

Clark tried to help me out. "Man, it's a fight," he said. "It's going so fast, and you don't always decide right. And it was your first time." I nodded my head and fondled my still-sore elbow. A rookie mistake? I could live with that. But half my reason for taking the fight was to try to do a brave thing—to redeem myself, at least in my own eyes, for all the times I'd flinched when I was young. What if I'd ruined everything by taking a coward's way out? Here's what I wanted to know: had I shot the second time because I preferred losing a wrestling match to trying to win a fistfight? I wasn't sure then, and I'm still not sure now.

On my way home from Johnstown I concluded that I was not a fighter and never would be a fighter. By this I don't just mean that I lack mastery of technique. I mean I don't have the disposition—courage laced with a little meanness—and will never develop it. In the lead-up to the fight, Coach Shrader seized me by both shoulders and stared hard into my eyes: "Listen. You need to get in that cage ready to tear off that guy's head and shit down his throat." When he saw the blank look on my face, he added, "Don't worry. When it's done you can buy him a beer and be best friends."

But I couldn't make contact with the darkness inside me. Far from trying to kill Justin (or poop on him), I hadn't really even tried to *fight* him. I'd tried to *frolic* him. I'd tried to wrestle him down the way I used to wrestle my brothers. I wanted to do the MMA equivalent of holding a little brother's face in the snow until he whined. I threw only one punch in the fight. And I threw that punch, a jab, purely as a fake to set up my takedown. I was going to punch Justin—really punch him—only in a dire self-defense emergency. In the lead-up to a fight, all fighters feel fear. But I felt almost as much fear for my opponent as I did for myself. Two nights before the fight I had a bad dream. I was in a stadium cage savaging a young man with punches. I hit him tirelessly and hard and very, very often. And the young man just ate the punches, blow after clubbing blow to his skull. The young man would not quit, and the ref would not stop me, and the bell would not ring. And I wouldn't stop killing him with my gory fists.

I'VE SAID I took up fighting partly in hopes of getting fired. But that's only half-true. Becoming a real college professor has been the great ambition of my adult life, and a big part of me is still reluctant to give up on it. In truth, I probably feared being fired as much as I hoped for it. And that's why, for most of a year, I religiously observed the first and second rules of fight club: *You do not talk about fight club!* But if you train in MMA, it's hard to stay in the closet about it. I kept showing up for work on crutches, or limping in a walking boot, or with red gouges on my face and angry handprints running up and down my arms. One day I ran into my department chair, Linda, between classes. We stood out in the cold autumn sunshine chatting, as the college kids parted around us. I can't recall what we talked about. I just recall wishing that I'd remembered to put on my sunglasses. And I remember the way she tried not to stare at my eye while we spoke—how I could see her decide to look away, then look back in spite of herself. The eye was indeed interesting to look at. It was a liverish blob of deep purples, yellows, and browns, all encircling a bloodshot sclera. Linda didn't pry about the eye, and I was grateful for that, because I wasn't ready to explain. The whole episode reminded me of that moment in the film *Fight Club* where the narrator (played by Edward Norton) is talking to his horrified boss while straining a mouthful of blood back and forth between his bared teeth.

Eventually I had to tell people. And nothing happened. No one cared. I think this was partly because MMA was so quickly losing its renegade edge and becoming a mainstream sport. But it was mainly because my colleagues are simply very nice people and not nearly as small-minded or intolerant as I'd hoped. I owe them all an apology. (Sorry, all, I was having a hard time).* No one seemed disgusted. No one was scandalized. And no one offered to assist with my career suicide. In fact, my colleagues seemed far more amused than appalled by my project, and they regularly checked in to see how it was going. They even kept inviting me to faculty parties.

Which is how, a month after losing my fight in Johnstown, I found myself at that party at the poet's house. And Nobu was there, and I argued with him about the martial arts. And since I was in a bit of a puppy-stomping mood, I asked him if he'd like to step out into the yard.

As we squared off in the grass, I felt a shiver of mildly drunken excitement. I was confident that Nobu was dead wrong in his defense of the traditional martial arts. I was confident I would win. I faced bigger, stronger guys all the time at the gym, and I was still in fighting trim. True, Nobu had a kicker's chance against me. But only if I was dumb enough to get into a kickboxing fight with him. I wasn't. I was going to put him on the ground and put my weight on him. I was going to twist him up in knots and make him quit. It wasn't that I was so confident in my grappling. My MMA fight had taught me (as if I needed teaching) that there were tons of things about ground fighting that I didn't even know I didn't know. But raw as my grappling was, I knew that Nobu's would be worse. And I knew that size mattered.

But then I looked across at Nobu and saw from his relaxed face and movements that he seemed even more confident than me! And for the first time it hit me: maybe *I'm* not the smart guy in this story. If this were the climax of a martial arts movie, Nobu would be the undersize hero, and I'd be the villain who was trying—first verbally, now physically—to strip him of the beliefs that underpinned his whole sense of himself as a man. If this were a movie, I'd stand for the soulless, win-at-all-costs ethic of the Cobra Kai, and Nobu would represent the humble spirituality of

---

* In the fall of 2012, after most of the action in this book transpired, I voluntarily left my teaching job to focus on writing. However, I maintain an affiliation with Washington & Jefferson as a research fellow.

Mr. Miyagi and Daniel-san. And Nobu would lay me out stiff with a crane kick to the face.

Watching Nobu dancing nimbly in the grass, and seeing how slight he was, and realizing how much was at stake for him, I almost hoped it could end that way. But it didn't.

"You ready?" I called to him.

"Yes."

"Okay, but let's not kick each other in the nuts."

"Okay."

"Or poke each other's eyes out."

"Okay."

"Ready?"

"Okay."

"Okay, then—"

"But wait," Nobu said. "When you punch me, is it okay if I punch your fist in order to break your pinkie?"

"That's okay."

"Ready?"

"Okay."

Nobu sprang forward, snapping a front kick at my belly. The kick was very pretty and very fast. But it was also six inches too short.

I had chosen exactly the wrong game plan to fight Justin McCloskey. But it was exactly the right plan for Nobu. When his kick came up short, I replied by throwing a jab at his face that was also too short, but that made him flinch enough for me to shoot in low, scoop up his left leg, and kick his right leg out from under him. I dumped him on his back and came down on top in side control. This is exactly how I'd opened up against McCloskey. But unlike McCloskey, Nobu immediately made the Jiu-jitsu 101 mistake of extending his arms to try to push me off. When he straightened his left arm enough, I applied a Jiu-jitsu 101 lock (an Americana) and cranked until his shoulder threatened to tear. He tapped my back frantically with his free hand. It was all over in fifteen or twenty seconds.

Nobu rose to his feet, seemingly unflustered. "One moment, please," he said, and he paced through the long shadows lying on the lawn. Like a professor puzzling his way through an equation that didn't make sense, he was running his hands through his black hair again and again, murmuring, "Interesting . . . interesting."

I squatted in the grass and waited. I was feeling crisply alert and sober, and Nobu looked clearheaded, too. He said, "During your takedown I could have kicked you in the belly. But I didn't want to hurt you, and I don't think I can hold you off without hurting you."

"Don't worry about it," I said. "Hit me. Kick me. It's no different than at the gym."

"Can we try again?"

"Definitely."

This time Nobu circled nimbly outside my range, wary of my grappling. But eventually he had to move forward and throw something, and when he did, I was waiting there with that same ground fighter's ambush I'd set in Johnstown. (My game is not versatile.) When Nobu stepped in and lashed out with his left hand, I ducked under it, buried my shoulder in his gut, and tackled him hard to the ground. In the scramble I ended up straddling his waist. I quickly shimmied up his torso until my knees were under his armpits and I was bothering his face with the light punches of a bullying big brother. Nobu tried to wave the punches away, tried to buck me off by driving upward with his hips. But he couldn't dislodge me, and I kept pecking him with little punches until he made the Jiu-jitsu 101 mistake I was waiting for. He instinctively rolled onto his belly to protect his face, and I snaked my right arm under his chin, locked it together with my left, and pinched off the arteries piping blood to his brain. Before he blacked out, Nobu smacked the grass in surrender.

I helped Nobu up, and he began to pace again, finger combing his hair and murmuring, "Interesting . . . interesting."

I was beginning to feel ashamed. "This really isn't fair," I called out to him. "I'm three weight classes heavier than you are."

Nobu waved this consolation away. "I train to fight bigger guys. That's what martial arts are for. Can we try one more time?"

We tried not one more time, but four. Each time we squared off, I had Nobu on his back within seconds, cranking his neck or his arm until he had to tap out. Nobu was game and athletic and a lot stronger than he looked, but he simply had no idea how to resist a takedown, and once he was on the ground, he was helpless.

By the end, his perfect composure had cracked open, showing some of his embarrassment and shock. He'd been forced to submit six times in the space of three or four minutes of total action. All the skills he'd honed in nearly three decades of training had been utterly negated—and by a newbie. So I felt both relieved and wildly frustrated when I learned—sitting there in the dewy grass with our drinks, waiting for our sweat to dry—that Nobu hadn't conceded my point at all. He had lost a battle, but he wasn't surrendering in our war. Nobu was struggling with a classic case of cognitive dissonance: he knew his martial arts worked, and yet he couldn't deny that he'd been utterly dominated. At times he almost agreed that the contest had exposed gaping holes in his martial arts education, but then he backed off, arguing that our test was artificial and inconclusive. He pointed out that he wasn't going all-out. I replied that neither was I. He said that in a real fight he could have raked at my eyes when we were rolling on the ground. I said that I could out-gouge him from the top position. He said that in a real fight he could have fractured my skull as I came in for my takedowns, pointing out how much bone-powdering force there is in a strong karate kick. "Nobu," I said, "I've seen hundreds of cage fights. Nothing like that ever happens."

We debated back and forth, but we were now fairly well exhausted in our opposing trenches, and so I asked him, "Can you take anything away from our experiment?"

"Oh, sure," he said. "I learned a lot. I learned about my limitations, about my shortcomings."

"Come on, Nobu," I cried, raising my voice in exasperation. "It didn't show your limitations; it showed your *style's* limitations. It has nothing to do with *you* and everything to do with *it*."

He considered for a moment. "I feel that the system did not fail," he said. "It was me that failed." He studied the blade of grass he was twisting in his fingers. "You can quote me on that."

We went back inside the poet's house, where I spent the next two hours trying to drub Nobu into admitting that I was right in my critique of the martial arts and he was wrong. The poet sat and drank with us, and seeing how aggressive I was being, he occasionally joined the debate on Nobu's side. They kept returning to imperfections in the experiment and alleging vague spiritual benefits associated with martial arts training. Here's what I told Nobu in my closing argument: "For all the katas you've done and all the chops you've thrown into mirrors, you really aren't much better equipped to win a fight than the average tennis player. In fact, you may be worse off. So much of the lore-based 'knowledge' of the traditional martial arts, like the madness that it's a good idea to try to intercept an incoming punch with a punch of your own that breaks your assailant's pinkie—which incapacitates him in what universe?—is worse than useless. It puts you at risk."

Nobu told me later that he lay awake deep into that night. He couldn't sleep because his neck ached from my chokes and cranks. He couldn't sleep because he kept replaying the action of our contest over and over again in his mind, wondering how he could have done better.

And across town I was lying awake in my bed, too, already a little hungover and struggling with a guilty conscience. I'd set out on my journey into MMA to try to learn how to slay Goliath. But I never did. Goliath—in the body of Mark Shrader or Mike Nesto or Nick Talarico or Clark Young or Tony DiPietro or, finally, Justin McCloskey—always slew me. Against half-decent cage fighters, I had zero success. But against a gentle, slightly built chemistry professor—a man who hadn't been in constant fight training for sixteen months; a man who hadn't been preparing even longer for a debate about martial arts training—I was Goliath. I was the big guy on the beach, using my bully body and my bully logic to show Nobu that he was no stronger than Mac. I'd literally forced my beliefs onto my friend, trying to strip him of a conviction that was at the core of his identity: that he was a man who knew how to fight.

Oh, yes, I had a dark side. I'd just made contact with it a month too late.

That night at the poet's house, I kept dismissing Nobu's main point as evasive, spiritual mumbo jumbo. He said he would have been disappointed by his showing against me "if the point of martial arts is to be stronger. But the main point is not to be stronger. The main point is to be happier and healthier. To be stronger in spirit." Lying there sleepless in bed, I suddenly realized that although Nobu's training might not have made him a better fighter, it had indeed made him a better man—happier, healthier, braver, more serene. On the other hand, MMA training had made me tougher, but judging by my behavior at the poet's house, I wasn't sure it had improved me otherwise.

IN THE END, Justin McCloskey came up behind my cageside seat with a plastic cup of beer in each hand. I took one, and we hiked up to a deserted section of the stands. (Opponents sharing a postfight beer is one of the nice rituals of small-time MMA shows in western Pennsylvania. The practice reminds me of seventeenth-century peasant duelists in Amsterdam, who after slashing each other in knife fights would "drink away" the trouble with a shared pot of beer.) We drank and relived the fight, and the anxious time leading up to it. We shared our initial reasons for getting into MMA—me because I was a writer in need of a challenge, him because he was a fat ex–football player in need of exercise. (Looking at his perfectly chiseled frame, I couldn't imagine him larded with fifty extra pounds.) He complimented me on my takedowns, and I thanked him. I'd worked those takedowns relentlessly—in the gym and in shadow bouts on my living room carpet—and they are the one part of my performance that I still feel proud of. I asked him to explain how he'd locked me up so tightly in that arm bar. He asked me how old I was, and

Justin McCloskey and the author.

I told him: thirty-nine years and eight months. I asked him how old he was, and he told me: twenty-four. We admitted to each other that we had been afraid going in. He said that he'd feared me because he knew I was a writer and a professor, and therefore that I must be smart. And I thought: *How smart is* that, *to fear the raw intelligence of your opponent.* Justin also confirmed what I already knew: I'd screwed up royally taking the fight to the ground. He modestly told me that jiu-jitsu was his thing. And one of the other fighters that night looked at me like I was crazy and asked, "What were you thinking—shooting against McCloskey?" It was the equivalent of throwing rock against scissors: a doomed strategy. Everyone had known that except me. Justin told me that he would fight again, but he needed to take a break to focus on finishing college. I told him that I was officially retired. Part of me wanted to do it all again, to see if I could do better—to see if I could fight smarter and braver. But at my age that would be dumb, probably even pathetic.

When we ran out of things to say, we shook hands and clapped shoulders, and I sat there alone in the steep stands, watching Justin make his way back to his people: his friends and family members, his trainers and gym mates. They absorbed him with hugs and fist bumps, then pressed another beer on him. I felt a tremendous sense of liking and respect for Justin, and I felt lucky that I'd been beaten by this sweet, skilled kid instead of by one of the other sweet kids who might have had to really hurt me to beat me.

As he walked away, I realized that Justin hadn't told me what he was studying in school. I called out the question, and he called back the answer with a sheepish smile. He paused for a moment to see if I'd crack a joke, but I just returned his smile. It was too perfect. Justin McCloskey, the MMA fighter who'd whipped my ass, was going to be a nurse when he grew up.

ACKNOWLEDGMENTS

This book benefited from five editors. The first was Colin Dickerman, who within hours of receiving my book proposal, wrote back to my agent: "Who else has it? I want to know so I can begin the process of elbowing them out of the way." Colin threw a few spinning elbows, cleared out the competition, and secured this book for the Penguin Press. When Colin moved on to a different job, he passed me over to Scott Moyers with this reassurance: "Scott is much more macho than I am, and I'm sure he could beat me in a cage fight." Scott's belief in this book helped me believe in it, and his input—on the smallest matters of language and the largest matters of narrative strategy—greatly improved the final product. A third editor at Penguin, Mally Anderson, made many artful improvements to the manuscript and also guided an exceptionally clueless author through the minefields of copyright law. The fourth editor was Barbara Jatkola, who poured a staggering amount of expert labor into copyediting this book. I'm both grateful for Barb's efforts and slightly mortified that I needed so much help even after making eighty-seven editing passes of my own. This is the second book I've worked on with Barb, and I hope there will be many more. Finally, my brother Robert served as a de facto fifth editor. The book has been a constant topic of conversation between us for years, and Robert showed great stamina—and skill—in doctoring draft after draft. More important, by always being available to strategize about my writing or to listen to me bitch about it, the guy keeps me sane.

Thanks to my agent, Max Brockman—and all his associates at Brockman, Inc.—for helping me craft the proposal and guiding it through the shoals of publication. I'm proud to be associated with one of the best and most influential literary agencies in the world.

Thanks to Mike Kessling and the other guys at Complete Devastation MMA for running safe, efficient, and entertaining events and for working hard to get an old guy into a cage fight. Special thanks to Complete Devastation's photographer, Rob Lynn—a devilishly handsome and not even slightly balding camera samurai—for allowing me to use his photos in the book so long as I pointed out that he was devilishly handsome and not going bald (that he is a camera samurai is my own observation). Thanks also to all of the other organizations and individuals who allowed me to use images, often free of charge.

Thanks to my colleagues at Washington & Jefferson College for their friendship and support. Special thanks to that warrior-philosopher Nobu, and to the poet—who knows how fond I am of him, even if we are on the rocks. To the horn blower: I'm sorry I called you Muppet-headed. But you will admit to something Muppety about your haircut. And you did steal the poet, for which I could have challenged you to swordplay at dawn. So who should be apologizing to whom?

Thanks to all my friends and training partners at Mark Shrader's Mixed Martial Arts, especially Nick Talarico, Clark Young, Mike Richie, Tim Gilbert, Adam Corwin, Jeremy Brunst, Temur Abrorov, Miguel Francisco, Coni Francisco, Max Mastrean, Matt Singo, Jake Magill, Tony DiPietro, Kellie Nesto, and Mike Nesto. Above all, thanks to Mark Shrader for inviting me into his gym and for treating me like one of the guys. Mark is a terrific natural trainer, and I'm grateful to him for teaching me how to fight. At least a little.

Thanks to my mother, Marcia, who has been my first reader for almost everything I've written since college. Thanks to my father, Jon, who read and commented on a draft of this book and has been a model of masculinity—strength without bravado—for me and my brothers.

Thanks to Steven Pinker for his encouragement and for allowing me to see a prepublication draft of his monumental book on the decline of violence, *The Better Angels of Our Nature* (2011). Thanks to my new friends Robert Deaner and David Puts for giving expert opinions on the manuscript and for rescuing me from many embarrassing errors. Thanks also to my old friends Marcus Nordlund and Brian Boyd for good input (and extra thanks to Brian for not *completely* melting down over my random approach to hyphenation).

Thanks to my brothers—Richard, Robert, and David—for being my first, and still my favorite, training partners in all varieties of ritual combat. And love to our big sister, Deidre, who doesn't join in our games but is still the best and truest of the Gottschall brothers.

Thanks to my daughters, Abigail and Annabel, and to my wife, Tiffani—"best of wives, best of women." For this book Tiffani put up with my usual absentminded professor nonsense, compounded by the absentmindedness that comes from being punched in the head a lot. One day last year, after I had done something quite staggeringly stupid, she asked me, with real curiosity and no meanness, "How can you function? How can you get through your life?" That's easy, wife. I can get through my life because of you.

NOTES

CHAPTER ONE: THE RIDDLE OF THE DUEL

7 *"The trouble with this country":* From a conversation with the poet James Dickey, quoted in Sheehan 1978, 8.

7 *history of the Ultimate Fighting Championship:* Wertheim 2009; Snowden 2008; Krauss and Aita 2002.

7 *"combat in its":* *Ultimate Fighting Championship Classics, Volume 1.* Santa Monica, CA: Lionsgate, 2006. DVD.

7 *The creators considered:* Krauss and Aita 2002.

7 *"The rules are simple":* *Ultimate Fighting Championship Classics, Volume 2.* Santa Monica, CA: Lionsgate, 2006. DVD.

11 *Before dawn on November 23:* Details of the duels of Philip and Alexander Hamilton are from Fleming 1999; Freeman 2001; Hendrickson 1976; Rogow 1998; and Hopton 2007. Details of Philip Hamilton's state of mind are speculative.

12 *"beggared all description":* Quoted in Hendrickson 1976, 543.

12 *"the brightest":* Quoted in Rogow 1998, 209.

12 *"the grave of his hopes":* Quoted in Hendrickson 1976, 535.

13 *knowing he was in the wrong:* "It is not to be denied," Hamilton wrote, "that . . . on different occasions, I, in common with many others, have made very unfavorable criticisms on particular instances of the private conduct of this gentleman." Hamilton went on to say that those criticisms "were accompanied with some falsehoods" (quoted in Rogow 1998, 252).

13 *"almost intolerable":* Quoted in Hendrickson 1976, 637.

13 *"damned rascal":* Ibid., 534.

14 *"my friend Hamilton":* Quoted in Rogow 1998, 198.

14 *"a religious duty":* Quoted in Fleming 1999, 100.

14 *"nigger ball":* Quoted in Rogow 1998, 259.

14 a *"profligate"* and a *"voluptuary in the extreme":* Quoted in Freeman 2001, 162.

14 *"best of wives":* Quoted in Fleming 1999, 311.

15 *their personal honor:* Appiah 2010; Bowman 2006.

15 *Muscular cultures of honor:* Brown and Osterman 2012; Anderson 1999; Nisbett and Cohen 1996; Appiah 2010; Bowman 2006; Leung and Cohen 2011.

16 *Consider the case of Jimmy Lerner:* Lerner 2002, 51–52, 170.

17 *"You can tell the rabbits":* Earley 1992, 141.

18 *"If we were truly brave":* Quoted in Fleming 1999, 331.

20 *"the monkey look":* Toole 2005.

20 *"All warfare is based":* Sun Tzu 2005, 4.

20 *twelve-pound mallet:* Altha et al. 1985.

20 *one hundred Gs of force:* Barrow 2012, 68.

23 *literally great-hearted:* Noakes 2004, 35.

25 *inner-city drive-bys:* On America's inner-city cultures of honor, see Anderson 1999. The sociologist Randall Collins (2008, 465) proposes that establishing a culture of boxing duels might control honor-based killings in inner-city neighborhoods.

25 *"I cannot impress":* Quoted in Hopton 2007, 96.

26 *"He looked at":* Maupassant 1889, 35–36.

28 *the journalist Matt Polly:* Polly 2011.

28 *Sam Sheridan's incisive book:* Sheridan 2007.

28 *George Plimpton had written:* Plimpton 1977.

29 *columnist Joel Stein:* Stein 2012.

30 *"When it was over":* Gallico 1992, 44–45.

CHAPTER TWO: MONKEY DANCE

33 *"The male disposition":* Locke 2011, 60.

35 *"relatively common social adaptation":* Volk et al. 2012. On the evolution of bullying, see also Sherrow 2011; Powell and Ladd 2010; and Underwood 2004. On bullies being assassinated by their victims, see Boehm 1999.

37 *one of the hardest things:* Hamil 2011.

40 *working-class Brits:* It is a myth that duels were limited to the aristocratic classes. For sources on peasant dueling cultures, see Boschi 1998; Spierenburg 1998a; Dyck 1980; and Davies 2002.

40 *"[If two men have a disagreement]":* Saussure 1902, 180. For descriptions of other working-class fistic dueling cultures, see Dyck 1980 and Mee 1998.

42 *Olympic pistol dueling:* Madigan and Delaney 2009, 42; Mather 2012.

43 *Boxing was dangerous:* Gorn 1986; Lindholm and Karlsson 2009.

45 *institutionalized in the Mensur.:* McAleer 1994.

45 *"a pretty little":* Holland 2003, 232.

46 *no one likes backing down:* Collins 2008; Luckenbill 1977; Polk 1999.

47 *On the rare occasions:* For a description of female forms of aggression, see Campbell 2002. See also Cross and Campbell 2011, 393; Campbell and Cross 2012; and Fisher, Garcia, and Chang 2013.

48 *the duel between the Russian poet:* Binyon 2003.

49 *actual violence is comparatively rare:* As the primatologist Frans de Waal explains, for every fight in one chimp troop he was studying, "literally hundreds of displays and nonviolent conflicts took place" (2007, 105).

49–50 *stunningly diverse array:* Sherrow 2012.

50 *explicitly compare them:* See, for example, Eibl-Eibesfeldt (1989, 375): "The tournament fights of animals are fully comparable to culturally ritualized human duels."

51 *"The Monkey Dance":* Miller 2008, 42. Miller is speaking strictly from personal experience,

but social science has reached the same conclusions about the strongly stereotyped patterns in men's fights. See, for example, Polk 1999; Luckenbill 1977; Collins 2008; and Felson 1982.

51 *as researchers used to believe:* Lorenz 1996.

51 *leading cause of male mortality:* Dennett 1995, 478.

51 *"altercations of a relatively trivial origin":* Daly and Wilson 1988, 125.

52 *Different forms of the duel:* On duels among the Samurai, see Musashi 2002. On the Yanomamö, see Chagnon 1992. On the Ona and the Inuit, see Fry 2005, 75–76. On the state of Truk, see Gilmore 1990.

53 *in the main we aren't:* Collins 2008.

54 *"lost the fight":* Toback 2008.

55 *People are masters:* Knapp and Hall 2010, 336.

56 *our direct eye contact is glancing:* Bordwell 2007.

56 *too much eye contact:* Knapp and Hall 2010, 355; Ellsworth, Carlsmith, and Henson 1972; Ellsworth and Carlsmith 1973.

56 *men are literally:* On men's tendency to size up each other's formidability, see Sell et al. 2009. On male size and strength as the best predictor of winning a fight, see ibid. and Von Rueden, Gurven, and Kaplan 2008.

57 *It's different for women:* Knapp and Hall 2010.

58 *"staring endurance":* Terburg et al. 2011.

58 *Sustained eye contact:* Grumet 2008, 121.

58 *When lab subjects are shown:* Terburg et al. 2011. See also Brooks, Church, and Fraser 1986.

59 *Nonverbal elements:* Andersen 2008, 456.

59 *Obama made the submissive move:* Sussman 2012.

60 *"At times, the thinly veiled":* Kaufman 2012.

61 *Obama almost invariably looked away:* Tecce 2012.

CHAPTER THREE: TOUGH MEN

63 *"The greater size":* Darwin 1871, 298.

67 *an arbitrary cultural ideal:* For predominantly social-constructivist positions on masculinity, see Connell 2005; Kimmel 1996, 2008; Faludi 1999; Mosse 1996; Pollack 1998; Kindlon and Thompson 1999; and Miedzlan 1991.

68 *"boying" and "girling":* Butler 1990, 1993.

68 *very much on their side:* Campbell 2002; Geary 2010; Ellis et al. 2008; Konner 2010; Seabright 2012. Sex differences in aggression behavior are particularly dramatic; see Archer 2009 and responses to Archer, *Behavioral and Brain Sciences* 32, no. 3–4 (2009): 266–311.

68 *turned out to be "not real":* Konner 2010, 263.

69 *very real and robust sex differences:* for reviews see Konner 2010, chap. 10; Archer 2009 and responses to Archer, *Behavioral and Brain Sciences* 32, no. 3–4 (2009): 266–311.

69 *"maximum reproductive rate":* Clutton-Brock and Parker 1992b; Clutton-Brock and Vincent 1991.

69 *the most fertile woman:* While *Guinness World Records* credits Vassilyev with sixty-nine children, medical authorities have been unable to verify that number: http://www .guinnessworldrecords.com/world-records/3000/most-prolific-mother-ever.

69 *An average man produces:* Cooper et al. 2010.

69 *there is sharp competition:* For an overview of the research on the stronger average sex drive of men relative to women, see Baumeister 2010, 223–33.

70 *"substantiated by empirical evidence":* Hudson and den Boer 2002, 12. See also Courtwright 1996 and Divale and Harris 1976.

70 *Among the Inuit:* Smith and Smith 1994.

70 *"boys will have to kill":* Quoted ibid., 607.

71 *Genetic studies show:* Wilder, Mobasher, and Hammer 2004; Shriver 2005. For an overview of genetic research, see Baumeister 2010, 63–65.

71 *An extreme example:* Baumeister 2010, 63–65; Mayell 2003; Zerjal et al. 2003.

71 *Women also had to compete:* Fisher, Garcia, and Chang 2013.

72 *typical sex roles may be reversed:* Darwin 1871; Andersson 1994, 177–83; Trivers 1972; Clutton-Brock and Parker 1992a, 1992b.

73 *across the animal kingdom:* Eibl-Eibesfeldt 1989, 276; Wilson 1975, 125–26, 324–30.

73 *powerfully shaped the males:* Major cross-species studies have found consistent links between large male size and success in dominance contests; see Andersson 1994 and Archer 2009, 262.

73 *The average man is only:* Archer 2009, 260.

74 *How large is the difference:* For differences between fat-free muscle mass in men and women, see Puts 2010. The quotation about the sex difference in upper-body muscle mass being similar in humans and gorillas is from Puts 2010, 161; see also Dixson 2009. For the difference between women and men in weightlifting, see Gaulin 2009, 280.

75 *In a study of thirty cultures:* Williams and Best 1982.

75 *the "WAW Effect":* Eagly and Mladinic 1989, 1994; Eagly, Mladinic, and Otto 1991. See also Baumeister 2010, 25.

75 *studies of what people think:* Campbell 2002, 104; Chick and Loy 2001, 3; Ellis et al. 2008, 927; Schmitt et al. 2008.

75 *Boy toddlers, for example:* Baillargeon et al. 2007. See also Hay 2005.

75 *zero-tolerance policies:* Tremblay and Nagin 2005, 84; Penny Holland 2003; Paley 1984.

75 *"differential treatment was virtually nil":* Campbell 2002, 3 (describing the findings of Lytton and Romney 1991). See also Maccoby 1998, 134.

76 *Studies of sex hormones:* Cohen-Bendahan, van de Beek, and Bernbaum 2005, 358; Auyeung et al. 2009. The quotation about female monkeys is from Cohen-Bendahan, van de Beek, and Bernbaum 2005, 355. For an overview of CAH, see Cohen-Bendahan, van de Beek, and Bernbaum 2005.

77 *cultural variation:* On variations in masculinity see Gilmore 1990.

81 *fearful rites of passage:* Gilmore 1990; Ong 1981; Vandello et al. 2008.

81 *Take Toughman:* The Toughman rites are entirely consistent with a cross-cultural pattern described by the scholar Ronald Grimes: "Male rites are . . . likely to require a demonstration of skills or an exhibition of prowess. The focus of boys' rites tends to be on assuming responsibility, the focus of girls' rites, on fertility and sexuality—in short, on men's productive role and women's procreative role" (2000, 109).

81 *Tough, violent societies:* Sosis, Kress, and Boster 2007.

82 *a lot of Don Quixote:* Ong 1981, 99.

82 *"the end of men":* Rosin 2012. See also Tiger 1999 and Dowd 2005.

84 *"taste for risk":* Campbell 2007, 367.

86 *"Positional wrestling":* Aldis 1975. See also Fry 2005, 57.

86 *competitors are overwhelmingly:* Deaner and Smith 2012.

87 *"only as comedic":* Beekman 2006, 31.

87 *"'Big Boobs,' 'Deep Crevice'":* Guttmann 2004, 45.

87 *"like a monkey riding a bicycle":* Barbara Holland 2003, 82.

88 *women are actually more likely:* Archer 2009.

88 *desperate form of family planning:* Hrdy 2009.

88 *Men have disputes with each other:* Daly and Wilson 1988; Geary et al. 2003, 449; Campbell 2005, 63; Archer 2009, 255.

88 *the much gentler sex:* Of the hundreds of studies of aggression collated by Ellis and colleagues, none found that women were more physically aggressive than men (Ellis et al. 2008, 706–7).

89 *"A girl that's been called":* Campbell 2002, 198. The sociologist Randall Collins reached the same conclusion: "Girls verbally bully others chiefly in terms of their low status in the sexual attractiveness/dating market; boys physically bully others chiefly for their perceived low standing in physical aggression" (2008, 160).

89 *aggression in female adolescents:* Campbell 2002. See also Cross and Campbell 2011, 393; Campbell and Cross 2012; and Fisher, Garcia, and Chang 2013.

89 *In legal records:* Muchembled 2012, 231.

89 *"Perhaps the real reason":* Quoted in Lansdale 2005, 76.

90 *hit by cars more often:* Zhu et al. 2012.

90 *Sex differences in risk tolerance:* Campbell 2002, 74. See also Harris, Jenkins, and Glaser 2006; Pawlowski, Rajinder, and Dunbar 2008; Cross, Copping, and Campbell 2011; and Cross 2010.

90 *differences between male and female death rates:* Kruger and Nesse 2006.

90 *a surprisingly small source:* Diamond 2012, 139–40; Pinker 2011.

90 *"[Young men] are killed":* Junger 2010, 238.

90 *Women are woods wary:* Cross and Campbell 2011, 392. On women's stronger physiological response to fear, see Campbell 2007.

91 *The Darwin Awards "commemorate":* "History and Rules," DarwinAwards.com, www .darwinawards.com/rules/.

92 *"Women's lives are precious commodities":* Cross and Campbell 2011, 391. See also Sear and Mace 2008.

92 *"The woman is life":* Campbell and Moyers 1991, 108.

CHAPTER FOUR: SLAYING GOLIATH

99 *upside to masculine energy:* Baumeister 2010 makes this case at book length.

99 *the humanities have been feminized:* Hunt 1997.

100 *"How can one successfully defend":* Danaher 2001, 2.

102 *not limited to the East:* For information on more than one thousand different martial arts styles from around the world, see Crudelli 2008.

104 *"We never had rules":* Quoted in Krauss and Aita 2002, 32.

108 *"These people":* Lorden 2000, 85.

109 *"[Oyama's] fighting principle":* "Sosai Masutatsu: Sosai's History," MasutatsuOyama.com, www.masutatsuoyama.com/masoyama.htm.

109 *cast serious doubt:* On skepticism regarding Oyama, see Smith 1999. For Jon Bluming's belief that Oyama never had a real fight and cheated when it came to board- and brick-

breaking exhibitions, see "Mas Oyama Stories," www.kyokushinkai.com.br/kyokushin-downloads/mas-oyama-was-a-fraud.pdf. For an interview with Jon Bluming, see Jose Fraguas, "A Classic Warrior," https://sites.google.com/site/jigokudojoscotland/founder-jon-bluming. For more debunking of Oyama myths, including the claim that Oyama had more than two hundred fights during his American tour, see Noble n.d.

110 *without actually touching them:* "5/7: The Fact of Yanagi Ryuken Daitoryu-Aikido," YouTube video, www.youtube.com/watch?v=mdUxPLIJVgI.

110 *If he was a faker:* YouTube video, www.youtube.com/watch?feature=player_embedded& v=7jf3Gc2a0_8&t=5. For an excellent treatment of Ryuken, see Sam Harris, "The Pleasures of Drowning," The Blog, SamHarris.org, www.samharris.org/blog/item/the-pleasures-of -drowning.

110 *semimythical founder:* For multiple examples of legendary martial arts founders, see Peterson 2003.

110 *"a record of fact":* Liang 1974, 95. For further discussion of tai chi's putative martial effectiveness, see Preston 2007.

111 *The most balanced of the Lee biographies:* Thomas 1994, 23.

111 *never questioning a senior:* To give one more example, a book about Mas Oyama tells a story about a karate student who was told to do push-ups as a punishment for some infraction. But the instructor forgot to tell the student to stop and found him wrenching out push-ups many hours later. "Why are you still doing pushups?" the instructor asked. The student replied that "he was instructed by a senior to do pushups, and if this meant all day and night he would do so. He went on to say that he would not question a senior and he would not dishonor Mas Oyama, Kyokushinkai, or his fellow *uchi-deshi* [students] by quitting his punishment" (Lorden 2000, 98–99).

114 *return to the true faith:* For a skeptical analysis of the myths of kung fu, see Meir Shahar's history of the Shaolin Monastery (2008).

114 *"reading this book":* Jōtarō 2009.

115 *"Monkey Steals the Peach":* Kim 1985, 132–33. See also Kim 1981.

115 *"the slaying of":* Huxley 2005, 244.

CHAPTER FIVE: SURVIVAL OF THE SPORTIEST

121 *"Gentlemen, you are":* Rawson and Miner 2006, 643. Jones was exhorting his team before the 1916 Harvard-Yale game.

122 *Why do people care:* In drawing my conclusions on the evolution of sport, I've drawn on accounts by researchers such as David Puts, Robert Deaner, Michael Lombardo, Andreas De Block, and Siegfried Dewitte.

122 *most scholars pay scant attention:* Zillmann, Bryant, and Sapolsky (1989, 246) describe "a nearly universal condemnation of sport spectatorship on the part of social scientists." As Wann and Melnick put it, "Everyone seems to like sport except the social scientists who comment about it" (2001, 155).

125 *unlikely to be a neutral trait:* Faurie and Raymond 2013.

125 *variety of health problems:* For a review of the data, see Llaurens, Raymond, and Faurie 2009a, 2009b. The data are cloudy and contested, but even researchers who are skeptical of arguments in favor of the evolutionary origins of left-handedness provisionally allow

that lefties seem to face increased health risks; see, for example, Schaafsma et al. 2012 and Groothuis et al. 2013.

125 *the biological mystery of southpaws:* Faurie and Raymond 2005, 2013; Llaurens, Faurie, and Raymond 2009a, 2009b.

126 *typically much more violent:* Pinker 2011; Diamond 2012; Gat 2006.

126 *For a recent book:* Brockman 2013.

127 *no evidence that lefties:* Schaafsma et al. 2012.

127 *Lefty genes may have survived:* Faurie and Raymond 2013.

127 *male-dominated preserve:* Deaner and Smith 2012; Guttmann 1991.

130 *the most common type of game:* Deaner et al. 2012.

132 *exercise scientists Loren Cordain and Joe Friel:* Cordain and Friel 2010, 271.

134 *ritualized insult wars:* Wald 2012; Locke 2011; Huizinga 1938; Parks 1990; Ong 1981.

134 *girls and women generally:* Wald 2012; Locke 2011. See also the linguist Deborah Tannen, who writes: "[Women] do not tend to engage in ceremonial combat to negotiate status and display their prowess. It is not fighting per se that is more often associated with men but agonism—ceremonial combat" (1998, 231). On sex differences in communication style, see Oberzaucher 2013.

135 *By the age of seventeen months:* Baillargeon et al. 2007.

136 *"Boys are not aggressive":* Maccoby 1998, 36, 37.

136 *fifty times more likely:* Maccoby 1998, 39. See also Campbell 2002, 105.

137 *over the past few decades:* Gottschall 2012, chap. 2; Paley 1984.

137 *Girls and boys self-segregate:* Maccoby 1998; Campbell 2002, 105; Bjorklund and Pellegrini 2004, 48; Geary 2010, 322–24; Paley 1984; Konner 2010.

137 *male rough-and-tumble play:* Ellis et al. 2008, 698–701; Pellegrini 2004; Pellegrini and Smith 2005; Konner 2010, 266; Bateson 2005; Smith 2010.

137 *Young male monkeys:* Meaney and Stewart 1985, 24; Geary 2010, 86. For female primates' fascination with infants, see Hrdy 1999 and Geary 2010, 86.

138 *"Perhaps the very existence":* Groos 1898, xx.

138 *clear-cut dominance:* Archer and Côté 2005, 434–35; Campbell 2002, 107; Golombok and Hines 2004, 120; Maccoby 1998, 38; Cummins 2005; Geary et al. 2003; Huntingford and Turner 1987, 331, 352.

138 *The social status:* Campbell 2002, 107. See also Archer and Côté 2005 and Collins 2008, 173.

139 *boys like play:* Panskepp 1998, 284. See also Fry 2005, 79.

139 *"Getting Ahead":* This phrase is taken from the psychologist Robert Hogan (1985), who calls "getting ahead" and "getting along" the two great challenges of human social life.

139 *a form of ritual combat:* Ong 1981.

139 *"It would be a mistake":* Zahavi and Zahavi 1997, 63.

139 *The biologist David Barash:* quoted in Parks 1990, 17.

140 *an "ultra-social" species:* E.O. Wilson 2012.

140 *"gay porn for straight men":* Simpson 2008.

140 *"shrinkage":* "The Hamptons," *Seinfeld,* season 5, episode 20, May 12, 1994.

143 *Humans are inherently hierarchical:* Cummins 2005.

143 *duelists should part:* Frevert 1998, 46; Spierenburg 1998b, 9.

143 *After two chimps fight:* Pennisi 2012a.

145 *This is ass-backward:* For a wide-ranging overview of females as intensely active players in the mating game, see Fisher, Garcia, and Chang 2013.

145 *An elephant seal cow:* Cox and Le Boeuf 1977. See also multiple studies cited in Borgia 2006, 251.

145 *cooperate with the winners:* Puts 2010.

145 *the Persians were shocked:* Herodotus, *History*, 8.26.3. See also Kyle 2007, 7.

146 *do better with the ladies:* See, for example, Lombardo 2012, 13; Campbell 2002, 107; Faurie, Pontierb, and Raymond 2004; Brewer and Howarth 2012; and Schulte-Hostedde 2008.

146 *lavish their attention:* Turton 2002.

146 *the boys get drunk and fight:* Gilmore 1990, 71.

146 *winning wrestlers attract:* Llaurens, Raymond, and Faurie 2009a; Guttmann 1996, 22.

146 *gladiators were sex-symbols:* Baker 2000; Wisdom 2001; Fagan 2011.

146 *attraction to athletic physiques:* Frederick and Haselton 2007. See also Honekopp et al. 2007.

147 *men seek physical beauties:* Puts 2010.

148 *the average male cares more:* For a review of the research, see Deaner, et al. 2012.

149 *men's favorite TV network:* Thompson 2013.

150 *greater male interest:* Deaner, et al. 2012.

150 *2012 study of dozens of cultures:* Deaner and Smith 2012.

150 *"have far greater inborn":* Deaner, et al. 2012.

150 *Since passage of the amendment:* The Women's Sports Foundation gives these statistics in support of the notion that girls are just as interested in playing sports as boys ("Title IX Myths and Facts," n.d., www.womenssportsfoundation.org/home/advocate/title-ix-and -issues/what-is-title-ix/title-ix-myths-and-facts).

150 *female participation in sports has increased 560 percent:* Women's Sports Foundation, http://www.womenssportsfoundation.org/home/advocate/title-ix-and-issues/what-is-title-ix/title-ix-myths-and-facts.

152 *studies show that female athletes:* Findlay and Bowker 2009; Gill and Dzewaltowski 1988; Gill 1988; Hellandsig 1998; Jamshidi, et al. 2011.

152 *This difference in competitiveness:* Deaner 2006a, 2006b.

153 *"Lisa, if the Bible":* "Lisa on Ice," *The Simpsons*, season 6, episode 8, November 13, 1994.

154 *some commentators:* See Rosin 2010, 2012, 2013.

154 *"age of testosterone":* Phrase from Rosin 2010.

154 *applies to women as well:* For a different evolutionary explanation of women's participation in sports, see Epstein 2013, chap. 4.

155 *what turns women on:* Campbell 2002, 120, 103.

155 *power in women:* Ibid., 120; Rhoads 2004, 152.

155 *men seek out fertility cues:* For more on the technical details, see Gottschall 2007.

CHAPTER SIX: WAR GAMES

158 *"you stupid Yinzers":* Yinz is Pittsburghese for "you 'uns" (or "you ones"). It basically means "you guys." Pittsburghers proudly refer to themselves as Yinzers, but foreigners such as Mr. Stiletto use the term as a slur.

159 *duel forms such as purring:* On purring, see Couch 2004. On rough-and-tumble fighting, see Gorn 1985.

159 *"you just got to be able":* Katz 1987.

160 *a strange, strange bird:* For various perspectives on sports fandom, see Guttmann 2004; Quinn 2009; Wann et al. 2001; St. John 2004; Winegard and Deaner 2010; and Hugenberg, Hardiakis, and Earnheardt 2008.

161 *avid sports spectators:* Guttmann 1986. The description of the Greek vase appears on page 17.

161 *In Roman times:* Cameron 1976, 54.

161 *"some maniacal drug":* Quoted in Guttmann 1986, 18.

161 *"Loyalty to any one sports team":* "The Label Maker," *Seinfeld*, season 6, episode 12, January 19, 1995. Comics are notorious joke thieves, and Seinfeld seems to have ripped off Pliny the Younger, who beat him to this insight by a couple thousand years: "It surprises me all the more that so many thousands of adult men should have such a childish passion for watching galloping horses and drivers standing in chariots, over and over again. If they were attracted by the speed of the horses or the drivers' skill, one could account for it, but in fact it is the racing colors they really support and care about, and if the colors were to be exchanged in mid-course during a race, they would transfer their favor and enthusiasm and rapidly desert the famous drivers and horses whose names they shout as they recognize them from afar. Such is the popularity and importance of a worthless shirt" (Quoted in Guttmann 1986, 30).

162 *"I adjure you, demon":* Harris 1972, 235.

163 *It explains why the crowds:* Fagan 2011; Cameron 1976.

163 *promoted as clashes:* Gorn 1986, 87.

163 *"terrible Turks":* Randazzo 2008, 68. See also Beekman 2006.

164 *if they weren't so offended:* Writers objecting to comparisons of sports and warfare include Palantonio 2008; Granderson 2010; Carpenter 2009; and Lipsyte 2003.

164 *flung rocks made:* See battle scenes in Homer's *Iliad*.

164 *"War was an exercise":* Quoted in Cornell 2002, 25.

164 *Among peoples as far-flung:* Blanchard and Cheska 1985, 175–87.

164 *"sham warfare":* Chick, Loy, and Miracle 1997.

164 *winners simply inflicted more damage:* For team dodgeball in the Marquesas Islands, see Chick and Loy 2001, 7. For stone-fighting games in Italy, see Chick and Loy 2001; in Kurdistan, Davis 1994, 1998; and in Korea, Saunderson 1895, 314.

165 *Aché tribesmen from:* Hill and Hurtado 1996.

165 *shield-bearing mobs:* Blanchard and Cheska 1985, 141.

165 *Dani men ran about:* Blanchard and Cheska 1985; Knauft 2002.

165 *I think the actual relationship:* Other scholars also have argued for a deep relationship between sports and war; see, for example, Elias and Dunning 1986, 659; Pinker 2003, 317; Cornell 2002; Symons 1978, 186–87; Guttmann 2004, 7; and Marples 1954, 1.

165 *mobs of Italian workingmen:* Davis 1994, 1998.

165 *medieval knights competed:* Kaeuper 2001; Keen 1984.

166 *one tournament in Neuss:* Keen 1984, 87.

166 *people blew their noses:* Pinker 2011, 69–72.

166 *Take football:* On the evolution of football, see Magoun 1938; Marples 1954; Palantonio 2008; Braunwart and Carroll 1997; Watterson 2000; and Bernstein 2001.

166 *"a ball full of wynde":* Quoted in Marples 1954, 33.

168 *like a running gang fight:* Football games were really excuses for "semi-institutionalized fights between local groups arranged on certain days of the year, particularly on Saints'

Days and Holy Days . . . Playing with a football was one of the ways of arranging such a fight. It was, in fact, one of the normal annual rituals of these traditional societies . . . Football and other similar encounters in those times were not simply accidental brawls" (Elias and Dunning 1986, 179).

168 *"a freendly kinde of fight":* Quoted in Braunwart and Carroll 1997, 1.

168 *mutated form of rugby:* Braunwart and Carroll 1997.

168 *Massed play was:* Watterson 2000.

168 *"got a running start":* Bernstein 2001, 28.

168 *three strikes:* Ibid., 34.

169 *a war game played avidly:* For details on lacrosse, see Vennum 1994 and Blanchard and Cheska 1985.

170 *"A person standing two-thirds":* Quoted ibid., 27.

170 *According to the National Center:* Cited in McGrath 2011, 49.

171 *football's essential character:* Magoun 1938; Marples 1954. See also Richard Carew, who wrote in 1602 about "hurling to country," which is one of many strange variants on the football theme, this one including men on horseback as well as on foot. Carew noted resemblances between the violent game and "the feats of warre": battle lines, flanking maneuvers, rear guards, cavalry racing like mad, men lying in ambush at bridges. And he commented on the aftermath of games, with the men limping home "as from a pitched battaile, with bloody pates, bones broken, and out of joint, and such bruses as serve to shorten their daies" (quoted in Elias and Dunning 1986, 185–87).

171 *"whoop or get whooped":* Gene Chizik in ESPN documentary Depth Chart Auburn, http://vimeo.com/49812057.

173 *"I regret to observe":* Quoted in Gorn 1986, 101.

173 *"Whoever learns not":* Quoted in Nye 1998, 220.

175 *"the Warrior Ethos":* "Official Home of Modern Army Combatives," U.S. Army Maneuver Center of Excellence, U.S. Army Combatives School, www.benning.army.mil/infantry/197th/combatives/.

176 *"The main function of sport":* Lorenz 1996, 280.

177 *it's a myth:* Guttmann 2002; Young 2004.

177 *societies with a lot:* Sipes 1973; Chick and Loy 2001.

177 *"ritualized non-lethal combat":* Knauft 2002, 138.

177 *"orgies of hatred":* Orwell 1945, 10.

179 *Animals rarely engage:* Pennisi 2012b.

179 *"competing military parades":* Wilson 2010, 86.

180 *"The entire bloodless performance":* Hölldobler and Wilson 1994, 70.

180 *one side in a "nothing fight":* Knauft 2002.

181 *team-based hitting duels:* Chagnon 1992, 178–89.

CHAPTER SEVEN: BLOODLUST

183 *"After the kill":* Mueller 1996, 72.

187 *greedily slurp up:* For varied perspectives on entertainment violence, see Eric Wilson 2012; King 1982; Goldstein 1998; Schechter 2005; Bok 1998; and Ehrenreich 1997.

187 *the wrong idea:* Kyle 2007, 315. See also Fagan 2011.

188 *fond of creative butchery:* For overviews of European blood sports, see Elias 1939; Pinker 2011; Schechter 2005; Hackwood 1907; and Malcolmson 1973.

188 *"a very rude":* Quoted in Guttmann 2004, 90.

189 *eighteenth-century tossing:* Blackmore 2000, xxiii.

189 *Emperor Leopold I:* Blanning 2007, 403.

189 *"The executioner tied":* Pinker 2011, 24.

189 *"into a sort of huge":* Fagan 2011, 54–55.

190 *On October 13, 1660:* Pepys 1904, 260.

190 *around the world:* For non-Western examples of viciousness and sadism as entertainment, see Fagan 2011. On animal cruelty as a cross-cultural phenomenon, see Patterson-Kane and Piper 2012.

191 *"sadistic gaiety":* Horowitz 2001, 2.

191 *Imagine that you find:* The opening of this section is adapted from a blog I wrote; see "Fiction Addiction: Why Do We Love Stories?" *Psychology Today,* May 30, 2012, www .psychologytoday.com/blog/the-storytelling-animal/201205/fiction-addiction.

194 *"Blood and gore sold":* Muchembled 2012, 263.

194 *much subsequent research:* Pinker 2011.

194 *Harold Schechter points out:* Schechter 2005.

194 *"Maybe we need the catharsis":* Quoted in Bok 1998, 13.

194 *Stephen King has:* King 1982.

195 *duels regulated by unwritten rules:* Bernstein 2006. The quotation is from Probert and McLellan-Day 2010, 18.

196 *"The evidence concerning":* Zillmann 1998, 186.

196 *The evidence for the alternative:* Ferguson 2010; Pinker 2003.

196 *determined, decades-long effort:* Gottschall 2012, chap. 2; Penny Holland 2003; Paley 1984; Tremblay and Nagin 2005, 84.

196 *In a fascinating 2008 study:* Benenson, Carder, and Geib-Cole, 2008.

197 *"I had to admit":* Broyles 1984.

198 *violence is for protecting:* For a full treatment of this argument, see Gottschall 2012, chap. 6.

199 *Men love-hate war:* In his massive study of the history of war, Azar Gat (2006, 39) explains that warriors typically feel both strong revulsion and attraction to war: "These antithetical emotional arrays . . . are the reason why through the ages artists, thinkers, and ordinary folk of all sorts have claimed with conviction that people rejoice in war, whereas others have held with equal self-persuasion that people regard it as an unmitigated disaster." Sebastian Junger makes similar arguments in *War* (2010), his account of life in a frontline army unit in Afghanistan. See also Hedges 2002.

199 *"It is well war":* Quoted in Sanborn 1966, 158.

199 *admits that he was happier:* Caputo 1977, 81.

199 *When the writer Henri de Man:* Livingstone 2007, 213.

199 *"mad monkey" inside:* Marlantes 2010, 560.

200 *chimpanzees love to kill:* Goodall 2000, chap. 8; Wrangham and Peterson 1997.

206 *Most of us think:* Wilson, Daly, and Pound 2009.

206 *"long ago the meek":* Symons 1978, 156.

206 *"We are nothing":* Quoted in Smith 2009, 81.

CHAPTER EIGHT: WHAT A FIGHT MEANS

211 *Fear is useful:* Wise 2009; De Becker 1997.

214 *"Mĕricon [faggot]":* Dundee and Sugar 2008, 94.

214 *"seeking to demonstrate":* Mailer 2002, 237.

214 *"[Boxing is] a religion of blood":* Ibid., 238.

214 *"a human experience":* Oates 2006, 197.

216 *"super-emotional climax":* Hemingway 1960, 239.

216 *"takes a man out":* Ibid., 206.

216 *"all matadors are gored":* Ibid., 166.

217 *the literature of boxing:* See the collected articles in Silverman 2002 and Kimball and Schulian 2011.

217 *"If boxing is a sport":* Oates 2006, 16.

218 *"Across that embattled":* Mailer 1975, 195.

219 *Heliogabalus's favorite thing:* Bloom 2004, 82.

226 *"Ah, me":* Quoted in Gorn 1986, 155.

227 *"The notion of":* James 1984, 352.

227 *"the horror makes":* Ibid., 355.

227 *The stereotypical fight fan:* The fight fans I've met aren't in it primarily for the carnage. My impression is backed up by a survey of 2,700 MMA fans that found few MMA fans were drawn to the sport primarily because of the violence or the blood. Most fans, the study concluded, are drawn to MMA because they "enjoy the competition and the technical aspects of the sport." (Cheever 2009, 25).

228 *there were aristocrats:* Gorn 1986.

231 *"other than boxing":* Oates 2006, 154.

EPILOGUE

242 *"drink away" the trouble:* Spierenburg 1998a, 115.

BIBLIOGRAPHY

Aldis, Owen. *Play Fighting*. New York: Academic Press, 1975.

Altha, J., M. Yeadon, J. Sandover, and K. Parsons. "The Damaging Punch." *British Medical Journal* (Clinical Research Edition) 291 (1985): 1756–77.

Andersen, Peter. "Positions of Power: Status and Dominance in Organizational Communication." In *The Non-Verbal Communication Reader*, edited by Laura Guerrero and Michael Hecht, 3rd ed., 450–67. Long Grove, IL: Waveland Press, 2008.

Anderson, Elijah. *Code of the Street: Decency, Violence, and the Moral Life of the Inner City*. New York: Norton, 1999.

Andersson, Malte. *Sexual Selection*. Princeton, NJ: Princeton University Press, 1994.

Appiah, Kwame Anthony. *The Honor Code: How Moral Revolutions Happen*. New York: Norton, 2010.

Archer, John. "Does Sexual Selection Explain Human Sex Differences in Aggression?" *Behavioral and Brain Sciences* 32 (2009): 249–66.

Archer, John, and Sylvana Côté. "Sex Differences in Aggressive Behavior: A Developmental and Evolutionary Perspective." In *Developmental Origins of Aggression*, edited by Richard Tremblay, Willard Hartup, and John Archer, 425–46. New York: Guilford Press, 2005.

Auyeung, B., S. Baron-Cohen, E. Ashwin, R. Knickmeyer, K. Taylor, G. Hackett, and M. Hines. "Fetal Testosterone Predicts Sexually Differentiated Childhood Behavior in Girls and in Boys." *Psychological Science* 20 (2009): 144.

Baillargeon, R. H., M. Zoccolillo, K. Keenan, S. Côté, D. Pérusse, H. X. Wu, and R. E. Tremblay. "Gender Differences in Physical Aggression: A Population-Based Survey of Children Before and After Two Years of Age." *Developmental Psychology* 43 (2007): 13–26.

Baker, Allen. *The Gladiator: The Secret History of Rome's Warrior Slaves*. New York: Da Capo, 2000.

Barr, John, and Josh Gross. "UFC Fighters Say Low Pay Simply Brutal." *ESPN Outside the Lines*, January 15, 2012. http://espn.go.com/espn/otl/story/_/page/UFCpay/ufc-fighters-say-low-pay-most-painful-hit-all.

Barrow, John. *Mathletics: A Scientist Explains 100 Amazing Things About the World of Sports*. New York: W. W. Norton, 2012.

Bateson, Patrick. "The Role of Play in the Evolution of Great Apes and Humans." In *The Nature of Play: Great Apes and Humans*, edited by Anthony Pellegrini and Peter Smith, 13–26. New York: Guilford Press, 2005.

Baumeister, Roy. *Is There Anything Good About Men?* Oxford: Oxford University Press, 2010.

Beekman, Scott. *Ringside: A History of Professional Wrestling in America*. Westport, CT: Praeger, 2006.

Benenson, Joyce, Hassina Carder, and Sarah Geib-Cole. "The Development of Boys' Preferential Pleasure in Physical Aggression." *Aggressive Behavior* 34 (2008): 154–66.

Bernstein, Mark. *Football: The Ivy League Origins of an American Obsession*. Philadelphia: University of Pennsylvania Press, 2001.

Bernstein, Ross. *The Code: The Unwritten Rules of Fighting and Retaliation in the NHL*. Chicago: Triumph Books, 2006.

Binyon, T. J. *Pushkin: A Biography*. New York: Alfred A. Knopf, 2003.

Bjorklund, David, and Anthony Pellegrini. "Evolutionary Perspectives on Social Development." In *Blackwell Handbook of Childhood Social Development*, edited by Peter Smith and Craig Hart, 44–59. Malden, MA: Blackwell, 2004.

Blackmore, Howard. *Hunting Weapons: From the Middle Ages to the Twentieth Century*. Mineola, NY: Courier Dover Publications, 2000.

Blanchard, Kendall, and Alyce Taylor Cheska. *The Anthropology of Sport: An Introduction*. South Hadley, MA: Bergin and Garvey, 1985.

Blanning, Tim. *The Pursuit of Glory: Europe 1648–1815*. New York: Penguin, 2007.

Bloom, Paul. *Descartes' Baby: How the Science of Child Development Explains What Makes Us Human*. New York: Basic Books, 2004.

Boehm, Christopher. *Hierarchy in the Forest: The Evolution of Egalitarian Behavior*. Cambridge, MA: Harvard University Press, 1999.

Bok, Sissela. *Mayhem: Violence as Public Entertainment*. Reading, MA: Addison-Wesley, 1998.

Bordwell, David. *Poetics of Cinema*. New York: Routledge, 2007.

Borgia, Gerald. "Preexisting Male Traits Are Important in the Evolution of Elaborated Male Sexual Display." *Advances in the Study of Behavior* 36 (2006): 249–303.

Boschi, Daniele. "Homicide and Knife Fighting in Rome, 1845–1915." In *Men and Violence: Gender, Honor, and Rituals in Modern Europe and America*, edited by Pieter Spierenburg, 128–58. Columbus: Ohio State University Press, 1998.

Bowman, James. *Honor: A History*. New York: Encounter Books, 2006.

Braunwart, Bob, and Bob Carroll. *The Journey to Camp: The Origins of American Football from Ancient Times to 1889*. East Huntingdon, PA: Professional Football Researchers Association, 1997.

Brewer, G., and Sharon Howarth. "Sport, Attractiveness, and Aggression." *Personality and Individual Differences* 53 (2012): 640–43.

Brockman, John, ed. *This Explains Everything: Deep, Beautiful, and Elegant Theories of How the World Works*. New York: Harper Perennial, 2013.

Brooks, Charles, Michael Church, and Lance Fraser. "Effects of Duration of Eye Contact on Judgments of Personality Characteristics." *Journal of Social Psychology* 126 (1986): 71–78.

Brown, Ryan, and Lindsey Osterman. "Culture of Honor, Violence, and Homicide." In *The Oxford Handbook of Evolutionary Perspectives on Violence, Homicide, and War*, edited by Todd Shackelford and Vivian Weekes-Shackelford, 218–32. Oxford: Oxford University Press, 2012.

Broyles, William, Jr. "Why Men Love War." *Esquire*, November 1984.

Butler, Judith. *Bodies That Matter: On the Discursive Limits of Sex*. New York: Routledge, 1993.

————. *Gender Trouble: Feminism and the Subversion of Identity.* New York: Routledge, 1990.

Cameron, Alan. *Circus Factions: Blues and Greens at Rome and Byzantium.* Oxford: Clarendon Press, 1976.

Campbell, Anne. "Aggression." In *The Handbook of Evolutionary Psychology,* edited by David Buss, 628–52. Hoboken, NJ: Wiley, 2005.

————. *A Mind of Her Own: The Evolutionary Psychology of Women.* Oxford: Oxford University Press, 2002.

————. "Sex Differences in Aggression." In *The Oxford Handbook of Evolutionary Psychology,* edited by Robin Dunbar and Louise Barrett, 365–82. Oxford: Oxford University Press, 2007.

Campbell, Anne, and Catharine Cross. "Women and Aggression." In *The Oxford Handbook of Evolutionary Perspectives on Violence, Homicide, and War,* edited by Todd Shackelford and Vivian Weekes-Shackelford, 197–217. Oxford: Oxford University Press, 2012.

Campbell, Joseph, and Bill Moyers. *The Power of Myth.* New York: Anchor Books, 1991.

Caputo, Philip. *A Rumor of War.* New York: Henry Holt, 1977.

Carpenter, Les. "NFL Orders Retreat from War Metaphors." *Washington Post,* February 1, 2009.

Carroll, Joseph. "The Extremes of Conflict in Literature: Violence, Homicide, and War." In *The Oxford Handbook of Evolutionary Perspectives on Violence, Homicide, and War,* edited by Todd Shackelford and Viviana Weekes-Shackelford, 413–34. Oxford: Oxford University Press, 2012.

Chagnon, Napoleon. *Yanomamö.* 4th ed. Santa Barbara: University of California Press, 1992.

Cheever, Nancy. "The Uses and Gratifications of Viewing Mixed Martial Arts." *Journal of Sports Media* 4 (2009): 25–53.

Chick, Garry, and John Loy. "Making Men of Them: Male Socialization for Warfare and Combative Sports." *World Cultures* 12 (2001): 2–17.

Chick, Garry, John Loy, and Andrew Miracle. "Combative Sport and Warfare: A Reappraisal of the Spillover and Catharsis Hypotheses." *Cross-Cultural Research* 31 (1997): 249–67.

Clutton-Brock, T., and G. Parker. "Potential Reproductive Rates and the Operation of Sexual Selection." *The Quarterly Review of Biology* 67 (1992a): 437–56.

————. "Sexual Coercion in Animal Societies." *Animal Behaviour* 49 (1992b): 1345–65.

Clutton-Brock, T., and C. Vincent. "Sexual Selection and the Potential Reproductive Rates of Males and Females." *Nature* 351 (1991): 58–60.

Cohen-Bendahan, Celina, Cornelieke van de Beek, and Sheri Bernbaum. "Prenatal Sex Hormone Effects on Child and Adult Sex-Typed Behavior: Methods and Findings." *Neuroscience and Biobehavioral Reviews* 29 (2005): 353–84.

Collins, Randall. *Violence: A Micro-Sociological Theory.* Princeton, NJ: Princeton University Press, 2008.

Connell, R. W. *Masculinities.* 2nd ed. Cambridge, UK: Polity Press, 2005.

Cooper, Trevor G., Elizabeth Noonan, Sigrid von Eckardstein, Jacques Auger, H. W. Gordon Baker, Hermann M. Behre, Trine B. Haugen, Thinus Kruger, Christina Wang, Michael T. Mbizvo, and Kirsten M. Vogelsong. "World Health Organization Reference Values for Human Semen Characteristics." *Human Reproduction Update* 16 (2010): 231–45.

Cordain, Loren, and Joe Friel. "The Paleolithic Athlete: The Original Cross-Trainer." In *The*

Anthropology of Sport and Human Movement, edited by Robert Sands and Linda Sands, 267–76. Lanham, MD: Lexington Books, 2010.

Cornell, T. "On War and Games in the Ancient World." In *War and Games*, edited by T. Cornell and T. B. Allen, 37–58. San Francisco: Boydell Press, 2002.

Couch, Jason. "Purring." *Journal of Manly Arts*, August 2004.

Courtwright, David. *Violent Land: Single Men and Social Disorder from the Frontier to the Inner City*. Cambridge, MA: Harvard University Press, 1996.

Cox, Cathleen R., and Burney J. Le Boeuf. "Female Incitation of Male Competition: A Mechanism in Sexual Selection." *American Naturalist* 111 (1977): 317–35.

Cross, Catharine. "Sex Differences in Same-Sex Direct Aggression and Sociosexuality: The Role of Risky Impulsivity." *Evolutionary Psychology* 8 (2010): 779–92.

Cross, Catharine, and Anne Campbell. "Women's Aggression." *Aggression and Violent Behavior* 16 (2011): 390–98.

Cross, Catharine, Lee Copping, and Anne Campbell. "Sex Differences in Impulsivity: A Meta-analysis." *Psychological Bulletin* 137 (2011): 97–130.

Crudelli, Chris. *The Way of the Warrior: Martial Arts and Fighting Skills from Around the World*. London: DK Publishing, 2008.

Cummins, Denise. "Dominance, Status, and Social Hierarchies." In *The Handbook of Evolutionary Psychology*, edited by David Buss, 676–97. Hoboken, NJ: Wiley, 2005.

Daly, Martin, and Margo Wilson. *Homicide*. Hawthorne, NY: Aldine de Gruyter, 1988.

Darwin, Charles. *The Descent of Man and Selection in Relation to Sex, Volume II*. New York: D. Appleton and Company, 1871.

Davies, Julian. *Street Fighters: Real Fighting Men Tell Their Stories*. Bury, UK: Milo Books, 2002.

Davis, Robert. "The Police and the Pugni: Sport and Social Control in Early-Modern Venice." *Stanford Humanities Review* 6 (1998).

———. *The War of the Fists: Popular Culture and Public Violence in Late Renaissance Venice*. Oxford: Oxford University Press: 1994.

Deaner, Robert. "More Males Run Fast: A Stable Sex Difference in Competitiveness in U.S. Distance Runners." *Evolution and Human Behavior* 27 (2006a): 63–84.

———. "More Males Run Relatively Fast in U.S. Road Races: Further Evidence of a Sex Difference in Competitiveness." *Evolutionary Psychology* 4 (2006b): 303–14.

Deaner, Robert, and Brandt Smith. "Sex Differences in Sports Across 50 Societies." *Cross-Cultural Research*. Published online before print, October 29, 2012. doi:10.1177/1069397112463687.

Deaner, Robert O., David C. Geary, David A. Puts, Sandra A. Ham, Judy Kruger, Elizabeth Fles, Bo Winegard, and Terry Grandis. "A Sex Difference in the Predisposition for Physical Competition: Males Play Sports Much More Than Females Even in the Contemporary U.S." *PLOS One* 7, no. 11 (2012): e49168. doi:10.1371/journal.pone.0049168.

De Becker, Gavin. *The Gift of Fear*. Boston: Little, Brown, 1997.

De Block, Andreas, and Siegfried Dewitte. "Darwinism and the Cultural Evolution of Sports." *Perspectives in Biology and Medicine* 52 (2009): 1–16.

Dennett, Daniel. *Darwin's Dangerous Idea: Evolution and the Meanings of Life*. New York: Simon & Schuster, 1995.

de Waal, Frans. *Chimpanzee Politics: Power and Sex Among the Apes*. Rev. ed. Baltimore: Johns Hopkins, 2007. First published 1982.

Diamond, Jared. *The World Until Yesterday: What We Can Learn from Traditional Societies.* New York: Viking, 2012.

Divale, William, and Marvin Harris. "Population, Warfare, and the Male Supremacist Complex." American Anthropologist 78 (1976): 521–38.

Dixson, Alan. *Sexual Selection and the Origins of Human Mating Systems.* Oxford: Oxford University Press, 2009.

Dowd, Maureen. *Are Men Necessary? When the Sexes Collide.* New York: G. P. Putnam's Sons, 2005.

Dundee, Angelo, and Bert Randolph Sugar. *My View from the Corner: A Life in Boxing.* New York: McGraw-Hill, 2008.

Dyck, Noel. "Booze, Barrooms and Scrapping: Masculinity and Violence in a Western Canadian Town." *Canadian Journal of Anthropology* 1 (1980): 191–98.

Eagly, A., and A. Mladinic. "Are People Prejudiced Against Women? Some Answers from Research on Attitudes, Gender Stereotypes, and Judgments of Competence." *European Review of Social Psychology* 5 (1994): 1–35.

———. "Gender Stereotypes and Attitudes Toward Women and Men." *Personality and Social Psychology Bulletin* 15 (1989): 543–58.

Eagly, Alice, Antonio Mladinic, and Stacey Otto. "Are Women Evaluated More Favorably Than Men? An Analysis of Attitudes, Beliefs, and Emotions." *Psychology of Women Quarterly* 15 (1991): 203–16.

Earley, Pete. *The Hot House: Life Inside Leavenworth Prison.* New York: Bantam Books, 1992.

Ehrenreich, Barbara. *Blood Rites: Origins and History of the Passions of War.* New York: Metropolitan Books, 1997.

Eibl-Eibesfeldt, Irenäus. *Human Ethology.* New York: Aldine de Gruyter, 1989.

Elias, Norbert. *The Civilizing Process: The History of Manners.* Translated by Edmund Jephcott. New York: Urizen Books, 1979. First published 1939.

Elias, Norbert, and Eric Dunning. *Quest for Excitement: Sport and Leisure in the Civilizing Process.* Oxford: Basil Blackwell, 1986.

Ellis, Lee, Scott Hershberger, Evelyn Field, Scott Wersinger, Sergio Pellis, David Geary, Craig Palmer, Katherine Hoyenga, Amir Hetsrani, and Kasmer Karadi. *Sex Differences: Summarizing More Than a Century of Scientific Research.* New York: Taylor and Francis, 2008.

Ellsworth, Phoebe, and J. Merrill Carlsmith. "Eye Contact and Gaze Aversion in an Aggressive Encounter." *Journal of Personality and Social Psychology* 28 (1973): 280–92.

Ellsworth, Phoebe, J. Merrill Carlsmith, and Alexander Henson. "The Stare as a Stimulus to Flight in Human Subjects: A Series of Field Experiments." *Journal of Personality and Social Psychology* 21 (1972): 302–11.

Epstein, David. *The Sports Gene: Inside the Science of Extraordinary Athletic Performance.* New York: Current, 2013.

Fagan, Garret. *The Lure of the Arena: Social Psychology and the Crowd at the Roman Games.* New York: Cambridge University Press, 2011.

Faludi, Susan. *Stiffed: The Betrayal of the American Man.* New York: HarperCollins, 1999.

Faurie, Charlotte, Dominique Pontierb, and Michel Raymond. "Student Athletes Claim to Have More Sexual Partners Than Other Students." *Evolution and Human Behavior* 25 (2004): 1–8.

Faurie, Charlotte, and Michel Raymond. "The Fighting Hypothesis as an Evolutionary Explanation for the Handedness Polymorphism in Humans: Where Are We?" *Annals of the New York Academy of Sciences* 1288 (2013): 110–13.

———. "Handedness, Homicide and Negative Frequency-Dependent Selection." *Proceedings of the Royal Society B* 272 (2005): 25–28.

Felson, Richard. "Impression Management and the Escalation of Aggression and Violence." *Social Psychology Quarterly* 45 (1982): 245–54.

Ferguson, Christopher. "Media Violence Effects and Violent Crime: Good Science or Moral Panic?" In *Violent Crime: Clinical and Social Implications*, edited by Christopher Ferguson, 37–56. Los Angeles: Sage, 2010.

Findlay, L., and A. Bowker. "The Link Between Competitive Sport Participation and Self-Concept in Early Adolescence: A Consideration of Gender and Sport Orientation." *Journal of Youth and Adolescence* 38 (2009): 29–40.

Fisher, Maryanne, Justin Garcia, and Rosemarie Sokol Chang. *Evolution's Empress: Darwinian Perspectives on the Nature of Women*. Oxford: Oxford University Press, 2013.

Fleming, Thomas. *Duel: Alexander Hamilton, Aaron Burr and the Future of America*. New York: Basic Books, 1999.

Frederick, David, and Martie Haselton. "Why Is Muscularity Sexy? Tests of the Fitness Indicator Hypothesis." *Personality and Social Psychology Bulletin* 33 (2007): 1167–83.

Freeman, Joanne. *Affairs of Honor: National Politics in the New Republic*. New Haven, CT: Yale University Press, 2001.

Frevert, Ute. "The Taming of the Noble Ruffian: Male Violence and Dueling in Early Modern and Modern Germany." In *Men and Violence: Gender, Honor, and Rituals in Modern Europe and America*, edited by Pieter Spierenburg, 37–63. Columbus: Ohio State University Press, 1998.

Fry, Douglas. "Rough-and-Tumble Play in Humans." In *The Nature of Play: Great Apes and Humans*, edited by Anthony Pellegrini and Peter Smith, 54–88. New York: Guilford Press, 2005.

Gallico, Paul. "The Feel." In *The Norton Book of Sports*, edited by George Plimpton, 41–49. New York: Norton, 1992.

Gat, Azar. *War in Human Civilization*. Oxford: Oxford University Press, 2006.

Gaulin, Steve. "Biophobia Breeds Unparsimonious Exceptionalism." *Behavioral and Brain Sciences* 32 (2009): 279–80.

Geary, David. *Male, Female: The Evolution of Human Sex Differences*. 2nd ed. Washington, DC: American Psychological Association, 2010.

Geary, David, Jennifer Byrd-Craven, Mary Hoard, Jacob Vigil, and Chattavee Numtee. "Evolution and Development of Boys' Social Behavior." *Developmental Review* 23 (2003): 444–70.

Gill, D. L. "Gender Differences in Competitive Orientation and Sport Participation." *International Journal of Sport Psychology* 19 (1988): 145–59.

Gill, D. L., and Dzewaltowski, D. A. "Competitive Orientations Among Intercollegiate Athletes: Is Winning the Only Thing?" *The Sport Psychologist* 2 (1988): 212–21.

Gilmore, David. *Manhood in the Making: Cultural Concepts of Masculinity*. New Haven, CT: Yale University Press, 1990.

Goldstein, Jeffrey, ed. *Why We Watch: The Attractions of Violent Entertainment*. Oxford: Oxford University Press, 1998.

Golombok, Susan, and Melissa Hines. "Sex Differences in Social Behavior." In *Blackwell Handbook of Childhood Social Development*, edited by Peter Smith and Craig Hart, 117–36. Malden, MA: Blackwell, 2004.

Goodall, Jane. *Reason for Hope: A Spiritual Journey.* New York: Grand Central Publishing, 2000.

Gorn, Elliot. "'Gouge and Bite, Pull Hair and Scratch': The Social Significance of Fighting in the Southern Backcountry." *Journal of Manly Arts,* April 2001. First published in *American Historical Review* 90 (1985): 18–43.

——. *The Manly Art: Bare-Knuckle Prize Fighting in America.* Ithaca, NY: Cornell University Press, 1986.

Gosso, Yumi, et al. "Play in Hunter-Gatherer Society." In *The Nature of Play: Great Apes and Humans,* edited by Anthony Pellegrini and Peter Smith, 213–53. New York: Guilford Press, 2005.

Gottschall, Jonathan. "Greater Emphasis on Female Attractiveness in *Homo sapiens*: A Revised Solution to an Old Evolutionary Riddle." *Evolutionary Psychology* 5 (2007): 347–58.

——. *The Rape of Troy: Evolution, Violence, and the World of Homer.* New York: Cambridge University Press, 2008.

——. *The Storytelling Animal: How Stories Make Us Human.* Boston: Houghton Mifflin, 2012.

Granderson, L. "Sports Teams Are Not at War." ESPN, October 31, 2010. http://sports.espn.go.com/espn/commentary/news/story?id=5741408.

Gracie, Renzo, and Royler Gracie "Introduction." In *Brazilian Jiu-jitsu: Theory and Technique,* by Renzo Gracie and Royler Gracie. Montpelier, VT: Invisible Cities Press, 2001.

Grimes, Ronald. *Deeply into the Bone: Re-inventing Rites of Passage.* Berkeley: University of California Press, 2000.

Groos, Karl. *The Play of Animals.* New York: D. Appleton, 1898.

Groothuis, Ton, I. C. McManus, Sara Schaafsma, and Reint Geuze. "The Fighting Hypothesis in Combat: How Well Does the Fighting Hypothesis Explain Human Left-Handed Minorities?" *Annals of the New York Academy of Sciences* 1288 (2013): 100–109.

Grumet, Gerald. "Eye Contact: The Core of Interpersonal Relatedness." In *The Non-Verbal Communication Reader,* edited by Laura Guerrero and Michael Hecht, 3rd ed., 119–29. Long Grove, IL: Waveland Press, 2008.

Guttmann, Allen. *The Erotic in Sports.* New York: Columbia University Press, 1996.

——. *The Olympics: A History of the Modern Games.* 2nd ed. Urbana: University of Illinois Press, 2002.

——. *Sports: The First Five Millennia.* Amherst: University of Massachusetts Press, 2004.

——. *Sports Spectators.* New York: Columbia University Press, 1986.

——. *Women's Sports: A History.* New York: Columbia University Press, 1991.

Hackwood, Frederick. *Old English Sports.* London: T. Fisher Unwin, 1907.

Halpern, Jake. "Balls and Blood." *Sports Illustrated,* August 4, 2008.

Hamil, Pete. "Up the Stairs with Cus D'Amato." In *At the Fights: American Writers on Boxing,* edited by George Kimball and John Schulian, 312–17. New York: Library of America, 2011.

Hansen, Victor David. *The Western Way of War: Infantry Battle in Classical Greece.* Berkeley: University of California Press, 1994.

Harris, Christine, Michael Jenkins, and Dale Glaser. "Gender Differences in Risk Assessment: Why Do Women Take Fewer Risks Than Men?" *Judgment and Decision Making* 1 (2006): 48–63.

Harris, Harold. *Sport in Greece and Rome.* Ithaca, NY: Cornell University Press, 1972.

Hay, Dale. "The Beginnings of Aggression in Infancy." In *Developmental Origins of Aggres-*

sion, edited by Richard Tremblay, Willard Hartup, and John Archer, 107–32. New York: Guilford Press, 2005.

Hazlitt, William. "The Fight" [1822]. In *The Greatest Boxing Stories Ever Told: Thirty-six Incredible Tales from the Ring*, edited by Jeff Silverman, 23–27. Guilford, CT: Lyons Press, 2002.

Hedges, Chris. *War Is a Force That Gives Us Meaning*. New York: Public Affairs, 2002.

Hellandsig, E. T. "Motivational Predictors of High Performance and Discontinuation in Different Types of Sports Among Talented Teenage Athletes." *International Journal of Sport Psychology* 29 (1998): 27–44.

Hemingway, Ernest. *Death in the Afternoon*. New York: Charles Scribner, 1960. First published 1932.

Hendrickson, Robert. *The Rise and Fall of Alexander Hamilton, Volume 2, 1789–1804*. New York: Mason/Charter, 1976.

Hill, Kim, and Magdalena Hurtado. *Ache Life History: The Ecology and Demography of a Foraging People*. New York: Aldine de Gruyter, 1996.

Hogan, Robert. "Socioanalytic Theory: An Alternative to Armadillo Psychology." In *The Self and Social Life*, edited by B. R. Schlenker, 175–98. New York: McGraw-Hill, 1985.

Holland, Barbara. *Gentlemen's Blood: A History of Dueling*. New York: Bloomsbury Press, 2003.

Holland, Penny. *We Don't Play with Guns Here: War, Weapon and Superhero Play in the Early Years*. Philadelphia: Open University Press, 2003.

Hölldobler, Bert, and Edward O. Wilson. *Journey to the Ants: A Story of Scientific Exploration*. Cambridge, MA: Harvard University Press, 1994.

Honekopp, Johannes, Udo Rudolph, Lothar Beier, Andreas Liebert, and Constanze Muller. "Physical Attractiveness of Face and Body as Indicators of Physical Fitness in Men." *Evolution and Human Behavior* 28 (2007): 106–11.

Hopton, Richard. *Pistols at Dawn: A History of Duelling*. London: Portrait, 2007.

Horowitz, Donald. *The Deadly Ethnic Riot*. Berkeley: University of California Press, 2001.

Hrdy, Sarah. *Mother Nature: A History of Mothers, Infants, and Natural Selection*. New York: Pantheon, 2009.

Hudson, Valerie, and Andrea den Boer. *Bare Branches: The Security Implications of Asia's Surplus Male Population*. Boston: MIT Press, 2005.

Hugenberg, Lawrence, Paul Hardiakis, and Adam Earnheardt. *Sports Mania: Essays on Fandom and the Media in the 21st Century*. Jefferson, NC: MacFarland, 2008.

Huizinga, Johan. *Homo Ludens: A Study of the Play Element in Culture*. Boston: Beacon Press, 1950. First published 1938.

Hunt, Lynn. "Democratization and Decline? The Consequences of Demographic Change in the Humanities." In *What's Happened to the Humanities?* edited by Alvin Kernan, 17–31. Princeton, NJ: Princeton University Press, 1997.

Huntingford, Felicity, and Angela Turner. *Animal Conflict*. London: Chapman and Hall, 1987.

Huxley, Thomas. *Collected Essays of Thomas Huxley: Discourses Biological and Geological*. Whitefish, MT: Kessinger, 2005.

James, William. "The Moral Equivalent of War." In *William James: The Essential Writings*, edited by Bruce Wilshire, 349–61. Albany: State University of New York Press, 1984. First published 1910.

Jamshidi, A., T. Hossien, S. Sajadi, K. Safari, and G. Zare. "The Relationship Between Sport Orientation and Competitive Anxiety in Elite Athletes." In *2nd World Conference on Psychology, Counselling and Guidance—2011*, (Vol. 30), edited by D. E. Ongen, C. Hursen, M. Halat, and H. Boz, Amsterdam: Elsevier Science, 2011.

Jōtarō. *Shadow Warrior: Secrets of Invisibility, Mind Reading, and Thought Control.* New York: Citadel Press, 2009.

Junger, Sebastian. *War.* New York: Twelve, 2010.

Kaeuper, Richard. *Chivalry and Violence in Medieval Europe.* Oxford: Oxford University Press, 2001.

Katz, Donald. "The King of the Ferret Leggers." *Outside,* October 1987.

Kaufman, Sarah. "In Obama-Romney Rematch, Who Won the Battle of Body Language?" *Washington Post,* October 17, 2012. www.washingtonpost.com/entertainment/theater_dance/in-obama-romney-rematch-who-won-the-battle-of-body-language/2012/10/17/e4783b8e-189b-11e2-8bfd-12e2ee90dcf2_story.html.

Keen, Maurice. *Chivalry.* New Haven, CT: Yale University Press, 1984.

Kim, Ashida. *Ninja Mind Control.* New York: Citadel Press, 1985.

———. *Secrets of the Ninja.* Boulder, CO: Paladin Press, 1981.

Kimball, George, and John Schulian, eds. *At the Fights: American Writers on Boxing.* New York: Library of America, 2011.

Kimmel, Michael. *Guyland: The Perilous World Where Boys Become Men.* New York: Harper-Collins, 2008.

———. *Manhood in America: A Cultural History.* New York: Free Press, 1996.

Kindlon, Dan, and Michael Thompson. *Raising Cain: Protecting the Emotional Life of Boys.* New York: Ballantine Books, 1999.

King, Stephen. *Danse Macabre.* New York: Everest House, 1982.

Knapp, Mark, and Judith Hall. *Nonverbal Communication in Human Interaction.* 7th ed. Boston: Wadsworth, 2010.

Knauft, Bruce. "Not Just for Fun: Formalized Conflict and Games of War in Relation to Unrestrained Violence in Indigenous Melanesia and Other Decentralized Societies." In *War and Games,* edited by T. Cornell and T. B. Allen. San Francisco: Boydell Press, 2002.

Konner, Melvin. *The Evolution of Childhood.* Cambridge, MA: Harvard University Press, 2010.

Krauss, Erich, and Bret Aita. *Brawl: A Behind-the-Scenes Look at Mixed Martial Arts Competition.* Toronto, Canada: ECW Press, 2002.

Kruger, Daniel, and Randolph Nesse. "An Evolutionary Life-History Framework for Understanding Sex Differences in Human Mortality Rates." *Human Nature* 17 (2006): 74–97.

Kyle, Donald. *Sport and Spectacle in the Ancient World.* Malden, MA: Blackwell, 2007.

Lansdale, James. *The Last Duel: A True Story of Death and Honor.* New York: Canongate, 2005.

Lerner, Jimmy. *You Got Nothing Coming: Notes from a Prison Fish.* New York: Broadway Books, 2002.

Leung, Angela, and Dov Cohen. "Within- and Between-Culture Variation: Individual Differences and the Cultural Logics of Honor, Face, and Dignity Cultures." *Journal of Personality and Social Psychology* 100 (2011): 507–26.

Liang, T. *T'ai Chi Ch'uan for Health and Self-Defense.* New York: Vintage, 1974.

Lindholm, David, and Ulf Karlsson. *The Bare-Knuckle Boxer's Companion: Learning How to Hit Hard and Train Tough from the Early Boxing Masters.* Boulder, CO: Paladin Press, 2009.

Lipsyte, Robert. "Sports Metaphors Trivialize War." *USA Today,* April 6, 2003.

Llaurens, V., M. Raymond, and C. Faurie. "Ritual Fights and Male Reproductive Success in a Human Population." *Journal of Evolutionary Biology* 22 (2009a): 1854–59.

———. "Why Are Some People Left-Handed? An Evolutionary Perspective." *Philosophical Transactions of the Royal Society London B* 364 (2009b): 881–94.

Locke, John L. *Duels and Duets: Why Men and Women Talk So Differently.* New York: Cambridge University Press, 2011.

Lombardo, Michael. "On the Evolution of Sport." *Evolutionary Psychology* 10 (2012): 1–28.

Lorden, Michael J. *Oyama: The Legend, the Legacy.* Burbank, CA: Multi-Media Books, 2000.

Lorenz, Konrad. *On Aggression.* New York: MJF Books, 1996. First published 1963.

Luckenbill, David. "Criminal Homicide as a Situated Transaction." *Social Problems* 25 (1977): 176–86.

Lytton, Hugh, and David Romney. "Parents' Differential Socialization of Boys and Girls: A Meta-analysis." *Psychological Bulletin* 109 (1991): 267–96.

Maccoby, Eleanor. *The Two Sexes: Growing Up Apart, Coming Together.* Cambridge, MA: Harvard University Press, 1998.

Madigan, Tim, and Tim Delaney. *Sports: Why People Love Them.* Lanham, MD: University Press of America, 2009.

Magoun, Francis Peabody. *History of Football: From the Beginnings to 1871.* Bochum-Langendreer, Germany: Verlag Heinrich Poppinghaus O.H.G., 1938.

Mailer, Norman. "The Death of Paret." In *The Greatest Boxing Stories Ever Told: Thirty-six Incredible Tales from the Ring,* edited by Jeff Silverman, 235–40. Guilford, CT: Lyons Press, 2002.

———. *The Fight.* Boston: Little, Brown, 1975.

Malcolmson, Robert. *Popular Recreations in English Society, 1700–1850.* New York: Cambridge University Press, 1973.

Marlantes, Karl. *Matterhorn: A Novel of Vietnam.* New York: Grove Press, 2011.

Marples, Morris. *A History of Football.* London: Secker and Warburg, 1954.

Mather, Victor. "Longing for the Return of Dueling Pistol," 2012 London Olympics (blog), *New York Times,* May 21, 2012. http://london2012.blogs.nytimes.com/2012/05/21/longing-for-the-return-of-dueling-pistol/.

Maupassant, Guy de. "A Coward." In *The Odd Number: Thirteen Tales by Guy de Maupassant,* 19–38. New York: Harper and Brothers, 1889.

Mayell, Hillary. "Genghis Khan a Prolific Lover, DNA Data Implies." *National Geographic News,* February 14, 2003. http://news.nationalgeographic.com/news/2003/02/0214_030214_genghis.html.

McAleer, Kevin. *Dueling: The Cult of Honor in Fin-de-Siècle Germany.* Princeton, NJ: Princeton University Press, 1994.

McGrath, Ben. "Does Football Have a Future? The NFL and the Concussion Crisis." *New Yorker,* January 31, 2011, 40–51.

Meaney, M., J. Stewart, and W. Beatty. "Sex Differences in Social Play: The Socialization of Sex Roles." In *Advances in the Study of Behavior,* edited by J. Rosenblatt, 1–58. New York: Academic Press, 1985.

Mee, Bob. *Bare Fists: A World of Violence Where Only the Brutal Survive.* London: Collins-Willow, 1998.

Miedzlan, Myriam. *Boys Will Be Boys: Breaking the Link Between Masculinity and Violence.* New York: Doubleday, 1991.

Miller, Rory. *Meditations on Violence: A Comparison of Martial Arts Training and Real World Violence.* Boston: YMAA Publications, 2008.

Mosse, George. *The Image of Man: The Creation of Modern Masculinity.* Oxford: Oxford University Press, 1996.

Muchembled, Robert. *A History of Violence: From the End of the Middle Ages to the Present.* Malden, MA: Polity Press, 2012.

Mueller, Lisel. *Alive Together: New and Selected Poems.* Baton Rouge, LA: LSU Press, 1996.

Musashi, Miyamoto. *The Book of Five Rings.* Boston: Shambhala Publications, 2002.

Nisbett, Richard, and Dov Cohen. *Culture of Honor: The Psychology of Violence in the South.* New York: Westview Press, 1996.

Noakes, Timothy. *Lore of Running.* 4th ed. Champaign, IL: Human Kinetics, 2004.

Noble, Graham. "Mas Oyama in America," n.d. http://seinenkai.com/articles/noble/noble-oyama.html.

Nye, Robert. *Masculinity and Male Codes of Honor in Modern France.* Berkeley: University of California Press, 1998.

Oates, Joyce Carol. *On Boxing.* New York: Harper Perennial, 2006. First published 1987.

Oberzaucher, Elisabeth. "Sex and Gender Differences in Communication Strategies." In *Evolution's Empress: Darwinian Perspectives on the Nature of Women*, edited by Maryanne Fisher, Justin Garcia, and Rosemarie Sokol Chang, 345–67. Oxford: Oxford University Press, 2013.

Ong, Walter. *Fighting for Life: Contest, Sexuality and Consciousness.* Ithaca, NY: Cornell University Press, 1981.

Orwell, George. "The Sporting Spirit." First published *Tribune* (London), December 14, 1945, 10–11.

Palantonio, Sal. *How Football Explains America.* Chicago: Triumph Books, 2008.

Paley, Vivian. *Boys and Girls: Superheroes in the Doll Corner.* Chicago: University of Chicago Press, 1984.

Panskepp, Jaak. *Affective Neuroscience: The Foundations of Human and Animal Emotions.* Oxford: Oxford University Press, 1998.

Parks, Ward. *Verbal Dueling in Heroic Narrative.* Princeton, NJ: Princeton University Press, 1990.

Patterson-Kane, Emily, and Heather Piper. "Animal Abuse and Cruelty." In *The Oxford Handbook of Evolutionary Perspectives on Violence, Homicide, and War*, edited by Todd Shackelford and Vivian Weekes-Shackelford, 254–69. Oxford: Oxford University Press, 2012.

Pawlowski, B., Atwal Rajinder, and Robin Dunbar. "Sex Differences in Everyday Risk-Taking Behavior." *Evolutionary Psychology* 6 (2008): 29–42.

Pellegrini, Anthony. "Rough-and-Tumble Play from Childhood Through Adolescence: Development and Possible Functions." In *Blackwell Handbook of Childhood Social Development*, edited by Peter Smith and Craig Hart, 438–54. Malden, MA: Blackwell, 2004.

Pellegrini, Anthony, and Peter Smith, eds. *The Nature of Play: Great Apes and Humans.* New York: Guilford Press, 2005.

Pennisi, Elizabeth. "From War to Peace." *Science* 336 (2012a): 841.

———. "Preening the Troops." *Science* 336 (2012b): 828.

Pepys, Samuel. *The Diary of Samuel Pepys.* London: George Bell & Sons, 1904.

Peterson, Susan. *Legends of the Martial Arts Masters.* North Clarendon, VT: Tuttle, 2003.

Pinker, Steven. *The Better Angels of Our Nature: Why Violence Has Declined.* New York: Viking, 2011.

———. *The Blank Slate: The Modern Denial of Human Nature.* New York: Viking, 2003.

Plimpton, George. *Shadow Box.* New York: G. P. Putnam's Sons, 1977.

Polk, Kenneth. "Males and Honor Contest Violence." *Homicide Studies* 3 (1999): 6–29.

Pollack, William. *Real Boys: Rescuing Our Sons from the Myths of Boyhood.* New York: Random House, 1998.

Polly, Matthew. *Tapped Out: Rear Naked Chokes, the Octagon, and the Last Emperor: An Odyssey in Mixed Martial Arts.* New York: Gotham, 2011.

Powell, Melissa, and Linda Ladd. "Bullying: A Review of the Literature and Implications for Family Therapists." *American Journal of Family Therapy* 39 (2010): 189–206.

Preston, Brian. *Me, Chi, and Bruce Lee: Adventures in the Martial Arts from the Shaolin Temple to the Ultimate Fighting Championship.* Berkeley, CA: Blue Snake Books, 2007.

Probert, Bob, and Kirstie McLellan-Day. *Tough Guy.* Chicago: Triumph Books, 2010.

Puts, David. "Beauty and the Beast: Mechanisms of Sexual Selection in Humans." *Evolution and Human Behavior* 31 (2010): 157–75.

Puts, David, Coren Apicella, and Rodrigo Cardenas. "Masculine Voices Signal Men's Threat Potential in Forager and Industrial Societies." *Proceedings of the Royal Society London B.* Published online before print, July 13, 2011. doi:10.1098/rspb.2011.0829.

Puts, David, Carolyn Hodges, Rodrigo Cardenas, and Steven Gaulin. "Men's Voices as Dominance Signals: Vocal Fundamental and Formant Frequencies Influence Dominance Attributions Among Men." *Evolution and Human Behavior* 28 (2007): 340–44.

Quinn, Kevin. *Sports and Their Fans: The History, Economics and Culture of the Relationship Between Spectator and Sport.* Jefferson, NC: McFarland, 2009.

Randazzo, Matthew. *Ring of Hell: The Story of Chris Benoit and the Fall of the Pro Wrestling Industry.* Beverly Hills, CA: Phoenix Books, 2008.

Rawson, Hugh and Margaret Miner, eds. *The Oxford Dictionary of American Quotations.* Oxford: Oxford University Press, 2006.

Rhoads, Steven. *Taking Sex Differences Seriously.* San Francisco: Encounter Books, 2004.

Rogow, Arnold. *A Fatal Friendship: Alexander Hamilton and Aaron Burr.* New York: Hill and Wang, 1998.

Rosin, Hanna. *The End of Men: And the Rise of Women.* New York: Penguin, 2012.

———. "The End of Men." *The Atlantic,* July/August, 2010. http://www.theatlantic.com/magazine/archive/2010/07/the-end-of-men/308135/.

———. "The Patriarchy Is Dead: Feminists, Accept It." *Slate,* September 11, 2013. http://www.slate.com/articles/double_x/doublex/2013/09/the_end_of_men_why_feminists_won_t_accept_that_things_are_looking_up_for.html.

Sanborn, Margaret. *Robert E. Lee: A Portrait, 1807–1861.* Philadelphia: Lippincott, 1966.

Saunderson, H. S. "Notes on Corea and Its People." *Journal of the Anthropological Institute of Great Britain and Ireland* 24 (1895): 299–315.

Saussure, Cesar de. *A Foreign View of England in the Reigns of George I and George II.* New York: Dutton, 1902.

Schaafsma, Sara, Reint Geuze, Bernd Riedstra, Wulf Schiefenhovel, Anke Bouma, and Ton Groothuis. "Handedness in a Non-industrial Society Challenges the Fighting Hypothesis as an Evolutionary Explanation for Left-Handedness." *Evolution and Human Behavior* 33 (2012): 94–99.

Schechter, Harold. *Savage Pastimes: A Cultural History of Violent Entertainment.* New York: St. Martin's Press, 2005.

Schmitt, David, Anu Realo, Martin Voracek, and Juri Allik. "Why Can't a Man Be More Like a

Woman? Sex Differences in Big Five Personality Traits Across 55 Cultures." *Journal of Personality and Social Psychology* 94 (2008): 168–82.

Schulte-Hostedde, Albrecht. "Female Mate Choice Is Influenced by Male Sport Participation." *Evolutionary Psychology* 6 (2008): 113–24.

Seabright, Paul. *The War of the Sexes: How Conflict and Cooperation Have Shaped Men and Women from Prehistory to the Present.* Princeton, NJ: Princeton University Press, 2012.

Sear, Rebecca, and Ruth Mace. "Who Keeps Children Alive? A Review of the Effects of Kin on Child Survival." *Evolution and Human Behavior* 29 (2008): 1–18.

Sell, Aaron, Leda Cosmides, John Tooby, Daniel Sznycer, Christopher von Rueden, and Michael Guerven. "Human Adaptations for the Visual Assessment of Strength and Fighting Ability from the Body and the Face." *Proceedings of the Royal Society London B* 276 (2009): 575–84.

Shahar, Meir. *The Shaolin Monastery: History, Religion, and the Chinese Martial Arts.* Honolulu: University of Hawaii Press, 2008.

Sheehan, Andrew. *Running and Being: The Total Experience.* Emmaus, PA: Rodale, 1978.

Sheridan, Sam. *A Fighter's Heart: One Man's Journey Through the World of Fighting.* New York: Grove, 2007.

Sherrow, Hogan. "The Origins of Bullying." Guest Blog, *Scientific American*, December 15, 2011. http://blogs.scientificamerican.com/guest-blog/2011/12/15/the-origins-of-bullying/.

———. "Violence Across Animals and Within Early Hominems." In *The Oxford Handbook of Evolutionary Perspectives on Violence, Homicide, and War*, edited by Todd Shackelford and Vivian Weekes-Shackelford, 23–40. Oxford: Oxford University Press, 2012.

Shriver, M. "Female Migration Rate Might Not Be Greater Than Male Rate." *European Journal of Human Genetics* 13 (2005): 131–32.

Silverman, Jeff, ed. *The Greatest Boxing Stories Ever Told: Thirty-six Incredible Tales from the Ring.* Guilford, CT: Lyons Press, 2002.

Simpson, Mark. "Fight Club." *Out*, July 7, 2008. www.out.com/entertainment/2008/07/07/fight-club.

Sipes, Richard. "War, Sports, and Aggression: An Empirical Test of Two Rival Theories." *American Anthropologist* 75 (1973): 64–86.

Smith, David Livingstone. *The Most Dangerous Animal: Human Nature and the Origins of War.* New York: Macmillan, 2009.

Smith, Eric Alden, and S. Abigail Smith. "Inuit Sex-Ratio Variation: Population Control, Ethnographic Error, or Parental Manipulation." *Current Anthropology* 35 (1994): 595–659.

Smith, Peter. *Children and Play.* London: Wiley-Blackwell, 2010.

Smith, Robert. *Martial Musings: A Portrayal of Martial Arts in the 20th Century.* Erie, PA: Via Media, 1999.

Snowden, Jonathan. *Total MMA: Inside Ultimate Fighting.* Toronto, Canada: ECW Press, 2008.

Sosis, Richard, Howard Kress, and James Boster. "Scars for War: Evaluating Alternative Signaling Explanations for Cross-cultural Variance in Ritual Costs." *Evolution and Human Behavior* 28 (2007): 234–47.

Spierenburg, Pieter. "Knife Fighting and Popular Codes of Honor in Early Modern Amsterdam." In *Men and Violence: Gender, Honor, and Rituals in Modern Europe and America*, edited by Pieter Spierenburg, 103–27. Columbus: Ohio State University Press, 1998a.

———. "Masculinity, Violence, and Honor: An Introduction." In *Men and Violence: Gender,*

Honor, and Rituals in Modern Europe and America, edited by Pieter Spierenburg, 1–29. Columbus: Ohio State University Press, 1998b.

St. John, Warren. *Rammer Jammer Yellow Hammer: A Journey into the Heart of Fan Mania*. New York: Crown, 2004.

Stein, Joel. *Man Made: A Stupid Quest for Masculinity*. New York: Grand Central, 2012.

Sun Tzu. *The Art of War*. El Paso, TX: El Paso Norte Press, 2005.

Sussman, David. "Presidential Debates: How Body Language Reveals Who Really Wins and Loses." *PolicyMic*, October 13, 2012. www.policymic.com/articles/16427/presidential -debates-how-body-language-reveals-who-really-wins-and-loses.

Symons, Donald. *Play and Aggression: A Study of Rhesus Monkeys*. New York: Columbia University Press, 1978.

Tannen, Deborah. *The Argument Culture: Moving from Debate to Dialogue*. New York: Random House, 1998.

Tecce, Joseph. "How a Candidate's Blinking Habits May Win—or Lose—the Election." Obama-Romney Debate No. 3: Faceoff on Foreign Policy (blog), NYDailyNews.com, October 22, 2012. http://live.nydailynews.com/Event/Obama-Romney_debate_No_3_Faceoff_ on_foreign_policy?Page=0.

Terburg, David, Nicole Hooiveld, Henk Aarts, J. Leon Kenemans, and Jack van Honk. "Eye Tracking Unconscious Face-to-Face Confrontations: Dominance Motives Prolong Gaze to Masked Angry Faces." *Psychological Science* 22 (2011): 314–19.

Thomas, Bruce. *Bruce Lee: Fighting Spirit: A Biography*. Berkeley, CA: Frog, 1994.

Thompson, Derek. "The Global Dominance of ESPN." *Atlantic*, August 14, 2013.

Tiger, Lionel. *The Decline of Males*. New York: Golden Books, 1999.

Toback, James. *Tyson*. Los Angeles: Sony Pictures Classics, 2008.

Toole, F. X. "The Monkey Look." In *Million Dollar Baby: Stories from the Corner*, 61–102. New York: HarperCollins, 2005.

Tremblay, Richard, and Daniel Nagin. "The Developmental Origins of Physical Aggression in Humans." In *Developmental Origins of Aggression*, edited by Richard Tremblay, Willard Hartup, and John Archer, 83–106. New York: Guilford Press, 2005.

Trivers, Robert. "Parental Investment and Sexual Selection." In *Sexual Selection and the Descent of Man, 1871–1971*, edited by B. Campbell, 136–207. Chicago: Aldine, 1972.

Turton, David. "The Same Only Different: War and Dueling as Boundary Marking Rituals in Mursiland, Southwest Ethiopia." In *War and Games*, edited by T. Cornell and T. B. Allen, 171–92. San Francisco: Boydell Press, 2002.

Underwood, Marion K. "Sticks and Stones and Social Exclusion: Aggression Among Girls and Boys." In *Blackwell Handbook of Childhood Social Development*, edited by Peter Smith and Craig Hart, 533–48. Malden, MA: Blackwell, 2004.

Vaillancourt, Tracy. "Indirect Aggression Among Humans: Social Construct or Evolutionary Adaptation?" In *Developmental Origins of Aggression*, edited by Richard Tremblay, Willard Hartup, and John Archer, 158–77. New York: Guilford Press, 2005.

Vandello, J., J. Bosson, C. Hohen, R. Burnaford, and J. Weaver. "Precarious Manhood." *Journal of Personality and Social Psychology* 95 (2008): 1325–39.

Vennum, Thomas. *American Indian Lacrosse: Little Brother of War*. Washington, DC: Smithsonian Institution Press, 1994.

Volk, Anthony, Joseph Camilleri, Andrew Dane, and Zopito Marini. "Is Adolescent Bullying an Evolutionary Adaptation?" *Aggressive Behavior* 38 (2012): 1–17.

Von Rueden, Christopher, Michael Gurven, and Hillard Kaplan. "The Multiple Dimensions of

Male Social Status in an Amazonian Society." *Evolution and Human Behavior* 29 (2008): 402–15.

Wald, Elijah. *The Dozens: A History of Rap's Mama*. Oxford: Oxford University Press, 2012.

Wann, Daniel, Merrill Melnick, Gordon Russell, and Dale Pease. *Sports Fans: The Psychology and Social Impact of Spectators*. New York: Routledge, 2001.

Watterson, John Sayle. *College Football: History, Spectacle, Controversy*. Baltimore: Johns Hopkins University Press, 2000.

Wertheim, L. Jon. *Blood in the Cage: Mixed Martial Arts, Pat Miletich, and the Furious Rise of the UFC*. Boston: Houghton Mifflin, 2009.

Wilder, J., Z. Mobasher, and M. Hammer. "Genetic Evidence for Unequal Effective Population Sizes of Human Females and Males." *Molecular Biology and Evolution* 21 (2004): 2047–57.

Williams, John, and Deborah Best. *Measuring Sex Stereotypes: A Thirty-Nation Study*. Beverly Hills, CA: Sage, 1982.

Wilson, Edward O. *Anthill*. New York: Norton, 2010.

———. *On Human Nature*. Cambridge, MA: Harvard University Press, 1982.

———. *The Social Conquest of the Earth*. New York: Liveright, 2012.

———. *Sociobiology: The New Synthesis*. Cambridge, MA: Harvard University Press, 1975.

Wilson, Eric. *Everyone Loves a Good Train Wreck*. New York: Farrar, Straus and Giroux, 2012.

Wilson, Margo, Martin Daly, and Nick Pound. "Sex Differences and Intrasexual Variation in Competitive Confrontation and Risk Taking: An Evolutionary Psychological Perspective." In *Hormones, Brain, and Behavior*, edited by D. Pfaff, P. Arnold, A. Etgen, S. Fahrbach, and R. Rubin, 2nd ed., 2825–52. Amsterdam: Elsevier, 2009.

Winegard, Benjamin, and Robert Deaner. "The Evolutionary Significance of Red Sox Nation: Sport Fandom as a By-product of Coalitional Psychology." *Evolutionary Psychology* 8 (2010): 432–46.

Wisdom, Stephen. *Gladiators, 100 BC–AD 200*. Oxford: Osprey, 2001.

Wise, Jeff. *Extreme Fear: The Science of Your Mind in Danger*. New York: Palgrave Macmillan, 2009.

Wrangham, Richard, and Dale Peterson. *Demonic Males: Apes and the Origins of Human Violence*. Boston: Mariner Books, 1997.

Young, David. *A Brief History of the Olympic Games*. New York: Blackwell, 2004.

Zahavi, Amotz, and Avishag Zahavi. *The Handicap Principle: A Missing Piece of Darwin's Puzzle*. Oxford: Oxford University Press, 1997.

Zerjal, Tatiana, Yali Xue, Giorgio Bertorelle, et al. "The Genetic Legacy of the Mongols." *American Journal of Human Genetics* 72 (2003): 717–21.

Zhu, Motao, Songzhu Zhao, Jeffrey Coben, and Gordon Smith. "Why More Male Pedestrians Die in Vehicle-Pedestrian Collisions Than Female Pedestrians: A Decompositional Analysis." *Injury Prevention* (2012). doi:10.1136/injuryprev-2012-040594.

Zillmann, Dolf. "The Psychology of the Appeal of Portrayals of Violence." In *Why We Watch: The Attractions of Violent Entertainment*, edited by Jeffrey Goldstein, 179–211. Oxford: Oxford University Press, 1998.

Zillmann, Dolf, J. Bryant, and N. Sapolsky. "Enjoyment from Sports Spectatorship." In *Sports, Games, and Play: Social and Psychological Viewpoints*, edited by J. Goldstein, 2nd ed., 241–78. Hillsdale, NJ: Lawrence Erlbaum, 1989.

INDEX

Note: page numbers in italics indicate illustrations.

IMAGE CREDITS

Page vii: Michael T. Singo
Page 2: Gilberto Tadday
Page 13: Lord, John. *Beacon Lights of History, Volume XI.* 1902
Page 19: Mark Shrader
Page 21: Getty (need license)
Page 26: Tassart, Francois and Mina Round. Recollections of Guy de Maupassant. New York and London: John Lane and Co., 1912.
Page 29: Library of Congress
Page 35: Brenda Malloy
Page 42: Library of Congress
Page 44: Corbis
Page 48: Global Look/Corbis
Page 52: SPAARNESTAD PHOTO/Het Leven
Page 54: Rob Lynn Photography
Page 57: New York Public Library
Page 64: Cornell University Library
Page 70: University of Washington Libraries
Page 72: USFWS
Page 76: University of Washington Libraries
Page 80: Jerry Thomas
Page 83: Jason Meyer
Page 88: Library of Congress
Page 91: State Archives of Florida, *Florida Memory*
Page 94: "The Insult That Made A Man Out of Mac®" under license from Charles Atlas, Ltd. (www.CharlesAtlas.com)
Page 101: Osmar Schindler (1869-1927): David und Goliath, 1888
Page 106: Peter Gordon
Page 118: Courtesy of the author
Page 129: Abigail Gottschall
Page 134: Paul James Jones
Page 136: National Archives
Page 142: Courtesy of the author
Page 145: Lorenzo Calistri
Page 147: Ken O'Brien Collection/Corbis

Page 150: Eric Hibbard
Page 152: National Archives of the Netherlands
Page 161: Library of Congress
Page 167: Library of Congress
Page 169: National Media Museum
Page 176: National Guard
Page 178: National Library of France
Page 191: Nebraska Historical Society
Page 195: Library of Congress
Page 198: National Museum of Denmark
Page 200: G.H. Walker
Page 202: Nick Talarico
Page 204: Courtesy of the author
Page 215: National Archives
Page 216: George Eastman House Collection
Page 218: Johns Hopkins University Press
Page 221: Rob Lynn Photography
Page 223: Rob Lynn Photography
Page 225: Rob Lynn Photography
Page 243: Tiffani Gottschall
Page 244: Tiffani Gottschall